NEW TESTAMENT MESSAGE

A Biblical-Theological Commentary

Wilfrid Harrington, O.P. and Donald Senior, C.P.

EDITORS

New Testament Message, Volume 6

JOHN

James McPolin, S.J.

A Michael Glazier Book
THE LITURGICAL PRESS
Collegeville, Minnesota

The Bible text in this publication is from the Revised Standard Version of the
Bible, copyrighted 1946, 1952, © 1971, 1973 by the Division of Christian Educa-
tion of the National Council of the Churches of Christ in the U.S.A., and used
by permission.

6	7	8	9	10

Library of Congress Cataloging-in-Publication Data

McPolin, James.
    John / James McPolin.
       p.   cm. — (New Testament message ; v. 6)
    Includes bibliographical references.
    ISBN 0-8146-5129-1
    1. Bible. N.T. John—Commentaries. I. Title. II. Series.
BS2615.3.M388   1993
226.5'077—dc20   93-605
                                                       CIP

Contents

Index of Subjects

EDITORS' PREFACE

New Testament Message is a commentary series designed to bring the best of biblical scholarship to a wide audience. Anyone who is sensitive to the mood of the church today is aware of a deep craving for the Word of God. This interest in reading and praying the scriptures is not confined to a religious elite. The desire to strengthen one's faith and to mature in prayer has brought Christians of all types and all ages to discover the beauty of the biblical message. Our age has also been heir to an avalanche of biblical scholarship. Recent archaeological finds, new manuscript evidence, and the increasing volume of specialized studies on the Bible have made possible a much more profound penetration of the biblical message. But the flood of information and its technical nature keeps much of this scholarship out of the hands of the Christian who is eager to learn but is not a specialist. *New Testament Message* is a response to this need.

The subtitle of the series is significant: "A Biblical-Theological Commentary." Each volume in the series, while drawing on up-to-date scholarship, concentrates on bringing to the fore in understandable terms the specific message of each biblical author. The essay-format (rather than a word-by-word commentary) helps the reader savor the beauty and power of the biblical message and, at the same time, understand the sensitive task of responsible biblical interpretation.

A distinctive feature of the series is the amount of space given to the "neglected" New Testament writings, such as Colossians, James, Jude, the Pastoral Letters, the Letters of Peter and John. These briefer biblical books make a significant but often overlooked contribution to the richness of the New Testament. By assigning larger than normal coverage to these books, the series hopes to give these parts of Scripture the attention they deserve.

Because *New Testament Message* is aimed at the entire English speaking world, it is a collaborative effort of international proportions. The twenty-two contributors represent biblical scholarship in North America, Britain, Ireland and Australia. Each of the contributors is a recognized expert in his or her field, has published widely, and has been chosen because of a proven ability to communicate at a popular level. And, while all of the contributors are Roman Catholic, their work is addressed to the Christian community as a whole. The New Testament is the patrimony of all Christians.It is the hope of all concerned with this series that it will bring a fuller appreciation of God's saving Word to his people.

Wilfrid Harrington, O.P.
Donald Senior, C.P.

INTRODUCTION

THE FOURTH GOSPEL has been commonly rated the most theological of the gospels and very early in the history of the Church it came to be known as the "spiritual gospel." The evangelist was called "John the theologian" and in art he is the eagle for he has the most penetrating gaze into the mystery of God made man. Thus, reading this gospel means "flying high". It is also like climbing a spiral staircase for we are led from one level of meaning to the next. This quality and depth of reflection is the reason why many people say that they find themselves closer to God and to Christ in this gospel than in any other book they know.

I. John the Theologian

When we turn from any other gospel to John we feel instantly we are in a different world since Matthew, Mark and Luke are somehow more straightforward in describing the person and work of Jesus. Besides, the teaching of Jesus is interspersed with plenty of action and he himself emerges clearly as the Son of Man, preacher and prophet of the kingdom of God, a healer full of compassion for the sinful and the sick. On the other hand in the Fourth Gospel there are longer discourses with less action and many abstract themes keep cropping up, for example, "life," "light," "glory," "truth." Furthermore, the author demands from us a deeper level of reflection on the meaning of Christ for our lives. For example, when Jesus meets the Samaritan woman at the well of Jacob, he promises her living water and we think at first of fresh drinking water that quenches our thirst. But then we are asked to reflect on another level: "The water that I shall give him will become in him a spring of water welling up to eternal life." Here the water promised by Jesus now means the Holy Spirit who deepens within us an understanding of Jesus and his message for daily living.

The gospel often moves on two levels: on one level it describes real people, places and events but these realities also contain a further spiritual meaning when they become symbols which are reminders of Christ. The wind, water, light, darkness, the night, wine, the vine—all these are symbols, but this does not mean they have no reality; rather reality itself has further meanings. For example, Jesus gives Judas a morsel of food from the common dish at the Last Supper. Then Judas leaves the room "and it was night" (13:30). Here the darkness of the night outside makes the evangelist think of a more frightening reality, namely, the darkness of evil and unbelief and thus the night is also the darkness of Judas who betrays. Another instance is provided by John's use of the image of water which symbolizes the life of the Spirit, the new life which Jesus promises the Samaritan woman at the well and also the life that comes from the death of Jesus as he is pierced on the cross (19:34). Another image for the Holy Spirit is that of a wind for the Spirit is a mysterious power which comes from above, from God. Events, too, are real happenings which contain a symbolic meaning; for example, the action of Jesus in changing water into wine is an event that points to a deeper spiritual reality about the person of Jesus. Thus it is a "sign" of the abundant gifts that come to man with the death and resurrection of Jesus, in particular, the new life and the gift of the Spirit. Such "signs," which are described in the gospel, are miracles that reveal the mystery of the person of Jesus and invite readers to a deeper life of faith in him (20:30-31).

The gospel, which is itself a theological commentary on the meaning and message of Jesus, continues to inspire a vast plethora of commentaries and writings that shows no sign of slackening, so that any writer who adds anything, no matter how limited, to the impressive and massive literature on the Fourth Gospel is more conscious of what he has to leave unsaid than of what remains to be said. At various stages of the present commentary some central themes of the gospel will be developed in order to help readers glimpse in a more unified way the theology of the gospel as a whole. Throughout, the aim is not to obscure in any way the eagle-like, penetrating gaze of the author into the mystery of Christ but rather to help readers experience both the theological and reflective quality of the gospel with its various levels of meaning concerning Christ and his message, and that closeness to the Father and the Son which readers sometimes discover in it through the Holy Spirit for "he will guide you into the heart of the Truth" who is Jesus (Jn. 16:13).

II. The Theme of the Gospel

The present commentary does not intend to help people "wade through" the gospel but, instead, to guide them to see how one central theme evolves through all the events and words of the story: Jesus discloses himself as the expected one of his people and the Incarnate Son of God and those who respond to him receive a share in his life. This leitmotif is introduced, along with some other leading themes, at the opening of the gospel, in a prologue (1:1-18). Then in the historical introduction to the public life of Jesus (1:19-51) the identity of Jesus is already revealed by a "witness," John the Baptist, who invites people to believe in him and sets the first followers on their way to discovering the mystery of Jesus. This band of disciples, which constitutes the first christian community, gather around Jesus and share life together with him.

In the first stage of his public mission (2:1-4:54) Jesus reveals himself in the miracle at the wedding feast of Cana and through his action in the temple. In this part of his life some individual responses of faith, which are described in the form of dialogues, show a progressive growth in the response to him. Here the response to Christ is generally more positive compared with that in the second stage of his public self-revelation (5:1-10:42). Then after two miracles with their accompanying and explanatory discourses (chs. 5-6) the hostility mounts and the central section (chs. 7-10) of the first half of the gospel (chs. 1-12) is marked by intense controversy which prepares for the great, final revelation of Jesus in the events of his "hour," namely, his death and resurrection. This takes place in or around the centre of the old worship, the temple area and the conflict, division and rejection frequently remind us of Jesus' coming "hour." Following this controversy and conflict, the events at Bethany and Jerusalem more clearly prefigure and prepare for this "hour."

The second part of the gospel (chs. 13-20; ch. 21 is an addition) comments on and describes the high point of the mission and self-revelation of Jesus, which is the "hour" of his "glorification" when he passes to his Father through death and resurrection. In this "hour" he reveals himself and communicates the life of God as his Son to those who accept him and commit themselves to him in faith and love. However, in this second part of the gospel Jesus reveals himself only to a small group of believing disciples, and before the actual events of the "hour" unfold (chs. 18-20), a long farewell message of Jesus to this intimate group interprets the meaning of these events for all christian disciples (chs. 13-17).

III. The Origins of the Gospel

The author gives us a general clue about the origins of the gospel when he states the aim of his work: "that you may believe (this can mean: "come to believe" or "go on believing") that Jesus is the Christ, the Son of God, and that believing you may have life in his name" (20:31). That he is writing for those who already believe is suggested by the general perspective of the gospel itself. It is not a "missionary" document intended for those who are outside the christian community but rather seems to be designed to root believers deeper in their commitment to Christ. The striking manner in which the evangelist reinterprets the Jesus traditions of the early Church reflected in the

Synoptics (cf. Mk 1:1-20; Jn 1:19-51) seems to presuppose a prior knowledge of these traditions and makes it more likely that the gospel was written to strengthen the faith of christians by refocusing it more sharply on the person of Christ.

(i) A SITUATION OF CONFLICT

A significant part of the johannine message is addressed to a community which has been experiencing a conflict situation and which, therefore, needs to be encouraged and strengthened in the christian way of life. This conflict situation is dramatized in the story of the man born blind. His parents refuse to answer the questions of "the Jews" because "they feared the Jews, for the Jews had already agreed that if anyone should confess him to be the Christ, he was to be *put out of the synagogue*" (9:22). "Put out of the synagogue" is a technical expression used only by John (cf. 12:42; 16:2) to reflect a concrete situation when Jewish christians were expelled formally from the synagogue, that is, from the Jewish religious community. This had serious personal and social consequences for them; it was a blow to them since they saw their faith in Jesus, the Christ, as something they could hold while they continued their synagogue life along with their traditional Jewish practices. In fact, the gospel seems to refer to some Jews of that time who were drawn to faith in Christ but out of fear of the social consequences ("reputation") they did not want to confess their faith publicly lest they be excluded from the synagogue (12:42-43).

This divisive and painful situation which separated Jewish christians from their Jewish community roots came to a head about 85 A.D. The destruction of Jerusalem (70 A.D.) had left the Jewish people deprived of their religious centre, of their cult and national life and, therefore, Judaism, weakened as it was socially and politically, felt the need to preserve itself from disintegration. In order to preserve the unity of the remnant it was necessary to eliminate any source of division on the religious-doctrinal level. Faced, then, with a sect which confessed that Jesus of Nazareth was the Christ, the synagogue at Jabneh (the new teaching centre of Judaism some miles west of Jerusalem) called on faithful Jews to consider as excluded from their community all deviators, including christians, in the context of a prayer of the synagogue service, called the "eighteen benedictions". Anyone who failed to pray this benediction aloud was taken to believe that Jesus was the Christ and was to be "put out of the synagogue" (cf. Jn 9:22).

This situation of conflict between the community addressed in the gospel and the Jewish synagogue is reflected throughout the gospel. For example, "the Jews" is frequently used in a negative and hostile sense. Directly, the gospel envisages the community situation when the johannine christians had been excluded from the synagogue by "the Jews" and, indirectly, the lifetime of Jesus when he was in conflict himself with the chief priests and some of the scribes in the sanhedrin (Mk 15:1; Jn 18:28-31). The author deliberately uses the same term, "the Jews", for the Jewish authorities of Jesus' time and for the hostile inhabitants of the synagogue in his own time. In describing the conflict between Jesus and "the Jews" he is at the same time describing the tension and conflict between the johannine community and the synagogue. This conflict seems to have resulted in death for some (cf. 16:2). As long as christians were considered Jews they would not be forced to take part in emperor worship since Judaism was tolerated by the Roman authorities, but once they were expelled from the synagogues they were no longer considered to be Jews. Therefore, failure to adhere to pagan customs and to participate in emperor worship created problems, since they could be denounced publicly as no longer belonging to the Jewish community.

It is important to read the Fourth Gospel, especially the "anti-Jewish" passages, against this particular situation when Jewish christians were excluded from the synagogue and when they were emerging as a distinct community. In different areas and different times in the first century there were varying relations between Jews who believed in Jesus and Jews who did not, and these relations were not always hostile. In johannine christianity, because of its peculiar history, we see one of the most hostile relationships. Once this gospel with its hostile reference to "the Jews" was circulated among gentile christians it acquired an anti-Semitic potential that has been abundantly and tragically actualized in the course of christian history. Paradoxically, these hostile references testify to the Jewishness of the gospel; they express the sadness and anger of christians at being severed from their Jewish roots, since "salvation is from the Jews" (4:22). For the johannine community the conflict revolves around the person of Jesus (i.e. his origin and authority as Son of God) and the law as interpreted by the contemporary normative Judaism of the synagogue. In fact, for christian Jews, the Scriptures lead to the recognition of Jesus and, therefore, testify to the thorough Jewishness of their roots and of their own self-understanding.

(ii) COSMOPOLITAN ORIGINS

While at least part of the johannine message is directed towards a community struggling for survival in a hostile Jewish world, there is also a universal outlook which takes the reader beyond the Jewish-christian problem (4:42). Gentiles, too, have an important role in the perspective of the gospel (12:20). Much of the gospel is addressed to the christian believer whether his derivation is Jewish or gentile. It gives us the impression of having taken shape in a cosmopolitan world where the johannine community had the task of resolving the problem with Judaism and also of adjusting to the multi-cultural influences in which they lived. A very early tradition links the origins of the gospel with Ephesus in Asia Minor, a flourishing, cosmopolitan seaport where there is proof of a strong Jewish presence (Rev 2:9; 3:9; Acts 19:1-7). Addressing such a world with its hellenistic, Jewish and various religious views of the world, the evangelist must have been influenced by that pluralistic milieu in communicating the christian message.

For example, a Word made flesh would remind Jews of their traditions about the wisdom and creative, life-giving word of God and possibly gentiles of the hellenistic *logos*, a kind of cosmic mind of God giving structure and order to the universe. It is difficult to determine the cultural and religious milieu of the johannine community which influenced the gospel itself. In particular, many johannine terms and expressions appear in Gnostic documents such as the Mandaean texts (a Gnostic baptist sect in Syria) and the writings of Hermetism (a hellenistic, pagan Gnosticism). But the influence may have been from John to Gnosticism and not vice versa, since our first evidence of a Gnostic system comes from the second century after the composition of the gospel. There is a similarity between some johannine ideas and expressions (e.g. "I am . . . " statements of Jesus) and the language of the recently published Gnostic library from Nag Hammadi (edited in 1977). Perhaps Gnosticism was developing in the pluralistic world of Asia Minor and this may have led John to use some of the terms. But the gospel cannot be called Gnostic. Though recent studies on the influence of Gnosticism on the gospel are inconclusive, the evangelist does portray Christ with features that would speak to men and women of diverse cultural backgrounds in order to emphasize his universal appeal for anyone, Jew or gentile.

New interest in the Jewish Targums (Aramaic paraphrases of the Old Testament which show a special character of Palestinian, Jewish thought) has led some to claim that typically johannine ideas and expressions (e.g. word, glory) are rooted in the Palestinian traditions. Besides, there is a striking resemblance between some of John's expressions and the language of the Dead Sea Scrolls (found near the Essene monastery of Qumran, which came to an end with the Roman conquest about 70 A.D.), e.g. the dualist "light-darkness" language in an ethical context, or the unusual expression "witness to the truth" (cf. Jn 5:33; 18:37). These similarities need not imply that the author of the gospel was himself an Essene or personally familiar with the Qumran literature. Rather they indicate a more general familiarity with the thought and style of expression in the Qumran literature. The ideas of Qumran must have been fairly widespread in some Jewish circles in the early first century A.D. Some suggest that the author may once have been a follower of John the Baptist (cf. Jn 1:35-36), who himself may have been an Essene. The latter viewpoint is more likely than the former, however.

The origins of the gospel are to be found in that cosmopolitan world and the gospel seeks to strengthen the faith of a community of Jews and gentiles trying to live out their commitment to Christ in a situation of conflict with the synagogue and in a pluralistic culture. They recognise Jesus as saviour of that cosmopolitan "world" of people who are loved by the Father (3:16; 4:42) but the frequent, negative use of the term "world" (cf. chs. 14-17), which means their world of Jew and gentile, was experienced as hostile because of the conflict with the Jewish synagogue and probably also because of gentile unbelief. The gospel motifs of "world", "light", "darkness" probably reflect their situation. While the gospel does express a universal outlook and emphasizes the light of Christ which shines in the johannine community of faith, at the same time their "world" is divided into those who believe and those who do not believe in Christ, into those who prefer light and those who prefer darkness (cf. 3:17-21). They would identify themselves as believers and most of those outside the community are looked upon as more or less shadowed by darkness. It is also understandable how a christian community with this view of their "world" would feel the need of strengthening the bonds of love within the community. The gospel message of "love one another" would have special meaning for them.

Recent studies explore, on the evidence of the gospel, the nature and history of the johannine community and attempt to identify various groups, e.g. "the Jews" (of the synagogue), those who "believe" in Jesus but are afraid to confess their faith publicly for fear of expulsion from the synagogue (12:42-43), other Jewish-christians of inadequate faith in Jesus (cf. 6:60-66; 7:3-5), christians of other churches, represented by Peter and the Twelve (6:67-69) as distinct from the johannine community whose traditions are linked with someone who does not belong to the apostolic group, namely, the Beloved Disciple (cf. 20:2-10). We cannot be certain about these groupings but their existence is quite likely, especially if we take into account that the gospel is directly addressed to a concrete community towards the end of the first century and that, indirectly, it can give us an insight into the life of that community at the time when the gospel was composed.

(iii) INCULTURATED FAITH

The gospel also discloses the presence of certain earlier traditions about Jesus and his message which have developed and which are integrated into a new situation and a different culture. The Fourth Gospel is a good example of how christian faith is not simply "handed on" as a static body of truths but develops and reaches a distinctive form through being inculturated and contextualized in a different milieu.

Both the distinctiveness of the gospel and the links with the living heritage of the early Church are clear from a comparison with the Synoptics. Its distinctiveness is obvious: events central to the other gospels are omitted. We have no story of the temptation of Jesus, no struggle in the garden, no confession of faith at Caesarea Philippi, no institution of the eucharist. Still, the Fourth Gospel gives us hints of these events: in ch. 12 of the temptation and Gethsemane, in ch. 6 of Peter's confession (vv. 67-71) and of the institution of the eucharist (vv. 51-58). John is less concerned with frequent episodes, incidents and miracles; at the same time the miracles he recounts (as "signs" and "works"), though fewer in number, are more spectacular and reported dramatically. They lead to more discussion and serve as a springboard for long discourses (chs. 5-6). While the basic pattern of the other gospels divides the ministry of Jesus into two parts — a Galilean and a Judean ministry — John in no way adheres to such a pattern and has Jesus freely move back and forth between the two areas.

While the Fourth Gospel represents a unique form of early thought, it does share some material in common with the other gospels: the cleansing of the temple (2:13-22), the healing of the royal official's son (4:46-54), the multiplication of the loaves (ch. 6), the anointing of Jesus and the entry into Jerusalem (ch. 12) as well as the general outline of the Last Supper, the passion, death and resurrection and many isolated verses of the sayings of Jesus. How are we to explain the similarities and the great divergencies between the Synoptics and the Fourth Gospel? Generally there is almost no evidence of a purely literary character to suggest that the Fourth Evangelist actually borrowed from one or more of the Synoptics. Therefore, it seems best to accept the general solution that John followed an *independent tradition*, which at some stage of its development had contacts with and was influenced by the streams of tradition represented in the Synoptics. This tradition would have reached him in an oral form but it is likely that he had also written sources available. Some have attempted to identify and reconstruct these written sources (e.g. a "Signs Source") from within the gospel but the task of distinguishing between the editorial and creative work of the evangelist and the written sources from which he worked is beset with great difficulties.

The differences between the Fourth Gospel and the Synoptics illustrate very strikingly how the heritage of christian faith was shaped in a new and radical way by the community situation. The Christology of the Fourth Gospel is fashioned and determined by the real, lived situation of the community. In conflict with the synagogue, one of the basic charges against christians was that they worshipped two gods: the God of the Old Testament, who must be clearly "one," and a divine Christ who makes himself equal with God (5:16-20). The gospel replies in making clear that, though Christ is a divine Messiah, a real Son, equal to God, he is not a second God, a usurper of God's power, working independently of him. Rather he acts in complete dependence on him and in no way does he act of his own accord. As the one sent, his mission and his life come from God, so that "the Father is greater than I" (14:28). The words of Jesus reflect this contemporary situation of the community. Besides, the gospel presents Jesus as a stranger from heaven because the johannine community experience themselves as strangers in and at odds with their "world" of unbelief and hostility (1:11; 3:13-19; 15:18-19; 17:6-14). Thus the gospel is reactionary and radical since it refashions, in the light of a new situation, the heritage of christian faith. New insights interpret the old and, despite the advances of johannine thought, the community retains an imagery and vocabulary that it can share with other christians (cf. 10:1-18; 15:1-17). In the Synoptics eternal life and the life of christians as children of God are gifts to be received in the future (Lk 6:35; 20:36; Mk 10:30). For John they are granted here and now through faith in Jesus (1:12; 5:24).

(iv) THE BELOVED DISCIPLE

The Fourth Gospel, then, expresses an advanced stage in the development of early christian faith and yet maintains a continuity with earlier traditions. Primarily, it discloses to us a Christ as he was presented to a community towards the end of the first century. Secondarily, it discloses the presence of earlier traditions which have grown and are now integrated into a new situation and into a cosmopolitan culture. More clearly, it gives a theology of Jesus which confers on him an insurpassable status as a Son who is one with his Father and pre-existent with him. It offers some means, however limited, for getting in touch with the life and message of the historical Jesus. Since it emphasizes the presence of Christ in the contemporary community towards the end of the first century, it is less in touch with the historical Christ than the Synoptics. However, it wishes to convey that there is a continuity between the Jesus of Palestine and the contemporary Christ whom they worship as Lord and God (20:28) and the community understood itself as heir of a tradition based on some historical witness to Jesus (1:14).

The key link with the Jesus of history is the Beloved Disciple, the witness in faith to what the gospel has recorded (21:24). He may be called an "author" of the gospel in the sense that his authority stands behind traditions contained in the gospel. He is a symbolic figure who stands for all faithful disciples beloved by Jesus and who are sensitive in faith and love to his presence (13:23; 20:8). Even though he always remains incognito, he is not just a symbol; he is also a historical figure idealized by his admiring followers, namely, the interpreters and editors of the johannine traditions (21:24). They look on him as the model of true discipleship and their father in faith since he "witnessed" to the life, death and resurrection of Jesus. As such they can call him the one "whom Jesus loved" (13:23; 19:26; 20:2). In other parts of the gospel there is mention of a man who is called "the other disciple" (18:15-16; 20:3, 4, 8), also unnamed and reticent about himself, and at the beginning of the gospel there is mention of an unnamed disciple, "one of the two" disciples of John the Baptist who follow Jesus (1:35, 40). All these references probably indicate the same person; they represent various traditions and distinct stages in the development of the allusions to an eyewitness who stands behind the gospel traditions. He is explicitly called "the Beloved Disciple" only in "the hour" of Jesus (13:1, 23) when he achieves his identity as uniquely close to Jesus. "During his lifetime, whether in the period of Jesus' ministry or in the post-resurrectional period, the Beloved Disciple lived through the same growth in christological perception that the johannine community went through, and it was this growth that made it possible for the community to identify him as the one whom Jesus particularly loved" (Brown: *Community of the Beloved Disciple*, 33).

The Gospel does not identify him as one of the twelve. In fact, by setting the Beloved Disciple over against Peter (20:8-10; 21:7) it gives the impression that he was an outsider to the group of best-known disciples, a group that would have included John, son of Zebedee (cf. Acts 3:1; 4:13; 8:14). Besides, the sons of Zebedee seem to be explicitly distinguished from the Beloved Disciple (21:2, 7). The consistent and deliberate contrast between Peter and this disciple (13:23-26; 18:15-16; 20:2-10) serves to highlight the crucial importance of the Beloved Disciple as the source of traditions which are behind the gospel and suggests that the johannine community sees itself as distinct from the apostolic churches, those churches that venerate Peter and the twelve (6:67-68).

The gospel itself, then, implies that he is not John, the apostle, but that probably he is a former disciple of John the Baptist who began to follow Jesus in Judea when Jesus himself was in close proximity to the Baptist (ch. 1). He shared the life of the Master during Jesus' last stay in Jerusalem. He was known to the high priest and his connection with Jesus was different from that of Peter who represented the Twelve. The johannine community, therefore, could not lay claim to one of the twelve as the source of their traditions but in their eyes he was a very special and beloved disciple of Jesus, their hero and their supreme tradition bearer and witness to Jesus.

This evidence drawn from the gospel seems to clash with the strong tradition, initiated in the second century by Irenaeus, that the apostle, John, published his gospel at Ephesus. On the other hand, it is strange that St. Ignatius of Antioch, who died about 110 A.D., in writing to the Ephesians, links the foundation of their community to Paul without mentioning John the Apostle or the Fourth Gospel. The Gospel would have reached its final form between 90-100 A.D., since we have to take into account the stages of its development until it reached its distinctive form, its links

with earlier traditions represented in the other gospels a..
also a conflict situation connected with an official action of
Judaism in Jabneh (c. 85 A.D.) If Ignatius had heard of a
long residence and death of the Apostle John at Ephesus, it
is remarkable, given that Ephesus appears to be the most
likely place of origin for the Gospel, that he should make no
reference to it in that particular context. Besides, at a time
when Gnostics found great support for their positions in the
Fourth Gospel, perhaps the linking of the gospel to an
apostolic author at the close of the second century was one
of the means used to show that this gospel was truly a part of
the apostolic witness to Jesus and not just a Gnostic source-
book. This could be the main reason for insisting on John
the Apostle as its author. Yet we cannot conclude definitely
that the tradition for choosing John the Apostle as author is
wrong. Ultimately, our information is rather inconclusive as
regards the *identity* of the Beloved Disciple who stands
behind the traditions contained in the gospel. However, the
validity of these traditions does not hinge on apostolic
authorship.

(v) THE COMPOSITION OF THE GOSPEL

Though the Beloved Disciple is an "author" in the sense
that his authority stands behind the gospel traditions, yet he
cannot be identified with the *writer* of the gospel (21:24).
The literary complexities of the gospel clearly indicate that
additions have been made in the course of its composition
(e.g. cf. 14:31 with 18:1 and ch. 21) and that more than one
writer is involved. It seems that the gospel is the product of
several editorial stages, finally unified into a coherent literary and theological work in the context of a "johannine
school" — a group responsible for the composition of the
gospel and Epistles of johannine Epistles.

Recent works seek to identify these various stages of
composition and to link them with stages in the history of
the johannine community. However, it is difficult to form
clear conclusions about these stages. It is likely that the

traditions behind the gospel have their origins among Jews who found that Jesus met their messianic expectations (ch. 1). The interest in Samaria (cf. ch. 4) suggests links with Samaritan converts or with Jewish-christians who evangelized in Samaria. Traditions then develop through contact with gentiles. There is a shift from an original Jewish background and a more primitive Christology to a gentile setting and to a higher form of Christology which emphasizes the divinity and pre-existence of Jesus (chs. 1-4). Then the traditions develop further through the conflict and contact of the johannine community with "the Jews" and "the world".

A commonly held view is that one distinctive figure, a dominant or master preacher and theologian (the "evangelist") gave shape to these basic traditions or "johannine" material about Jesus' works and words. He may have made one or more editions of his gospel. His work corresponds substantially to the gospel as we know it, with the exception of some additions. After his death, one of his "disciples," belonging to a "johannine school" made a final edition of the gospel, incorporating other material that the evangelist had preached and taught and perhaps also some of the material of the evangelist's co-workers.

IV. Christ in the Fourth Gospel

(i) A CHRIST-CENTRED THEOLOGY

With the Fourth Gospel the view of Christ in early christian thinking made a giant leap forward in a direction which proved eventually to be the way the later Church would go in its statements about the person of Christ. In virtually every episode of the gospel the evangelist's reinterpretation highlights the person of Jesus almost to the exclusion of any consideration of Jesus' message. Besides, we distort the features of the johannine Christ once we try to separate Christology from the rest of the gospel, from its theology of the Church, sacraments, Holy Spirit, from ecclesiology or even Mariology. The person and work of Christ is the heart of the gospel from which all other concepts are sustained.

Christ constantly discloses himself in statements about who he is, where he comes from. He has the courage to say 'I': "I am the bread of life., the light of the world., the door of the sheep., the good shepherd., the resurrection and the life., the way, the truth and the life., the true vine". But these statements are not essential definitions of Jesus or static titles of autodoxology. They describe Jesus in his activity towards community, towards the world of humanity and also towards the individual. They express the revelation of the divine commitment involved in the Father sending his Son: he is the one sent by the Father to show and to share the life of the Father, to lay down his life in love for his friends and to draw them through faith and love into the life of communion with God.

Besides, he applies to himself an Old Testament refrain: "I am he" (Is 41:4; 43:10, 13, 25 etc.). This expressed that Yahweh was the one and only liberator and Lord of the history of his people. In this way it is conveyed to a Jewish audience that Jesus has authority and power on a level with God, as the deliverer of his people, particularly through his death leading to resurrection. He is not another rival god beside Yahweh; rather he acts in union with and is dependent on his Father (13:16, 19; 8:24, 28, 58; 4:26; 6:20; 18:5, 6, 8).

(ii) JESUS, THE CHRIST AND SON OF GOD

The centre of attention is not the pre-existent Word and divine Son, but Jesus of Nazareth, the Incarnate Son sent by the Father on his mission to the world of humanity. "I came from the Father and I have come into the world; again I am leaving the world and going to the Father" (16:28). In these words the evangelist summarizes Christology as a circular movement with the focus on: "I have come into the world". He has taken his place among men and women in history; he is a Son who came from the Father as from the spring of the deity and who returns to his Father, still an Incarnate but transformed, risen Lord and Son.

The most comprehensive name or title for the person of Jesus throughout the gospel is: Son of God. But this is not just a title statically describing the nature of Jesus. Rather it is a dynamic expression of his personality in action and in his relationship to people and to God, his Father. First of all, it describes Jesus in his mission on earth in his "working" relationship with his Father for humanity. Like a son he reproduces the thought and action of his Father by *revealing* his Father and by *communicating* the divine life of his Father. This "working" relationship in union with and in dependence on his Father is also a loving relationship in which the Father takes the initiative and he himself shows loving obedience. Being a Son is an ongoing, dynamic process of belonging more and more to his Father in such a way that his death on the cross appears to be the most supreme expression of his life as a loving Son of his Father. In addition, the meaning of his name, "Son of God," is to be understood in the light of all these sayings about his oneness with his Father (cf. chs. 3, 5, 10): He is one with his Father as Son since in him the Father is revealed and salvation or life offered to believers.

"Son of God" also describes him as the glorified Jesus who has passed through suffering and death to the presence of his Father in glory and who continues his mission as a beloved Son, as he still exercises his life-giving power and reveals the Father through the power of the Spirit (ch. 17). In addition, he is a Son who is loved by the Father before the foundation of the world; the title includes his life as pre-existent Son of God who has come into the world to reveal the Father (1:14; 17:24). It is the most comprehensive name for this all-embracing, dynamic, Father-Son relationship, pre-existent, incarnate and continued in the glorification of Jesus with his Father through his cross. Other titles or names are not as comprehensive: "Son of Man" focuses more on the suffering, human Jesus exalted on the cross. Jesus is called "the Word" when his pre-existent state is the centre of attention; it describes him as pre-existent, present to God the Father outside of history and as God's self-communication to humanity in history.

The sonship of Jesus is the basis of his union of love with the Father. It is also the basis of his mission as the true messiah of his people, that is, he is the Christ because he is the Son of God (10:24-25; 20:31). Throughout the gospel various individuals confess their faith in him as the Messiah or messianic Son of God in ways which clearly show they have a limited understanding of who he is (1:49-51; 11:27, 38, 41; 4:25-26). Others guess about who he is and force their own messianic expectations on him. The gospel makes it clear that these guesses and confessions of faith in Jesus as Messiah are inadequate (cf. 1:51; 7:26-27, 40-43; 11:41). Jesus corrects them in order to show that he can be understood as the Christ who comes from the Father, who is in close relationship with him as the Son. The gospel is addressed to Jewish-christians who are separated from their roots in the synagogue because they confess that Jesus is the Christ (cf. 9:22). But writing for a community which includes gentiles and which has to find its feet in the syncretistic world of Asia Minor, the evangelist sees that Jesus is more than "the Christ" and he has to inform the title with a new content. Consequently, Jesus is a divine Son of God / Messiah who transcends the limits of all Jewish messianic expectations. Thus the johannine Messiah breaks the bounds of the limitations which Jewish hopes wished to impose on him because his being Messiah consists in his being, above all, the Son of God in union with his Father. The heart of faith for the johannine community is the commitment to Jesus of Nazareth as the Son of God.

(iii) THE HUMAN GOD AND THE DIVINE HUMAN

As the sonship of Jesus is so central, johannine Christology has been sometimes characterized as a uniquely "high" Christology, for Jesus seems to move consistently in the sphere of the divinity. Yet the evangelist sustains in tension the contrast of the mystery of Jesus as a human God and divine human. The gospel does not permit us to focus attention exclusively either on the human or transcendent Jesus or to accentuate the God in Jesus to the detriment of the man or vice versa. The human God and the divine human are inseparable even in thought for the evangelist. For when he seems to stress the humanity of Jesus by highlighting that he is a "*man*," at the same moment he underlines that he is more, that he has a special relationship with God (4:6, 29; 8:40; 10:30; 19:5). On the other hand, when the emphasis seems to be on the divine, his humanity is simultaneously noted. In his risen state and also when he describes his relationship with his Father we see his humanity in the affective, humane way he relates to his Father and to disciples (1:18; 13:23; 20:17; 21:15-17). Even in his human aloneness, abandoned by disciples, he is in loving union with his Father (16:32; 8:29).

V. The Gospel as a Community Drama

Jesus in the Fourth Gospel is the protagonist in a cosmic drama larger than historical life. The self-disclosure of Jesus and the response of people, which forms the central theme of the gospel, moves along progressively and dramatically from the very beginning (2:4) to the "hour" of Jesus when he passes to his Father through death and resurrection (13:1). The tension and conflict between light and darkness reflects the life-situation of a johannine community trying to live out their commitment to Christ. Besides, many chapters in the gospel are dramatically structured as dialogue, with strong theological content, and the action progresses towards a dramatic climax (chs. 4, 9, 11, 20). The dialogues move through a dynamic of ambiguity, misunderstanding and clarification so that the reader is held in suspense while certain issues are clarified by the evangelist through the characters involved (3:1-15; 6:25-71; 4:17-26; 14:1-11). Many of these characters are not simply historical figures, since they personify certain types of people encountered by Christ and by the johannine community. The community could recognize themselves in and identify with them; they (and we, too) could see their own life-story of faith played out through them (e.g. ch. 4; ch. 9; 12:42-43; 6:60-66; 13:23).

Dramatic irony of word and action is a feature of the gospel; ironically, statements or situations are often true and more meaningful than the characters realise (11:50; 4:12; 7:35, 42; 8:22; 19:5). There are ironical reversals of roles: the blind man is the one who sees, Jesus under interrogation becomes the interrogator, in being judged he emerges as the judge and there is a dramatic change of mood and movement as we shift from the agitated activity at the praetorium to the stillness of Calvary (cf. chs. 18-19). All these dramatic qualities of the gospel express not only the story of Jesus but also the story of the community in a dramatic, literary form which would have been a very suitable means of communication for christians in a hellenistic milieu where theatre would have been a form of entertainment frequented by all classes of society. Today, christian readers will not find it difficult to identify with this dramatic form and to see their own lives of faith also played out on stage in the Fouth Gospel. The gospel does have a certain universal, timeless and transcultural appeal. It is remarkably free of explicit mention of Church offices and structures (except, perhaps ch. 21), it seeks to root christians solidly in the person of Jesus. It faces all readers with a free and personal choice between light and darkness which must affect their personal and public life. The drama continues to be lived out in the conflict between faith and unbelief in its various forms, such as injustice and violence. The widespread violence and injustice in today's world are contemporary manifestations of the unbelief challenged by the author of the Fourth Gospel — and an understanding of the gospel helps us to situate ourselves in relation to our world just as it helped the johannine community to relate to its milieu.

Part I.
PROLOGUE, "OVERTURE."
1:1-18

OVERTURE:

1:1-18.

A WORD OF LIFE AND LIGHT.
1:1-11.

1 In the beginning was the Word, and the Word was with God, and the Word was God. [2]He was in the beginning with God; [3]all things were made through him, and without him was not anything made that was made. [4]In him was life, and the life was the light of men. [5]The light shines in the darkness, and the darkness has not overcome it.

[6]There was a man sent from God, whose name was John. [7]He came for testimony, to bear witness to the light, that all might believe through him. [8]He was not the light, but came to bear witness to the light.

[9]The true light that enlightens every man was coming into the world. [10]He was in the world, and the world was made through him, yet the world knew him not. [11]He came to his own home, and his own people received him not.

LEADING MOTIFS of the gospel are sounded in the prologue, which is a type of musical overture. These will unfold gradually and we shall be able to appreciate the overture only after hearing the whole work through. Thus already we are prepared for some recurring themes of the gospel, for example: Jesus is the truth and the source of life for man; opposed to darkness, he is light for the world; John the Baptist is a witness who summons people to faith in Jesus; as Son of God Jesus manifests his glory and through him believers become children of God.

Brief, dense phrases, sometimes similar in thought or vocabulary, give this introduction a poetic ring not equalled elsewhere in the gospel. Whether or not it originally goes back to a hymn about the Word or Jesus Christ, its purpose is to introduce the theme tune which is sustained throughout the gospel, from beginning to end (20:30-31): Jesus Christ is the saving revealer, as the Incarnate Son of God, who communicates the gift of life, a share in his Sonship, to those who give a positive response.

Some see a descending (vv. 1-10) and ascending (vv. 15-18) movement in the prologue with a kind of crescendo in the centre (vv. 11-14): those who welcome and commit themselves to the Incarnate Son of God receive God's greatest gift — they become children of God. But it is more likely that it moves in three parallel developments. The first section opens with a consideration of the Word in God and his revealing role (vv. 1-5). The central section focuses on the insertion of the Word into the history of salvation (vv. 6-14), and a conclusion treats of the revealing role of the Word, Jesus Christ, in the history of all of us who believe (vv. 15-18). The second and third of these sections (vv. 6-14, 15-18), both of which are concerned with the Word in history, open with a reference to John the Baptist and thus the prologue is firmly anchored in human history. Even when we contemplate the life of the Word in God, it remains clear to whom the Word refers. John stresses this fact by emphasizing that all that has been said applies to the man who is the Word.

Verses 1-11 speak about the Son in rather abstract terms as a "Word" who brings "life" from God and as "light" insofar as he is the revealer of God. Here the negative response Jesus received from man is stressed. But vv. 12-18 use more concrete language (Jesus, the Christ, the Father) and describe the positive response to Christ and the life of christians as children of God.

into our world. John the Baptist is a witness to Jesus in so far as he summons people to faith in Jesus as the divine revealer of God who ranks before John himself in dignity and power (v.15).

Furthermore, the christian community have come to share in the "fullness" of "grace and truth" which appeared in Jesus, the Word made flesh (vv. 14, 16). "Grace and truth" means that gift which *is* the truth, namely the revelation given in and by Christ in the fullness of time. In the Fourth Gospel "truth" is a term of revelation. It indicates the divine mystery revealed in Jesus; Jesus reveals God the Father by revealing himself as Son. Christ here is that revelation which replaces the law. Therefore, children of God share in the "fullness" of Jesus, the Word made flesh, by believing in him as the Son.

The reason why the Incarnate Son is able to reveal God and communicate his life, why he *is* the revelation of God is that he has a unique relationship with his Father. Thus no other being knows the Father directly except the Incarnate Son who is constantly "turned towards the bosom of the Father." Just as the Beloved Disciple was an intimate friend because he rested on the breast of Jesus (13:23), likewise the Incarnate, only and beloved Son is turned towards a loving Father and responds to him in loving obedience all through his life on earth. This final thought (v.18) is a good lead into the gospel which dwells on the relationship of Jesus to his Father and on the faith of disciples as they gradually discover in Jesus the only Son and the perfect reflection of the Father.

The overture had begun with the eternal Word "turned towards God" and now ends with the eternal Incarnate Son in a communion of love with his Father, in order to show that Jesus alone is capable of revealing and communicating the divine life and thus making us children of the Father. The way in which the thought develops in this overture is typical of the gospel as a whole and resembles waves breaking on the shore; each wave rises and repeats the preceding one. Similarly, the one theme is developed progressively, namely, the meaning of Jesus for man as a Word, an Incarnate Son of God, who brings saving light and life to those willing to respond. This is clarified in successive waves or stages: the Word as God's revealer brings light and life (vv. 1-5); the Incarnate, revealing Word and man's response (vv. 6-14); the gift of complete revelation and full life in Jesus (vv. 15-18).

This is the only place in the gospel where Jesus is called "the Word" because nowhere else is the pre-existent state of Jesus explicitly taught or described. However, even here John's attention is on the historical Jesus of Nazareth and by means of this title he wishes to convey that Jesus is the embodiment of divine revelation and that he cannot be understood unless one accepts his pre-existence with the Father whom he claims to reveal to humanity. As the Word-made-flesh he embodies in himself the complete revelation of God (v. 14) and the choice of the title "Word" shows that the prologue is concerned with God-man communication. But since Jesus is *the Word* who became flesh (v. 14) and who is present, turned towards God in a personal, loving and inseparable communion with him (v. 1), "the Word" primarily expresses his pre-existent state.

Thus Jesus is the perfect revelation of God's nature made to man through the man ('flesh') Jesus, because he is pre-existent Word and all that God is the Word is. His pre-existent state, as he turns towards his Father in loving union, is *outside* time. This Word, which will be spoken to humanity in the person of Jesus of Nazareth, is none other than the fullness of God himself. The "Word," then, is used exclusively to speak of Jesus' presence with the Father outside history and once we are told that the Word became flesh (v. 14) the titles of Jesus change. Now he is called "the only Son from the Father" (v. 14), "Jesus Christ" (v. 17) and "the only Son" (v. 18), which suggests that John used "the Word" to speak exclusively of the pre-existence of Jesus.

This use is close to the Old Testament "Word of God," through which God creates and which comes to the prophets. There is also a similarity between the Word of

God and the Wisdom of God in the Old Testament. Wisdom is often personified and is present with God from the beginning, an active agent in creation (Ecclus 1:1; Prov 8:22-23; Wisd 9:9). In Jewish tradition the law (Torah) is also closely linked with the Word of God and is seen as created before all things. Besides, in the Targum, the Aramaic Bible, "memra" (the word) describes God in his dealings with men. It could well be that these various strains of Jewish thought form the background of the prologue: the Word of God that came to the prophets has become personal in Jesus Christ; he is the divine Wisdom, pre-existent, but now come to teach and to give life; he is the "memra," God's presence among men. Perhaps, too, a Word made flesh would remind gentiles of the hellenistic *logos*, a kind of cosmic mind of God giving structure and order to the universe. But John's choice of "Word" rather than Wisdom implies that he is more influenced by the Old Testament Word of God. Besides, it is more in line with his own theology of the "word" understood as God's message spoken by Jesus (e.g. 17:14) and for him there is a very close connection between the word and the person of Jesus (cf. 17:17). He who speaks the revealed word of God is himself the unique source of revelation about God, the Word made flesh.

PART II.
THE PUBLIC MINISTRY OF JESUS.
1-12.

A. HISTORICAL INTRODUCTION:

The Witness of John the Baptist and the Call of Disciples

1:19-51

The Witness—John the Baptist
1:19-34

NEGATIVE TESTIMONY.
1:19-28.

[19] And this is the testimony of John, when the Jews sent priests and Levites from Jerusalem to ask him, "Who are you?" [20] He confessed, he did not deny, but confessed, "I am not the Christ." [21] And they asked him, "What then? Are you Elijah?" He said, "I am not." "Are you the prophet?" And he answered, "No." [22] They said to him then, "Who are you? Let us have an answer for those who sent us. What do you say about yourself?" [23] He said, "I am the voice of one crying in the wilderness, 'Make straight the way of the Lord,' as the prophet Isaiah said."

[24] Now they had been sent from the Pharisees. [25] They asked him, "Then why are you baptizing, if you are neither the Christ, nor Elijah, nor the prophet?" [26] John answered them, "I baptize with water; but among you stands one whom you do not know, [27] even he who comes after me, the thong of whose sandal I am not worthy to untie." [28] This took place in Bethany beyond the Jordan, where John was baptizing.

THE GOSPEL PROPER begins with the mission of John the Baptist and first spells out the description of his mission given in the prologue. The first part of John's witness to Jesus is negative: John himself was not the light and thus he says who he is not (vv.8,15,19-28). Then he positively witnesses to the light by revealing to others the mystery of the person of Jesus (vv.7,29-34) so that "all might believe in him" and subsequently sends his own disciples to Jesus (vv.7,35-37).

In the other gospels the Baptist is mainly a forerunner and a preacher of conversion, whereas in the Fourth Gospel the title "witness" epitomizes his life (5:33). He is a witness because out of his own special faith experience, a gift of God (v.35), he communicates to others the mystery of the person of Jesus and invites them to commit themselves to him in faith. Usually all testimony to the person of Jesus throughout the gospel takes place against a negative background of hostility and unbelief (15:26-27; 18:36-37). Thus there is a certain inquisitorial tone here about the interrogation of the Baptist by the Jewish authorities (vv.19,24), who are described as people who do not "know" Jesus (v.26) - this is a foreshadowing of Jesus' later accusations against those who reject him (8:19). Here John gives open witness before the Jewish authorities (vv.19-28), before the people of Israel (v.31) and, finally, before disciples (vv.35-37).

If John seems to speak very negatively about himself, it is because he is the great example of the man prepared to obliterate himself so that Jesus may be seen. At first most of his statements about himself are: "I am not . . ." or "no," so that he is not the Messiah, nor Elijah, whose return some expected (2 Kgs 2:11; 1 Mac 4:41-50; 14:41), nor the prophet like Moses who was to come (6:14; 7:40,52). Never does John make his own person the centre of his mission but rather he witnesses to another. Moreover, angels were thought of as preparing a way through the desert for the people of Israel to return from captivity in Babylon (Is 40:3); like a modern bulldozer they were to level hills, fill in valleys and thus prepare a superhighway. Similarly, the Baptist prepares a road for God to come to his people in and whose life and death results in liberation. Since there is little in the gospel which suggests that Jesus is conceived as an expiation from sin, it is likely that the evangelist wanted the liberating qualities of Christ to be understood in broader terms than that of an expiatory death.

The Call of Disciples.
1:35-51.

'COME AND SEE.'
1:35-42.

35The next day again John was standing with two of his disciples; 36and he looked at Jesus as he walked, and said, "Behold, the Lamb of God!" 37The two disciples heard him say this, and they followed Jesus. 38Jesus turned, and saw them following, and said to them, "What do you seek?" And they said to him, "Rabbi" (which means Teacher), "where are you staying?" 39He said to them, "Come and see." They came and saw where he was staying; and they stayed with him that day, for it was about the tenth hour. 40One of the two who heard John speak, and followed him, was Andrew, Simon Peter's brother. 41He first found his brother Simon, and said to him, "We have found the Messiah" (which means Christ). 42He brought him to Jesus. Jesus looked at him, and said, "So you are Simon the son of John? You shall be called Cephas" (which means Peter).

The witness, John, now leads his own disciples to Jesus by revealing to them who Jesus is and they, in turn, "followed Jesus." Here the "call" of disciples by Jesus is not described as a sudden happening, a peremptory summons to drop everything and follow out of an unreflected response. Throughout this scene we see Jesus taking the initiative and disclosing the mystery of who he is to disciples while they, in turn, discover who he is, confess their faith in him and follow him. However, this call to follow Jesus is not exclusively the initiative of Jesus, for even before Jesus invited them to "come and see" they had already "followed Jesus" (v.37). Thus it is implied here and also frequently throughout the gospel that following Jesus is a response not only to a call from Jesus but also from the Father, for the disciples are the Father's gift to Jesus and the Father himself is the source of every call to faith in Jesus (17:2,6,9).

"What do you seek,? . . . Come and see": "seeking" often expresses the quest and following of Jesus in faith (5:44;6:24,26). Besides, the gospel begins with the first disciples "seeking" Jesus and it ends with Mary Magdalene seeking in faith her risen Lord (20:15). Furthermore, to "come to" Jesus (3:18-21) and to "see" him (14:9) is the active movement towards the person of Jesus and the understanding in faith of who he is. When the evangelist wishes to draw attention to the importance of some event, he will sometimes mention the time it happened (v.39;4:6) and thus "about the tenth hour" marks how memorable is the time when the first two disciples found Jesus. About four o'clock on an afternoon in Galilee, the disciples' new life of faith, the christian community itself, begins. One of these disciples, Andrew, expresses his response of faith in Jesus the Messiah but attention focuses on the initiative of Jesus who discloses himself by revealing Simon's future and by giving him a new name. This change of name (Gen 17:5,15) means that Peter takes up a new way of life and that he will exercise a special position of support for the christian community.

PHILIP AND NATHANAEL.
1:43-51.

> ⁴³The next day Jesus decided to go to Galilee. And he found Philip and said to him, "Follow me." ⁴⁴Now Philip was from Bethsaida, the city of Andrew and

ing such a charge with the claim that Jesus is in an entirely different category than the Baptist.

B. FIRST STAGE OF JESUS' SELF-REVELATION.

2:1-4:54

THE "SIGN" OF THE WINE.
2:1-11.

2 On the third day there was a marriage at Cana in Galilee, and the mother of Jesus was there; ²Jesus also was invited to the marriage, with his disciples. ³When the wine gave out, the mother of Jesus said to him, "They have no wine." ⁴And Jesus said to her, "O woman, what have you to do with me? My hour has not yet come." ⁵His mother said to the servants, "Do whatever he tells you." ⁶Now six stone jars were standing there, for the Jewish rites of purification, each holding twenty or thirty gallons. ⁷Jesus said to them, "Fill the jars with water." And they filled them up to the brim. ⁸He said to them, "Now draw some out, and take it to the steward of the feast." So they took it. ⁹When the steward of the feast tasted the water now become wine, and did not know where it came from (though the servants who had drawn the water knew), the steward of the feast called the bridegroom ¹⁰and said to him, "Every man serves the good wine first; and when men have drunk freely, then the poor wine; but you have kept the good wine until now." ¹¹This, the first of his signs, Jesus did at Cana in Galilee, and manifested his glory; and his disciples believed in him.

JESUS, having promised disciples that they will "see greater things," now in the first part of his public ministry (chs. 2-4) discloses the mystery of his person in a miracle at Cana (2:1-11) and in his authoritative action in the temple in Jerusalem (2:12-22). This leads on to the description of the various responses of individuals, Nicodemus, the Samaritan woman and an official at Cana, to the self-revelation of Jesus (2:23-4:54). In this way the central motif of the gospel unfolds: Jesus reveals himself as the Messiah and the Incarnate Son of God and those who respond to him in faith receive a share in his life.

The meaning of this miracle at Cana comes at the end of the account as a reflection of the evangelist himself (2:11), for whom it is a "sign" through which Jesus manifests his "glory" and disciples come to believe in him. A "sign," according to its most characteristic use in the gospel, is a miracle which symbolizes a spiritual reality about Jesus, reveals who he is and brings or strengthens faith in him (20:30-31). However, there is less emphasis on the concrete details and results of the miracle than on its spiritual symbolism. Here the changing of water into wine at the marriage feast symbolizes the abundant gifts that come with the "hour" of Jesus' death leading to resurrection. This symbolic meaning goes back to the Old Testament where wine in abundance is a symbol of the richness and overflowing plenty that God promises for the days of messianic deliverance (Amos 9:13; Hos 2:24; Joel 3:18; Is 25:6).

There are pointers to this deeper meaning all through the account, even in the introductory setting (vv.1-2). For example, the wedding celebrations, which would have gone on for seven days in the groom's home, and which Jesus, his mother and disciples attended, may already be a reminder of the gifts that Jesus brings in his "hour" since a wedding feast is symbol of the days of happiness and the abundant gifts which the Messiah brings (Is 54:4-8;62:4-5). Besides, Mary is called "the mother of Jesus" and also "woman" (v.4) in the only two scenes where she appears in the gospel, that is, here and in the "hour" beside the cross (19:25-27;6:42). She is never called "Mary" in the gospel but preferably "mother of Jesus," a title which focuses on her Son and on her relationship with him as mother. In the Orient it was also a complimentary title for a woman who has been fortunate enough to bear a son.

The dialogue, too, between Jesus and his mother, which prepares for the miracle (vv.3-5) suggests its inner meaning. "Has my hour yet come?": this is, more probably, a question and resembles those questions typical of the gospel which invite different responses (7:35; 8:22). At Cana, in one sense, the "hour" of Jesus has arrived and thus the question could be answered in the affirmative, for here with full authority Jesus begins his mission, that is, the work given to him by his Father (4:34; 17:4). It is a time when he reveals his "glory" (2:11), for in working this miracle he manifests his divine power and life as Son of God. However, in another sense, the "hour" of Jesus, so frequently associated with his death and resurrection (7:6,8,30; 8:20; 13:1) has not arrived yet. Only then will Jesus give true "wine" of a different brand, that is, all those gifts promised for the days of salvation and which come through his death, for example, the new life and the Holy Spirit (19:34). Consequently, that "glory" which Jesus manifests at Cana looks forward to the hour when he is "glorified" (12:23; 13:31-32; 17:1,5) and when he reveals his glory, namely, his life, his power and his love for his Father as a loving and beloved Son.

In addition, the first question of Jesus to his mother shows that what happens at Cana receives its full meaning at the hour of his death: "Woman, what have you to do with me?" This form of question, also suggestive of different responses, asks about the nature of a relationship between two persons (Josh 22:24-25; Judg 11:12; 1 Kgs 17:18): "What is the relationship between you and me?" This reply of Jesus to his mother is not discourteous or harsh; neither is it a refusal, because she did not ask any-thing of him; nor is it a reproach, because Jesus takes the initiative and works a miracle and Mary is not put off, for she asks the servants in words also found in Gen 41:55 to do all that Jesus will ask.

Moreover, the question is open to a negative and a positive response both of which are true for there is and there is not a rupture in the relationship between them. In questioning the relationship which united him so far with his mother, Jesus suggests that a change is to take place in this relationship. Negatively, a family relationship by which she can influence him as a mother and expect him to help, ceases. But positively, there is a new relation-ship between them which transcends any human tie of flesh and blood (Lk 2:49; Mk 3:31-35; Lk 11:27-28). In this new relationship Mary allows herself to be influenced by him and her reaction to Jesus' question is precisely this: she does not exercise her influence on him as a mother any more but she gives instructions to the waiters, thus allowing herself to be influenced by him and placing herself at his service. In that way she shows her disponibility of faith and hope as regards her Son and, by accepting this imposed renunciation, foregoes her privileged position as mother and even invites others to be docile to her Son. Thus her position as mother of Jesus in the flesh gives place to a spiritual motherhood of the faithful and the "mother of Jesus" becomes "woman." This title of honor expresses the dignity of her new relationship with Jesus in the order of faith and hope and therefore is far from being an offensive expression of undue reserve or distance on the part of Jesus towards Mary.

In addition, this changed relationship points to the "hour" of Jesus, so that the implications of his question are: "My relationship with you as my mother, in which I should be influenced by you, has changed and will change even more in my hour when you will be influenced by me in a special way." In the "hour" in its full sense, as she

stands by the cross, the "mother of Jesus" is addressed
again by Jesus as "woman" (19:25-27) and thus on his
initiative her relationship with him is transformed. His
death now puts an end to her physical motherhood as
regards Jesus but instead she becomes mother of the
Beloved Disciple. However, there is not a total break in
her relationship with him for she received from him the
Beloved Disciple and, more important, she received the
gift of "life," which is symbolised by the water flowing
from the side of Jesus (19:34). Thus she, who allowed
herself to be influenced by him through faith and hope
at Cana, now receives life, a gift flowing from the death
of her Son; she, who had given him physical life and
influenced him as a mother is, in turn, influenced by his
life-giving power. Thus the transformation of her relationship, already implied at Cana, is completed on Calvary
and she is no longer "mother" but "woman." Now she
has a relationship of a new kind with Jesus and with
other believers which is implied in the title "woman."
This recalls Eve who "shall be called 'woman' because
she was taken out of man" (Gen 2:23), and who is also
"mother of all living" (Gen 3:20). Therefore at Cana,
Mary's relationship with Jesus undergoes a transformation in so far as she believes and hopes in him, allowing
herself to be influenced by him, and thus she represents all
believers, the church. Implicitly, too, she is mother of the
faithful because she invites others to be docile in faith to
her Son (2:5). However, this will become more explicit in the
"hour" when she will be constituted mother of the Beloved
Disciple.

The relationship, then, between Mary and her Son looks
to the "hour" when new "wine," new life will be given by
Jesus. Besides, the descriptions of the miracle itself (vv.6-8)
and its consequences (vv.9-10) also convey a second level
of meaning for they highlight the quality, the abundance and
divine origin of the gifts, the new life or the new "wine"
which flows from the death of Jesus: the many large jars
are "filled to the brim" with wine which is "good" (vv.6-7,10)

but the steward did not know "where it came from" (v.9). Throughout the gospel the question of the divine origins of Jesus is posed in the form: "From where . . .?" (7:27;8:14; 9:29;19:9). Here the gift of new life which comes through the death of Jesus is rich and good for man, for it comes from a divine source, from the Son of God.

THE NEW TEMPLE.
2:12-22.

> [12]After this he went down to Capernaum, with his mother and his brothers and his disciples; and there they stayed for a few days.
> [13]The Passover of the Jews was at hand, and Jesus went up to Jerusalem. [14]In the temple he found those who were selling oxen and sheep and pigeons, and the money-changers at their business. [15]And making a whip of cords, he drove them all, with the sheep and oxen, out of the temple; and he poured out the coins of the money-changers and overturned their tables. [16]And he told those who sold the pigeons, "Take these things away; you shall not make my Father's house a house of trade." [17]His disciples remembered that it was written, "Zeal for thy house will consume me." [18]The Jews then said to him, "What sign have you to show us for doing this?" [19]Jesus answered them, "Destroy this temple, and in three days I will raise it up." [20]The Jews then said, "It has taken forty-six years to build this temple, and will you raise it up in three days?" [21]But he spoke of the temple of his body. [22]When therefore he was raised from the dead, his disciples remembered that he had said this; and they believed the scripture and the word which Jesus had spoken.

The scene changes from the joyful wedding celebrations, where Jesus is surrounded by believers, that is, by his mother and disciples, to the temple in Jerusalem where there is conflict, menace and incredulity of the "Jews," who are probably the religious authorities hostile to Jesus (vv. 18,20; Mk 11:15-19,27 par.; 2:12 bridges two scenes). Their unbelief contrasts with the faith of disciples (vv. 11,22) and already the gulf of misunderstanding and unbelief opens between Jesus and the religious authorities, so that at the end it is only disciples who believe (2:22: for the meaning of "the Jews" in the gospel cf. p. 251). Again an action of Jesus is the subject of a special reflection of the evangelist (vv. 11, 21-22) and the events of the "hour" of Jesus are recalled (vv. 17-22). In fact, throughout the whole scene John directs our attention from the Jerusalem temple to the new temple, which is the person of the glorified Jesus (v. 19).

Once the scene is set, the first part of the account focuses on the action and words of Jesus and also gives a comment of the evangelist himself (vv. 14-17). Then the reaction of the "Jews" is described for they draw an enigmatic response from Jesus and do not understand (vv. 18-20) and once again there is a comment of the evangelist (vv. 21-22). In this atmosphere of hostility, the first of the three Passovers mentioned in John (6:4; 11:55), along with the implications about his death and resurrection (vv. 19-22), look ahead to the Passover time of his death. This forceful action of Jesus takes place in "my Father's house" (v. 16), in the temple, which in the Old Testament is called "the house of God" (Mk 2:26; Lk 2:49) and therefore Jesus is a divine Son in communion with his Father. Besides, it is already implied that he will become a new temple after his resurrection, when he draws disciples into a life of communion with himself and his Father (14:2-3).

It is only after his resurrection, with the help of the Spirit (14:26), that disciples grasp in the light of Scripture (Ps 69:10) the meaning of Jesus' action in the temple. Moreover, his concern for the temple, which he expresses here so dramatically, will antagonize the religious leaders and contribute to his death (v. 17) because for them his authoritative action is equivalent to a claim to be Messiah. The prophets, too, had protested against the secularization of the temple and had promised that in the days of the Messiah "all will be holy in Jerusalem and no merchant will be found in the temple" (Zech 14:21; cf. Jer 7:11; Mal 3:1). That is why his opponents demand a proof, a "sign" that he was the Messiah, authorized by God to act with such forcefulness.

Jesus, therefore, promises a "sign" which is that of his risen body, for his body will be destroyed and in three days Jesus will raise himself. His statement is ambiguous since "destroy" and "raise up" can refer to a building as well as to the body of Jesus. It could, therefore, have been understood by the audience as a messianic claim to be the one who replaces the temple in three days, that is, in a short time (Hos 6:2). Besides, the Old Testament had foretold a rebuilding of the temple (Ezek chs. 40-46; Tob 13:10-12). But after the resurrection, with the help of the Spirit who "brings to remembrance" the teaching of Jesus (14:26), disciples will interpret the words of Jesus with reference to his death and resurrection: Jesus, through his power as Son, will raise himself in three days from the dead and become a new temple in so far as through him believers enter into a living communion with the Father (vv. 19-20; 10:17-18; 1 Cor 15:4). Thus the risen Jesus is the "place" of a new worship, and through faith in him, which is the interior work of the Spirit, believers enter into a new relationship with God their Father (4:23-24; 14:2-3). Consequently, the Incarnate Jesus, who clears out the temple, is a sign of a new temple who is the glorified Jesus; in other words he is both the sign and what is signified. However, only later will disciples come to understand the meaning of Jesus' words and to see that his death and resurrection were confirmed by Scripture (Pss 69:10; 16:10).

A Book of "Signs."

The "signs" described in the gospel are miracles which receive their explanation through the words of Jesus, and if they are understood or "seen" in faith, they reveal who Jesus is (6:26). Thus they reveal Jesus and are also a call to faith in him (20:30-31). Besides, they are both real and symbolical for they are events which point to a deeper, spiritual reality about his person. For example, Jesus changes water into wine, he multiplies the loaves, he heals a blind man and raises Lazarus from the dead. All these point to the mystery of Jesus as one who brings a new "wine," who is the bread of life, the light of the world, the resurrection and the life.

Besides, there are three kinds of reaction to the "signs" or miracles of Jesus: no faith (12:37), partial and imperfect faith (2:23;3:2;4:48) and that true faith which discovers the mystery of Jesus as the Messiah and Incarnate Son of God (2:11;20:31). Consequently, "sign" sometimes has a negative sense in order to reflect that imperfect faith or attitude with regard to the miracles of Jesus in those people who look for "proofs" of faith (2:18;6:30) or for the sensational without looking beyond the meaning of the miracle to the reality of who Jesus really is (2:23-25;4:48;6:26).

The resurrection appearances of Jesus are also "signs" for they are miraculous events and actions of Jesus calling people to believe in him as Lord and God (cf. 20:29-31). Finally, in the Old Testament God also worked "signs" which were considered miraculous and revealed the presence of God. In addition, they were intended to confirm the faith of the people in their God or in Moses as his authentic representative (Ex 3:12;10:1-2). Likewise in the gospel they reveal and confirm the person of Jesus as a Messiah and Son sent by the Father. Finally, they are somewhat similar to but also different from "works" (cf. p. 150).

The Dialogue of Jesus with Nicodemus: 2:23-3:21.

SEEKING SIGNS.
2:23-3:2

> [23]Now when he was in Jerusalem at the Passover feast, many believed in his name when they saw the signs which he did; [24]but Jesus did not trust himself to them, [25]because

> he knew all men and needed no one to bear witness of
> man; for he himself knew what was in man.
> 3 Now there was a man of the Pharisees, named Nico-
> demus, a ruler of the Jews. ²This man came to Jesus by
> night and said to him, "Rabbi, we know that you are a
> teacher come from God; for no one can do these signs
> that you do, unless God is with him."

Nicodemus, who is the first of three people selected to
illustrate various responses to Jesus, was a "teacher" of
the law and probably a member of the Sanhedrin (3:10;
7:50). The lead-up to his conversation with Jesus shows that
his view of Jesus was typical of "many" who were impressed
in a superficial way by his "signs" (probably his miracles:
v.23). These looked on Jesus as a wonder-worker, a teacher
of the law with a mission from God to communicate true
and right teaching according to God's will. People would
have said about such a man: "God is with him" (3:2).

But since God is "with" Jesus in a much deeper sense,
this kind of faith, which is preoccupied with signs, was
very partial as far as Jesus was concerned. Therefore, he
did not accept their homage which was offered for the
wrong reasons. Their faith in him, "in his name," that is, in
his person as revealed and grasped in faith, was far from
true faith in him as the beloved Son of God (cf. 3:18). Thus
he was not willing to have them as genuine disciples and
companions, and his reserve in the face of this kind of
acceptance was based on his experiential knowledge of their
shaky dispositions of faith (2:23-25). Consequently, his
purpose in this dialogue is to lead Nicodemus from that kind
of attitude to a more authentic faith in himself. Nicodemus
had come to him by night not only out of fear of his companions in authority but he also comes in the darkness of
such deficient faith to him who is the light (3:19-21;12:42;
19:38). For Jesus as the revealer of God's love and life is
the light: "he who is in the darkness comes to Jesus, the
light" (Augustine).

BORN OF THE SPIRIT.
3:3-10

> [3]Jesus answered him, "Truly, truly, I say to you, unless one is born anew, he cannot see the kingdom of God." [4]Nicodemus said to him, "How can a man be born when he is old? Can he enter a second time into his mother's womb and be born?" [5]Jesus answered, "Truly, truly, I say to you, unless one is born of water and the Spirit, he cannot enter the kingdom of God. [6]That which is born of the flesh is flesh, and that which is born of the Spirit is spirit. [7]Do not marvel that I said to you, 'You must be born anew.' [8]The wind blows where it wills, and you hear the sound of it, but you do not know whence it comes or whither it goes; so it is with every one who is born of the Spirit." [9]Nicodemus said to him, "How can this be?" [10]Jesus answered him, "Are you a teacher of Israel, and yet you do not understand this?"

The first part of this dialogue, whose theme is the meaning and origin of genuine faith in Jesus, gives the condition for (vv. 3-10), while the second part gives the content of authentic faith (vv. 11-21). Thus faith is first looked at from God's point of view, in so far as it is the work of his Spirit, and then from man's point of view, for it is also his activity directed towards the person of Jesus. The dialogue moves in typically johannine fashion as Jesus first makes a statement (v. 3), which is misunderstood (v. 4). Then he offers clarification (vv. 5-8) but this leads to further incomprehension (vv. 9-10) and the dialogue concludes with a final revelation of Jesus (vv. 11-21). One gets the impression at the end that Nicodemus is none the wiser and that his faith has not matured. However, later in the gospel we see a growth in his faith when at a moment of great conflict he speaks out that Jesus should get a hearing, and finally when he is a faithful follower at the tomb who helps to give Jesus an honourable burial (7:51; 19:38).

At the beginning Nicodemus seems so sure of his own position: "We know . . ." (v. 2) but after he has spoken with this unchallengeable ecclesiastical authority, Jesus challenges him about his need for that genuine faith which is the work of God's Spirit. Jesus then speaks about the condition for a life of faith and expresses it in two ways: it is a "begetting from above" (or "anew": 3:31;19:11,23), and a "begetting from water and Spirit" (vv.3,5). This life of faith is a new birth for it is an initial communication of new, divine life that brings one forth as God's child: more specifically it is a new relationship with God through Jesus, one not previously experienced. Moreover, the two basic principles of this new life are baptism (water) and faith (Spirit). Though it commences with baptism it is not a once and for all event for it is a continued life of faith and an ongoing life-giving communion with Jesus. But Nicodemus, who is captivated by Jesus as a great teacher, needs the gift of faith which is the ability to "see" in Jesus the presence of God's life, that is, the kingdom of God (v.3) and it is only through the Spirit that the believer "sees" the kingdom in Jesus and enters into the "kingdom," namely, into a life of communion through faith with Jesus (vv.3,5,36).

But man out of his own resources cannot rise to this life of faith in Jesus because it belongs to a completely different order of being, to the divine ("spirit") as opposed to the purely human which is weak ("flesh": 6:63-64). Rather it is an activity of the Spirit of God who is described as a wind in so far as we cannot fathom the operation of the Spirit, who is a mysterious power. Thus the person who shares the quality of the Spirit shares his life and his unfathomable quality. Yet the existence of him who is born through the Spirit to the life of faith in Jesus is a reality, though mysterious. Nicodemus, however, does not grasp what Jesus is saying for he interprets this regenerated person of faith on a physical level (v.4). As a teacher of Scripture he should have been familiar with the Spirit of Yahweh who interiorizes the law and renews life (Jer 31:31-34; Ezek 36:26-27; 37:9). Yet Nicodemus would have interpreted this with reference to the renewal of the community of Israel. Here the newness of Jesus' teaching is that each individual needs to be regenerated through the Spirit and it is at this point that Nicodemus stumbles, for in the case of the individual he can conceive only of a physical birth into the community (v. 10).

THE MEANING OF FAITH.
3:11-21.

> [11]"Truly, truly, I say to you, we speak of what we know, and bear witness to what we have seen; but you do not receive our testimony. [12]If I have told you earthly things and you do not believe, how can you believe if I tell you heavenly things? [13]No one has ascended into heaven but he who descended from heaven, the Son of man. [14]And as Moses lifted up the serpent in the wilderness, so must the Son of man be lifted up, [15]that whoever believes in him may have eternal life."
>
> [16]For God so loved the world that he gave his only Son, that whoever believes in him should not perish but have eternal life. [17]For God sent the Son into the world, not to condemn the world, but that the world might be saved through him. [18]He who believes in him is not condemned; he who does not believe is condemned already, because he has not believed in the name of the only Son of God. [19]And this is the judgment, that the light has come into the world, and men loved darkness rather than light, because their deeds were evil. [20]For every one who does evil hates the light, and does not come to the light, lest his deeds should be exposed. [21]But he who does what is true comes to the light, that it may be clearly seen that his deeds have been wrought in God.

The conversation switches from faith as a generation of new life by the Spirit to faith as a personal activity of man directed towards the person of Jesus and as a life-giving relationship with the Son of God. This faith is described in three stages:

(a) Faith is founded in the person of Jesus for he is the perfect revealer of God whose revelation reaches its climax in his exaltation on the cross (vv. 11-15). Thus faith is man's active response to Jesus as the true revealer of God who communicates what he experiences in his intimate life with the Father. As one who knows God he speaks to man God's own truth, not just the truth about man's own destiny and life of faith ("earthly things") but also the mystery of his own person ("heavenly things"). For no human being is able to know and reveal these "heavenly" things except the perfect revealer who came from God to reveal his own life with the Father (v. 12). Besides, the life-giving faith of the christian is directed towards him who was "lifted up" on the cross, just as Moses lifted up the image of the serpent on a pole so that those bitten by the serpents might see it and be cured (Num 21:4-9; Wis 16:6-7). Hence, Jesus is enthroned or "lifted up" like a king on the cross where he is a source of saving life for the person who believes in him (8:28; 12:32).

(b) The saving revelation of Jesus is the manifestation of God's love for the world which is not directed towards the "judgment" or condemnation of the world but towards the salvation of those who believe in the Son of God (vv. 16-18). Thus the breadth of God's love is the world of mankind for whom Christ died and the depth of his love is his most precious gift, his only beloved Son, whose whole life, especially his death, reveals how much God wants to share his own "eternal life" with mankind. Also the person of faith enters into a life-giving communion with Jesus and comes to share in this saving "life" through faith. But this must be a genuine faith as opposed to that faith which seeks signs (2:23; 3:18). Such faith is a movement towards the person of Jesus, the giving of oneself to him and accepting him as he has revealed himself, that is, as the only, beloved Son, generated from the Father and the supreme expression of God's love ("believing into the name . . ."). But the person who deliberately rejects Jesus, condemns himself.

(c) This revelation of God in Jesus, or the coming of the light into the world, evokes a double response: the majority remain incredulous while others respond in faith (3:18-21). First, the positive response of faith in Jesus is described

from various points of view. It is a "coming to the light" or
an active movement in faith towards Jesus as revealer of
God. In addition, faith is an internal self-appropriation of
the meaning and message of Jesus who is the truth, or self-
revelation of God. Thus "doing the truth" means making
this truth one's own or part of one's living. Faith is also a
question of "works" (rather than "deeds" in the RSV),
which are not to be identified with "good works" or actions
which are morally good. Rather they are personal responses
of faith, such as listening to the word of Jesus, seeing Jesus
as the Son of God, confessing faith in him, and they embrace
those various activities in the process of faith through which
the believer enters into communion with God through Jesus
(v. 29; cf. 6:29; 14:12; 2 Jn 8).

On the other hand, the negative response to Jesus is
judgment or self-condemnation for to reject Jesus is to
alienate oneself from a life-giving communion with him.
The reason why people did not believe in Jesus, that is, come
to the light, is because they made a deliberate choice against
Jesus which is manifested in their negative responses
("works" rather than "deeds" is the more correct rendering),
such as the refusal to accept his word and to acknowledge
their faith in Jesus as the Son of God (2 Jn 7). Moreover, because they are not willing to come to the light who is Jesus,
they do not see the evil of their own incredulity (v. 20).

A FINAL WITNESS.
3:22-30.

> [22]After this Jesus and his disciples went into the land
> of Judea; there he remained with them and baptized.
> [23]John also was baptizing at Aenon near Salim, because
> there was much water there; and people came and were
> baptized. [24]For John had not yet been put in prison.
> [25]Now a discussion arose between John's disciples and
> a Jew over purifying. [26]And they came to John, and said
> to him, "Rabbi, he who was with you beyond the Jordan,
> to whom you bore witness, here he is, baptizing, and all
> are going to him." [27]John answered, "No one can receive
> anything except what is given him from heaven. [28]You

yourselves bear me witness, that I said, I am not the Christ, but I have been sent before him. [29]He who has the bride is the bridegroom; the friend of the bridegroom, who stands and hears him, rejoices greatly at the bridegroom's voice; therefore this joy of mine is now full. [30]He must increase, but I must decrease."

At this stage the sudden appearance of John the Baptist confirms the special quality of the new life and baptism associated with Jesus (cf. v.5). John's mission is subordinate to him who baptizes with the Spirit (1:33), and the many who come to believe in Jesus are the Father's gift to his Son (v.27 could also mean: if only a few people have come to John, that is all God has given him). In describing his mission in relation to Jesus, the Baptist compares himself to the friend or best man of the groom whose duty is to arrange all for the wedding and prepare for the bride. Now that he has prepared the bride, who is the people of Israel, for the coming of Jesus, the messianic bridegroom, he must fall into the background with joy and dignity. Now he himself sees his hopes fulfilled through the coming of Jesus the Messiah whose presence is for him a source of true joy.

A UNIQUE REVEALER.
3:31-36.

[31]He who comes from above is above all; he who is of the earth belongs to the earth, and of the earth he speaks; he who comes from heaven is above all. [32]He bears witness to what he has seen and heard, yet no one receives his testimony; [33]he who receives his testimony sets his seal to this, that God is true. [34]For he whom God has sent utters the words of God, for it is not by measure that he gives the Spirit; [35]the Father loves the Son, and has given all things into his hand. [36]He who believes in the Son has eternal life; he who does not obey the Son shall not see life, but the wrath of God rests upon him.

A final reflection of the evangelist summarizes some of the leading ideas of the chapter: Jesus is transcendent and he alone can reveal the life of God which is manifest in himself as a Son. Yet he, the unique revealer, meets with a negative response. But the person who responds positively confirms that God, who does not deceive or disappoint man, is speaking through Jesus, and to listen to Jesus is to hear God himself because he has the fullness of the Spirit in order to communicate the word of God. Besides, that "generation" of faith in believers through the Holy Spirit, which Jesus discussed with Nicodemus, continues through the word of Jesus for this word is active and effective in them only through the power of the Spirit (cf. v. 6). But Jesus continues still to give the Spirit, that is, to "baptize with the Spirit" (1:33) and his words continue to be Spirit-filled and life-giving for he has received all power from his Father, in particular, the power to give life through his word to those who believe (vv. 35-36; cf. 6:63). But so long as people reject him who is the bringer of life, they cannot now or in the future share in the life of God, because to persist in unbelief is to remain in death, that is, in a state of alienation from God (v. 36).

The Gospel of Belief.

Faith is the key theme not only of Jesus' dialogue with Nicodemus and the rest of the chapter but also every chapter in the gospel is about faith, from beginning (1:9-13) to end (20:30-31). Therefore is has been rightly called the gospel of belief. Still, not once does the abstract word "faith" occur in the gospel because there is only the personal *activity* of believing which is almost exclusively directed towards the person of Jesus. One may believe something *about* Jesus, for example, that he is Messiah and Son of God (20:30-31) or give credence to him by accepting as true what he *says* (2:22). But the element of personal commitment to Jesus is expressed in the most frequent phrase: "believing into" Jesus: "He who believes in (to) me has eternal life" (6:47; 3:18).

This "believing in (to)" Jesus goes far beyond accepting his message for it is a movement towards the person of Jesus, an attachment to him as the promised one and Son of God in such a way that the believer appropriates the very life of

Jesus. Thus faith means to enjoy a life-giving relationship with him and to give oneself to Christ in dedication and full confidence. Besides, the reality of faith is expressed in other ways: to "follow," "receive" (welcome), to "come to" Jesus, to "hear" his "voice" (an active obedience to his word). Finally, "seeing" Jesus often includes more than physical vision since it also means to contemplate him in faith.

Furthermore, believing in Jesus leads to "knowing" him; but this knowledge extends beyond the understanding of faith (6:69) and includes the experience of the person of Jesus in understanding and love, and a fellowship and communion of life with him (17:3).

As regards the source of faith in Jesus, it is the activity of God and man. The Father himself is the origin of faith for it is his "work" as he draws people to faith through the word of his Son and through the inner action of the Holy Spirit (6:29,44;14:17,26). But Jesus also is a source of faith, as throughout the gospel he invites and brings people to commit themselves in faith to him. The Holy Spirit, too, is active in the life of faith for he "regenerates" man into the life of faith, and as the Spirit of truth he interiorizes the word and self-revelation of Jesus (16:13-15).

Faith not only originates from the Father and the Son but it is also directed towards Jesus and through him to the Father because in Jesus we come to know what the Father is like (14:9). But we come to know the Holy Spirit in a different way: through his working within us, "for he dwells with you and will be in you" (14:17).

Jesus and the Samaritan Woman.
4:1-42.

AT THE WELL.
4:1-6.

4 Now when the Lord knew that the Pharisees had heard that Jesus was making and baptizing more disciples than John ²(although Jesus himself did not baptize, but only his disciples), [3]he left Judea and departed again to Galilee. [4]He had to pass through Samaria. [5]So he came to a city of Samaria, called Sychar, near the field that Jacob gave to his son Joseph. [6]Jacob's well was there, and so Jesus, wearied as he was with his journey, sat down beside the well. It was about the sixth hour.

The Fourth Gospel is *the* gospel of personal relationships, for throughout Jesus not only speaks about his own relationship with his Father, with disciples, and the relationship of disciples with one another (e.g. 15:1-17), but he also reveals himself in his relationships with individual people, for example, with Nicodemus, with a blind man (ch. 9), with the Beloved Disciple and with other followers, both men and women. In these relationships he takes the initiative in so far as he discloses himself to people and they, in turn, discover who he is and what he means to them.

This meeting with the Samaritan woman is the story of Jesus progressively revealing himself and inviting her to faith. She gives a positive response and comes gradually to discover who he is and she not only comes to faith in him but also shares this faith with other Samaritans who, in turn, come to accept him and his message (vv. 27-42). Her response goes further than that of Nicodemus who represented official Judaism and orthodoxy. But she portrays schismatic Judaism which broke off from Jerusalem (v. 9). Her faith and the faith of the Samaritans are inspired by the words of Jesus (vv. 19,29,39,41,42) and thus the faith of these half-pagan Samaritans, who accept Jesus so wholeheartedly and welcome him to their homes, stands out in contrast to the superficial, miracle-hungry faith of the Jerusalem crowds (2:23-25) and to the bewilderment of Nicodemus.

A framework (vv. 1-3) before the actual introduction to the story (vv. 4-6) transfers the setting away from Judea, which appears throughout the gospel as an area of hostility for Jesus (7:1;11:7-8). Thus Jesus, turning away from the unbelieving Pharisees (v. 1), makes his way towards Galilee and on the journey he finds faith in Samaria. If this gospel stresses often that Jesus is a transcendent Son of God, there are also moments when we feel the touch of Jesus' humanity more closely than in any other gospel. Here, for example, Jesus sits down "exhausted" by the sweltering midday heat (the sixth hour) at Jacob's well. In the Old Testament, too, the well is a favourite setting for meetings and relationships between men and women which influence the course of salvation history (Gen 24:11-27: Abraham and Rebecca; 29:1-21: Jacob and Rachel; Ex 2:15-21: Moses and Seporah). Here such a setting along with the precise indications of time and place (cf. 1:39), underline the importance of this meeting for the Samaritan woman and for her people (v. 42).

THE GIVER OF LIVING WATER.
4:7-15.

[7]There came a woman of Samaria to draw water. Jesus said to her, "Give me a drink." [8]For his disciples had gone away into the city to buy food. [9]The Samaritan woman said to him, "How is it that you, a Jew, ask a drink of me, a woman of Samaria?" For Jews have no dealings with Samaritans. [10]Jesus answered her, "If you knew the gift of God, and who it is that is saying to you, 'Give me a drink,' you would have asked him, and he would have given you living water." [11]The woman said to him, "Sir, you have nothing to draw with, and the well is deep; where do you get that living water? [12]Are you greater than our father Jacob, who gave us the well, and drank from it himself, and his sons, and his cattle?" [13]Jesus said to her, "Every one who drinks of this water will thirst again, [14]but whoever drinks of the water that I shall give him will never thirst; the water that I shall give him will become in him a spring of water welling up to eternal life." [15]The woman said to him, "Sir, give me this water, that I may not thirst, nor come here to draw."

As in the dialogue with Nicodemus, Jesus progressively reveals himself to the Samaritan woman and invites her to faith. His statements are also punctuated by her interventions which show that she cannot grasp the level of meaning he intends (vv.11,15,25). But as Jesus clarifies them further, she gradually grows in her understanding of who he is. However, at first Jesus is just another "Jew" (v.9) and then she begins to wonder whether he is greater than the patriarch Jacob (v.12). Astonished at this stranger's knowledge of her hidden past, she admires him as a "prophet" (v.19;9:17), which is a general term expressing that he is a man of God. She even seriously thinks that he may be the Messiah (vv.25,29) for the Samaritans, too, expected a Messiah, a new Moses, priest and prophet who would overcome his opponents and restore true worship on Mount Gerizim. But the climax of the confession of faith in this scene is the firm acknowledgment by the Samaritan people that he is the universal Messiah-Saviour (v.42: "we know").

This pedagogy of faith, in which Jesus takes the initiative and the woman discovers the mystery of who he is, begins with Jesus revealing himself as a "giver" of "living water" (vv.7-15). But the starting-point of this relationship could not have been more unfavourable because Jesus was a Jew from the southern kingdom and she was a Samaritan. There was opposition between the northerners and the Jews of the south since the Samaritans refused to worship at Jerusalem and they had helped foreign powers (the Syrians) in their wars against the southern kingdom. Furthermore, communication between the two peoples was forbidden by law, probably even to the point that Jews placed a ritual taboo on eating or drinking from the same vessels and dishes (v.9). Later on, in a moment of great hostility, Jesus is accused of being a "Samaritan" and of "having a demon" as if they were one and the same thing (8:48). However, the disciples on their return from shopping are not so much shocked that Jesus is speaking to a Samaritan as by the fact that he is speaking to a woman (v.27).

But Jesus breaks through all these social and political taboos and discloses the mystery of himself and when he describes himself as the giver of living water he speaks on two levels. First, the fresh, flowing, spring water ("living") from the well is a symbol of his own special gift of "living water." This is "a gift of God" for "everyone" who wishes it and confers the gift of "eternal life." Now this living water is the Holy Spirit in so far as he interiorizes within the believer the self-revelation of Jesus. Consequently, it is closely linked with the person of Jesus. In the Old Testament the "gift of God" *par excellence* was the revealed word of God, the law of Moses, and in a parched climate such as that of Israel flowing, spring water was a frequent symbol for God's self-revelation, particularly his word, his law—this is "drink" for man (Sir 24:19-31; Prov 14:27). The water of which Jesus speaks "wells (bubbles) up to eternal life," i.e. in order to confer eternal life. This brings out the special vitality of the force of the Spirit which interiorizes Jesus' self-revelation, or his word, so that it becomes life-giving, for the Holy Spirit is the Spirit who deepens and enlivens faith in Jesus, who is the truth, that is, the revelation of God (vv. 23-24).

THE WORDS OF THE PROPHET.
4:16-19.

> [16]Jesus said to her, "Go, call your husband, and come here." [17]The woman answered him, "I have no husband." Jesus said to her, "You are right in saying, 'I have no husband'; [18]for you have had five husbands, and he whom you now have is not your husband; this you said truly." [19]The woman said to him, "Sir, I perceive that you are a prophet."

The next initiative of Jesus discloses further the mystery of who Jesus is. Here knowledge of the woman's life underlies his simple request to her to call her husband, and when she answers evasively that she has no husband he shows how well he knows her life-sory. This special knowledge of an individual's life, which evokes wonder and questions, is part of the picture of Jesus in the gospel (1:48). Thus by disclosing the secrets of her life Jesus leads her to discover more deeply who he is and she responds by calling him a prophet. Thus his efforts are not directed primarily to bringing the woman to abandon her sinful way of life, but he draws her first to believe in him after which she becomes aware of her guilt and of the low opinion which her fellow Samaritans have of her, for this is implied in her own comment (vv.29,39).

DAYS OF A NEW WORSHIP.
4:20-26.

> [20]"Our fathers worshiped on this mountain; and you say that in Jerusalem is the place where men ought to worship." [21]Jesus said to her, "Woman, believe me, the hour is coming when neither on this mountain nor in Jerusalem will you worship the Father. [22]You worship what you do not know; we worship what we know, for salvation is from the Jews. [23]But the hour is coming, and now is, when the true worshipers will worship the Father in spirit and truth, for such the Father seeks to worship him. [24]God is spirit, and those who worship him must worship in spirit and truth." [25]The woman said to him, "I know that Messiah is coming (he who is called Christ); when he comes, he will show us all things." [26]Jesus said to her, "I who speak to you am he."

Jesus goes on to speak to the woman of a new era, the advent of which will make the dispute concerning the place of true worship irrelevant. Jesus himself will usher in this new era. At present the Samaritans do not possess true knowledge of God, for their worship grew out of national and political ambitions, whereas the Jews have the legitimate worship of God and "salvation," that is, the Messiah and Saviour comes from the Jewish people (v.42).

However all such discrimination ceases because the true worship which Jesus proclaims will not be restricted to one place (Mal 1:11; Zeph 2:11), such as Mount Gerizim or Jerusalem, for its centre is the person of Jesus who is the truth in so far as he is the self-revelation of God (14:6). This new christian worship, which Jesus brings, is the worship of God as Father in a communion of faith with Jesus (the truth) through the interior action of the Holy Spirit. The believer comes to know the Father and to enter into a relationship with him through Jesus, the revealer of the Father, by accepting the word of Jesus (14:7). Thus the activity of the Holy Spirit brings believers into a communion of faith with Jesus so that the risen Jesus is the new "place" of worship, the new temple (2:19-21; 14:26; 16:13). This life of faith in Jesus is the work of God through his Spirit, for God is Spirit, that is, he acts, communicates himself through his Spirit.

The dialogue draws to a close as the woman expresses her hope in a Messiah who would "disclose" to her all those things which Jesus has been discussing with her. Jesus now replies in a solemn statement that he is such a Messiah and in addition that he is a divine, transcendent revealer of God: "I am he": this phrase of the Old Testament, expressing the transcendent power of God, is implied in Jesus' reply (cf. 6:20).

FOOD AND A HARVEST.
4:27-38.

> [27]Just then his disciples came. They marveled that he was talking with a woman, but none said, "What do you wish?" or, "Why are you talking with her?" [28]So the woman left her water jar, and went away into the city, and said to the people, [29]"Come, see a man who told me all that I ever did. Can this be the Christ?" [30]They went out of the city and were coming to him.

[31]Meanwhile the disciples besought him, saying, "Rabbi, eat." [32]But he said to them, "I have food to eat of which you do not know." [33]So the disciples said to one another, "Has any one brought him food?" [34]Jesus said to them, "My food is to do the will of him who sent me, and to accomplish his work. [35]Do you not say, 'There are yet four months, then comes the harvest'? I tell you, lift up your eyes, and see how the fields are already white for harvest. [36]He who reaps receives wages, and gathers fruit for eternal life, so that sower and reaper may rejoice together. [37]For here the saying holds true, 'One sows and another reaps.' [38]I sent you to reap that for which you did not labor; others have labored, and you have entered into their labor."

The conversation between Jesus and his disciples (vv. 27-38) and the response of the Samaritans (vv. 39-42) centre on Jesus' mission as revealer and on man's response of faith. Just as he had spoken about his "gift" on two levels of meaning through the image of living water, Jesus now describes his mission in terms of "food" (vv. 31-34), for the disciples had gone to buy food and wanted him to eat. He also describes his mission as a "harvest" (vv. 35-38) since this was suggested by the ripe grain-fields around Schechem. What directs and sustains Jesus ("the food") and claims him totally is doing the will of his Father and bringing to perfect completion the mission which he has received from his Father (17:4). Besides, his mission is a "work"—this is a term which describes his whole activity of revealing God, of leading people to faith and conferring on them his own gift of life (4:14).

The grain-fields ripe for harvesting are a symbol of Samaritans coming to believe in Jesus and the messianic days of salvation are harvest time which has arrived with the presence of Jesus, the Messiah (4:26; Joel 4:13). This "work" or the harvesting of Jesus consists in leading people to faith and into a communion of life with himself and the Father (4:23-24). Already the seed of faith which he has sown in Samaria is ripening and this is a source of joy: "Lift up your eyes" (v.35): the Samaritans are already coming to faith and thus the mission of Jesus is meeting with an enthusiastic response. But Jesus does not carry out his mission by himself because the Father (who sows) and Jesus (he reaps) together accomplish the work of leading them to faith through which they share in the "eternal life" of the Father and the Son (v.36). The disciples, too, after the resurrection, will continue the mission of Jesus and his Father and, in anticipation, the evangelist thinks of the later mission of "disciples" in Samaria. Their mission, also, is a work of harvesting, of leading to faith in Jesus and into a communion of life with him and they "reap" where the Father and Jesus have sown (v.37).

SAVIOUR OF THE WORLD.
4:39-42

> [39]Many Samaritans from that city believed in him because of the woman's testimony, "He told me all that I ever did." [40]So when the Samaritans came to him, they asked him to stay with them; and he stayed there two days. [41]And many more believed because of his word. [42]They said to the woman, "It is no longer because of your words that we believe, for we have heard for ourselves, and we know that this is indeed the Savior of the world."

The fields already ripe for the harvest remind Jesus of the Samaritans coming to faith in him through the word of the woman, who shares her experience of Christ with them, and also through the presence of Jesus himself among them. There is a progressive growth in their faith, too; they take their first step in faith when they believe because of the woman's testimony and this faith in Jesus spreads ("many more") and becomes firmer, because they no longer believe just because of her words and they "know" about Jesus with certainty (v.42). Their faith grows deeper, too, because they now believe in a universal Saviour-Messiah. Besides, it is a faith which comes from a personal encounter with Jesus. Just as the disciples came to faith by "staying" with Jesus when they were invited to "come and see," so also the faith of the Samaritans takes root when they invited him to "stay" with them and when "he stayed there two days" (v.40; 1:39).

This story (4:1-42), in the typically johannine style, begins with an initiative of Jesus. It is also constructed very dramatically. Both the dialogue and the action move progressively to a climax. It is divided into scenes by changes in conversation partners and the dialogue moves through a dynamic of ambiguity, misunderstanding and clarification. Besides, a series of christological titles progressively reveal Jesus' true identity (vv. 19, 25, 42). A similar chain to titles linked the discipleship stories in the first chapter (1:35-51).

The woman's responses reflect the belief of Samaritans that a prophet like Moses would come in the last days and decide questions about worship that were hotly debated between Samaritans and Jews (vv. 19-20). Jesus, the Messiah, responds to Samaritan expectations of a teacher and revealer to come but he makes it clear that he goes beyond such expectations since he also claims the title "I am he" (vv. 25-26). The story then culminates with the confession that Jesus is "the saviour of the world"; he is not only a saviour for Jews but also for gentiles. This title, widely used in early christianity (cf. Lk 2:11; 1 Jn 4:14; 2 Tim 1:10) can unite Jews and Samaritans in a single confession rather than separate them.

A SECOND SIGN AT CANA.
4:43-54.

> [43]After the two days he departed to Galilee. [44]For Jesus himself testified that a prophet has no honor in his own country. [45]So when he came to Galilee, the Galileans welcomed him, having seen all that he had done in Jerusalem at the feast, for they too had gone to the feast.

⁴⁶So he came again to Cana in Galilee, where he had made the water wine. And at Capernaum there was an official whose son was ill. ⁴⁷When he heard that Jesus had come from Judea to Galilee, he went and begged him to come down and heal his son, for he was at the point of death. ⁴⁸Jesus therefore said to him, "Unless you see signs and wonders you will not believe." ⁴⁹The official said to him, "Sir, come down before my child dies." ⁵⁰Jesus said to him, "Go; your son will live." The man believed the word that Jesus spoke to him and went his way. ⁵¹As he was going down, his servants met him and told him that his son was living. ⁵²So he asked them the hour when he began to mend, and they said to him, "Yesterday at the seventh hour the fever left him." ⁵³The father knew that was the hour when Jesus had said to him, "Your son will live"; and he himself believed, and all his household. ⁵⁴This was now the second sign that Jesus did when he had come from Judea to Galilee.

The healing of an official's son completes the first stage of Jesus' public ministry (vv. 43-45 bridge the scenes), as the account moves back to Galilee, once more to Cana. Here an official belonging to the staff of King Herod (either an administrative official or a soldier) along with all his household respond positively to Jesus. His faith contrasts with the unsatisfactory faith of the Galileans in general (vv. 44-45) for the welcome they give him is just as shallow as the reaction which had greeted him earlier in Jerusalem (2:23-25). Jesus, the prophet, expects no great gains in his homeland as his own countrymen were not open to the mystery of who he is and they remained fascinated merely by the prodigious quality of his miracles (4:48).

Against this background of partial faith, the official is picked out as an example of a positive response in faith to Jesus. Again Jesus discloses himself, in particular, his life-giving power, and the official responds in faith (v. 53). In spite of differences, the same incident probably lies behind this account and that of the Synoptics (Mt 8:5-13;

Lk 7:1-10) but John stresses the faith responses of the official and, in particular, the life-giving power of Jesus and the "sign" value of the miracle (vv.50,53-54). For John the miracle as a "sign" points to the mystery of who Jesus is.

The restoration of physical life through the word of Jesus, which is effective even at a distance (vv.50,53), along with the emphasis on death (vv.47,49) and life (vv.50,51,53), is a sign of a more profound reality about Jesus: Jesus, as Son of God, gives life to those who receive his word in faith. This official, a man of faith, had come down to Cana to ask Jesus to heal his child who was on the point of death, suffering from a serious fever, and now through him Jesus addresses the Galileans as a whole by pointing out the unacceptable quality of that faith which relies exclusively on the spectacular ("signs and wonders": v.48; cf. vv.44-45). Thus for Jesus the purely sensational is not a valid motive for faith and he wishes to lead the official to true faith based on what the miracle as a sign would tell him about Jesus. The repeated "your son will live" (vv.50,53) suggests Jesus' life-giving power through his word. The official who sets off full of confidence in this word of Jesus has a faith which goes beyond the level of those who are fascinated by the sensational and also beyond the level of faith in his word, since he and his household are led through this sign to believe in his person, just as disciples came to believe in Jesus as a result of the first sign at Cana.

The two signs at Cana are similar to one another, for in both Jesus returns to Galilee, there is a request, an apparent refusal, the questioner persists, a request is then granted with the consequence that a group of people (disciples, a household) believe in Jesus. Furthermore, the incident unifies three chapters (2-4) by recalling the first sign. Finally, "life" is the keynote of this scene which prepares for another healing story linked with the life-giving power of Jesus (ch. 5) and the account points even further ahead to the story of Lazarus where the physical miracle is a "sign" that Jesus is the resurrection and the life (11:25).

"Life" in the Gospel

God's greatest act of friendship towards man through Jesus is described as a sharing in his "life" and this is what it means to be a child of God (1:12-13). Besides, "life" permeates the whole gospel from beginning to end (1:14;20:31). This is not natural life but rather that divine life which the Father shares with his Son and which is communicated to those who through faith enter into a life-giving relationship with Jesus (3:16).

The "living" Father is the source of life (5:26;6:57) but life is most frequently linked with the person of Jesus whose mission is to give life (10:10). Also, the Holy Spirit, through whom men come to faith and grow in faith, generates this life within them by helping them make the word part and parcel of their lives (3:3-5;6:63). The communion of life with Jesus and the Father is described in terms of knowing, loving and mutual indwelling (10:14; 14:19:17:3). But this life is not a thing or quality that stands on its own, for it flows from a life-giving relationship with a person, that is, with Jesus and through him with the Father. Thus, being in relationship with them is to "live" in the fullest way possible for man.

The sharing in God's life is both a present and a future possession. Besides, this life is "eternal" not so much because it belongs to the next life but because it is indestructible, since it is God's own life which knows no death and which will continue beyond physical death (8:51; 11:25-26). In fact, eternal life in the gospel is an all-inclusive term for salvation because it takes in everything which the Saviour sent by God brings from God to man.

Natural life is man's most treasured possession and thus "life" is a suitable symbol for the most precious of divine gifts lying beyond man's reach. But the starting-point is the Old Testament idea of life which included the sum total of all that was good in life. However, the fullness of life was limited to earthly and material existence and consisted in a long life of peace and happiness in the promised land together with honour, riches, friends and a life of fidelity to God's word (Deut. 4:40). Only in later Jewish writings did it come to mean a new and transcendent life beyond the grave. But in the Fourth Gospel life is a present and a future divine gift. Most of all, it is knowing the Father and the Son with a vital, personal touch so that the existence and activity of the believer consists in that personal relation to God which is the supreme gift and carries with it all other gifts.

working." [18]This was why the Jews sought all the more
to kill him, because he not only broke the sabbath
but also called God his own Father, making himself
equal with God.

This healing, which points to the mystery of who Jesus
is, is a "work" which Jesus does along with his Father on the
sabbath (vv. 9-10,17;7:21) and here the physical healing is
linked with healing forgiveness: "See, you are well! Sin
no more that nothing worse may befall you" (v. 14). When
the paralyzed man receives forgiveness on the sabbath
through the saving "work" and mercy of Jesus and his
Father (v. 17), this restoring of vitality points to the life-
giving power which the Son possesses in fullness and exercises along with his Father (5:21). Anything "worse" implies more than physical death since it can also mean the
loss of true "life" which results from deliberately rejecting
Jesus and the life he offers (5:21) and which consists in self-
condemnation or that "judgment" to which Jesus refers in
his discourse (5:24). This story is similar to the account
of the blind man. For example, Jesus "sees" that the person
is in need of healing and he goes to "find" him after the
healing (vv. 6,14;9:1,35), while in the face of opposition the
man confesses that Jesus is his healer (v. 15;9:11). In both
scenes healing and sin go together (v. 14;9:1-3,40-41) and
Jesus is accused of violating the sabbath (v. 15;9:16). Finally,
both incidents point to the mystery of the person of Jesus
as the "light of the world" (ch. 9) and as the Son who
"works" together with his Father (5:17).

But there are noticeable differences. For example, the
paralyzed man does not show the same persistence and he
disappears from the scene quickly. But here the interest
centres on the sabbath setting and its implications as regards
Jesus so that the whole discourse hinges on the statement of
Jesus: "My Father is working still, and I am working"
(v. 17). The main points of this discourse are: (a) The relationship between Jesus and his Father. Vv. 19-30 are also
one of the gospel's key statements about Christ. (b) Eternal

life and judgment (also in vv. 19-30) and (c) the theme of "witness" (vv. 31-40).

First of all, Jesus defends his "work" of healing on the sabbath against "the Jews," who are probably the religious authorities hostile to Jesus (cf. 9:16), by reminding them of their own traditional belief that God "worked" on the sabbath. But since this sabbath privilege was special to God, Jesus was claiming to possess a divine prerogative, to be above the sabbath and to be divine in the strict sense when he asserted his right to work by healing or restoring life (with its deeper implications) just as God "my Father" worked. Therefore, his opponents accuse him of usurping divine power and authority - he, a mere creature, is setting himself up against the creator and Lord of the world. Besides, he also claimed that God was his Father.

FATHER AND SON.
5:19-30

¹⁹Jesus said to them, "Truly, truly, I say to you, the Son can do nothing of his own accord, but only what he sees the Father doing; for whatever he does, that the Son does likewise. ²⁰For the Father loves the Son, and shows him all that he himself is doing; and greater works than these will he show him, that you may marvel. ²¹For as the Father raises the dead and gives them life, so also the Son gives life to whom he will. ²²The Father judges no one, but has given all judgment to the Son, ²³that all may honor the Son, even as they honor the Father. He who does not honor the Son does not honor the Father who sent him. ²⁴Truly, truly, I say to you, he who hears my word and believes him who sent me, has eternal life; he does not come into judgment, but has passed from death to life.

²⁵"Truly, truly, I say to you, the hour is coming, and now is, when the dead will hear the voice of the Son of God, and those who hear will live. ²⁶For as the Father has life in himself, so he has granted the Son also to

have life in himself, [27]and has given him authority to execute judgment, because he is the Son of man. [28]Do not marvel at this; for the hour is coming when all who are in the tombs will hear his voice [29]and come forth, those who have done good, to the resurrection of life, and those who have done evil, to the resurrection of judgment.

[30]"I can do nothing on my own authority; as I hear, I judge; and my judgment is just, because I seek not my own will but the will of him who sent me."

In response to the hostile reaction of his audience, Jesus explains the special quality of his relationship with God, his Father. While he is a real Son ("my Father") and equal to God (vv. 17-18), he is not a usurper of God's powers, working independently of him, for he acts in complete dependence on his Father and in no way does he act out "of his own accord" (vv. 19,30; cf. 7:18;8:28). Rather he is one sent by the Father and he carries out his will in all that he does. Therefore, in all his actions he looks to ("sees") the Father from whom he receives the impulse of his action, as was the case in his healing of the paralyzed man (v. 19). Thus his action takes place at the same time as, along with that of his Father, particularly in the matter of "life-giving" and "judging" (cf. vv. 21-22,25-27). Consequently, the invisible, transcendent God works through the Incarnate Word in whom he is present with his will, work and word (1:1-3). The Incarnate Jesus is God and man alike and, therefore, he can carry out the saving work of God for man. In fact, such is the unity between Father and Son that the work of the one is also the work of the other and there is no action of the Son which is not the work of the Father, just as there is no activity of the Father which would go beyond or be independent of that of the Son (v. 19).

The relationship between Jesus and his Father, which is summarized in the expresson "my Father" (v. 17), is described in terms of mutual knowledge and love. The

Son "hears," "sees" while the Father "shows," "loves" (vv.19-20,30). The Father opens himself fully in love to his Son and gives him both the power and impulse to act. Thus he hands over, allocates his works to the Son ("shows"), associating him without reserve in his work and also in "greater works" to come (v.20). These probably refer to miracles such as the healing of the blind man (ch. 9) and the raising of Lazarus (ch. 11) in so far as these have for their inner meaning that they will manifest Jesus' true power to give "life" to those who believe. Jesus shares in this life-giving power of the Father in dependence on his will (v.21). Thus he has life in himself, like the Father, that is, in similar fullness and power, for this has been communicated to him from eternity and now as the Incarnate Son he will share it with believers.

This divine, eternal life has its source in the Father who communicates it to Jesus without losing anything of the richness of his own life (v.26). Therefore, the Son is due the same honour as his Father since he is sent by the Father himself and represents him (v.23). Judgment, too, a characteristic prerogative of God in the Old Testament is also shared by Jesus, so that God's dignity and power is also in Jesus (Dan 7).

Eternal Life and Judgment:
Already Realized and Yet to Come

Eternal life is a present as well as a future gift (vv.21, 24-25,29). Consequently, there is a "judgment" in this life (vv.22,24,27a) and in the future (v.29), "on the last day" (11:25). These two aspects of life and judgment, of which Jesus speaks, have been called "realized" (in the present) and "future eschatology." But the Fourth Gospel stresses realized eschatology even though the present (v.27a) and future (v.27b) judgment are merged together, since the mention of the "Son of Man" opens the horizon to the final coming.

Eternal or indestructible life is possessed by the disciple who commits himself now to the person of Jesus and accepts his word for living (v.24). Such life comes from the Father and is also the gift of Jesus to those who enter into communion with him through faith. The power of Jesus to give life to the believer is here called "raising the dead" (v.21), a phrase which was originally used in the christian community for the final raising from the dead but applied here by the evangelist to the present life-giving communion with Jesus through faith. Besides, this present sharing in the divine life through faith is called a "passing from death to life" because all are "dead" without Christ (v.24) and to hear "the voice of the Son of God" is man's active response to Jesus summoning him to faith through which he enters into a communion with Christ in this life (v.25). But eternal life is also a future possession for there is a "resurrection of life," that is, which consists in or leads to life, when those who have done good will be summoned by the "voice" of the glorious Son of Man from the tombs to enjoy eternal life forever (Mk 13:26; Mt 13:41; 25:31; Lk 21:36).

But there is also an obverse side of "eternal life" in the Fourth Gospel which is called "judgment." This, however, is not an action of God by which he discriminates between the good and the evil; neither is it a positive action of God or Jesus. Rather it is what happens to man when he deliberately rejects Jesus and the life-giving communion he offers (3:16-17). Besides, it is not a power of the Father or of Jesus as distinct from their power to give life, but it is a self-deserved reality, an action by which man condemns (judges) himself in rejecting Jesus. Thus "judgment" is self-condemnation, man's refusal of life either now or "on the last day" (vv.24,29;11:24). Yet Jesus has power to give life and to "judge" insofar as he reveals God and offers life so that a division takes place before him: some believe, others reject him and "judge" or condemn themselves (3:16-31). There is also a "resurrection of judgment" (that is, of final self-condemnation) at the end for those who have done evil (v.29). Yet the actual resurrection of "the body" is not described but it is presumed because of the mention of "tombs" (v.28) along the lines of the current Jewish tradition (Dan 12:2).

THE WITNESSES TO JESUS.
5:31-40.

> [31]"If I bear witness to myself, my testimony is not true; [32]there is another who bears witness to me, and I know that the testimony which he bears to me is true. [33]You sent to John, and he has borne witness to the truth. [34]Not that the testimony which I receive is from man; but I say this that you may be saved. [35]He was a burning and shining lamp, and you were willing to rejoice for a while in his light. [36]But the testimony which I have is greater than that of John; for the works which the Father has granted me to accomplish, these very works which I am doing, bear me witness that the Father has sent me. [37]And the Father who sent me has himself borne witness to me. His voice you have never heard, his form you have never seen; [38]and you do not have his word abiding in you, for you do not believe him whom he has sent. [39]You search the scriptures, because you think that in them you have eternal life; and it is they that bear witness to me; [40]yet you refuse to come to me that you may have life."

Jesus now explains to his hearers why they should accept all these claims he has made by appealing to a series of "witnesses" in his favour. "Witnessing," which is a major theme in the gospel, means to reveal something about the person of Jesus and thus invite others to believe in him. In Jewish law a man could not be condemned on the testimony of one person and here, in a matter concerning testimony in favour of himself, Jesus appeals to the witness of "another," namely, his Father (vv.31-32). In fact, the Father is at work giving witness to Jesus as the one sent by him, for the Father, as the source of all faith and all revelation, reveals Jesus and invites people to believe in him (cf. v.36). Though a series of different witnesses are brought forward in support of Jesus and his mission, they are all reduced to the testimony of the Father as their source (vv.32,37).

First, the Baptist's mission is recalled since he was a witness who called on people to believe in Jesus, the truth or the self-revelation of God, and his whole mission was directed to Jesus, the truth and the light (1:6-8,15,19-34). Yet John was only a lamp which shone only for a while as he was greeted with a temporary, passing acceptance. But his testimony originates from the Father who sent him and it is a call to faith from God even if it is a human testimony (v.34;1:7). The second witness is the "works" of Jesus, namely, all his activity of leading people to faith and to a life-giving communion with him. These, too, are the works of the Father who "assigned" them to his Son (v.36). Thus all these witnesses are the Father's way of inviting people to faith in his Son but, in fact, Jesus' listeners have no direct access to the Father and their only way of knowing God now is through Jesus for the person who "sees" the Son on faith "sees" the Father (v.37;14:9). However, they are not open to the various ways in which God calls them to believe in Jesus. The Scriptures, too, which are the words of the Father, witness to Jesus for not only individual sayings of Scripture are to be interpreted in the light of Jesus, but also the Old Testament as a whole is ordered to and speaks of him. His audience, however, is unreceptive as they are unwilling to come to Jesus in faith and enter into a relationship of faith that leads to life (vv.39-40;6:35).

REASONS AND CONSEQUENCES OF UNBELIEF. 5:41-47.

[41]"I do not receive glory from men. [42]But I know that you have not the love of God within you. [43]I have

come in my Father's name, and you do not receive me; if another comes in his own name, him you will receive. [44]How can you believe, who receive glory from one another and do not seek the glory that comes from the only God? [45]Do not think that I shall accuse you to the Father; it is Moses who accuses you, on whom you set your hope. [46]If you believed Moses, you would believe me, for he wrote of me. [47]But if you do not believe his writings, how will you believe my words?"

Facing such a distinctively negative response from his listeners, Jesus gives the reasons (vv.41-44) and the consequences of their unbelief (vv.45-47). Jesus is not seeking human approbation when he calls for faith for he seeks only the honour and the will of his Father. However, his experience of his audience (here probably the religious authorities) is that they are not open to God's love, since they do not welcome in faith him whom God himself has sent among them. But the root cause of their lack of faith and love is that they are too concerned about the approval of others and not sufficiently open to the manifestation of God's glory and divine life present in Jesus. They had supposedly defended Moses' law when they accused him of breaking the sabbath in healing the paralytic (v.45; cf. v.16). But now Moses himself is their accuser because they are rejecting someone who is sent by God. The Scriptures themselves, which represent Moses, give evidence in favour of Jesus and they should lead them to believe what Jesus says, for if they accept Moses' message, they must also accept his (Deut 18:15; Jn 6:14,30-33;8:56).

The "Witness" of the Gospel

Unlike other New Testament writers, this evangelist never calls his work or his message about Jesus a "gospel" ("good news": *euaggelion*). Rather, the Fourth Gospel is a "testimony," a witnessing about Jesus (21:24). This image of "witnessing" comes from the law court; we witness

or give evidence in favour of someone by declaring something we know about him or what we may have experienced of him and we ask people to believe the truth
about him. Similarly, any "witness" in the gospel *reveals*
something about who Jesus is and invites others to *faith*
in him. Though the image belongs to a legal background,
which constituted a central area in the life of the Jewish
people, the reality it expresses in the gospel concerns
revelation and faith.

The gospel presents the life of Jesus as a trial or a vast
lawsuit between Jesus and the forces of evil and unbelief,
a type of confrontation in court where Jesus is the central
figure and various "witnesses" in his favour come forward.
Besides, this conflict between Jesus and those who oppose
him, namely, the "world," still continues for John into the
time of the church when the Holy Spirit and disciples still
give witness to Jesus. However, "witness" is only one of
the terms which belong to the vocabulary describing the
life of Jesus as a lawsuit for the gospel abounds with
legal terms, for example, judge, judgment, confess, con-
vict, paraclete. Moreover, the roles are sometimes
reversed in the conflict as those who judge Jesus are
judged themselves and as he becomes their judge (8:15-16;
12:31). Similarly, those who accuse Jesus of violating
the law of Moses are themselves accused by Moses
(5:45).

There is a variety of witnesses in the gospel, some of
whom have been mentioned in ch. 5: the Father, John
the Baptist, Scripture, the "works" of Jesus. In addition,
Jesus himself gives witness for he reveals the mystery of
himself as the revealer of God and he invites people to
faith in him (18:37). But the witness of the Holy Spirit
is interior for within the hearts of believers he strengthens
faith in Jesus (15:26). Christians also give witness to Jesus
because their life of faith and love are an invitation
to others to follow him (15:27). The testimony of the
Beloved Disciple concerns something which he has experienced in faith about Jesus, for he saw the meaning of

the water and the blood which flowed from the side of Jesus, testifies about it and invites us to faith in the exalted Lord (19:34,37). Similarly, the Baptist has a vision of faith in which it is communicated to him that Jesus is the one to whom the Spirit is given and he then testifies that Jesus is the chosen one of God (1:34). The witnessing of disciples, too, is based on their faith experience of Jesus: "And you also are my witnesses because you have been with me from the beginning" (15:27). Likewise, Jesus gives testimony about what he himself has seen in the presence of his Father but his testimony differs from that of all other witnesses because it is based on a direct vision of his Father (3:32).

By way of summary, all testimony derives from the Father because he is the source of all revelation and of every call to faith in Jesus. However, Jesus himself is the sole object of every testimony in the gospel, for all witnesses give evidence in favour of Jesus as they reveal the mystery of his person and invite others to commit themselves to him in faith. But christians can give witness to Jesus only through the inner strength and enlightenment about Jesus which they receive from the Spirit. In this way testimony according to the Fourth Gospel is the work and an experience of the Father, Son and Spirit.

The Sign of the Bread.
6:1-59.

JESUS FEEDS HIS PEOPLE.
6:1-15

6 After this Jesus went to the other side of the Sea of Galilee, which is the Sea of Tiberias. ²And a multitude followed him, because they saw the signs which he did on those who were diseased. ³Jesus went up on the mountain, and there sat down with his disciples. ⁴Now the Passover, the feast of the Jews, was at hand. ⁵Lifting

up his eye, then, and seeing that a multitude was coming to him, Jesus said to Philip, "How are we to buy bread, so that these people may eat?" ⁶This he said to test him, for he himself knew what he would do. ⁷Philip answered him, "Two hundred denarii would not buy enough bread for each of them to get a little." ⁸One of his disciples, Andrew, Simon Peter's brother, said to him, ⁹"There is a lad here who has five barley loaves and two fish; but what are they among so many?" ¹⁰Jesus said, "Make the people sit down." Now there was much grass in the place; so the men sat down, in number about five thousand. ¹¹Jesus then took the loaves, and when he had given thanks, he distributed them to those who were seated; so also the fish, as much as they wanted. ¹²And when they had eaten their fill, he told his disciples, "Gather up the fragments left over, that nothing may be lost." ¹³So they gathered them up and filled twelve baskets with fragments from the five barley loaves, left by those who had eaten. ¹⁴When the people saw the sign which he had done, they said, "This is indeed the prophet who is to come into the world!"

¹⁵Perceiving then that they were about to come and take him by force to make him king, Jesus withdrew again to the mountain by himself.

Again Jesus performs a miraculous action (vv.1-15) whose inner meaning is spelled out at length (vv.25-59): this bread which he multiplies for the crowd is a "sign" which discloses Jesus as the one who sustains us with his living word and with the gift of his own life in the eucharistic bread. Not only the sign of the bread but also the reassuring words to disciples, "It is I" (v.20), along with the Christological "I am" statements (vv.25,35,41, 48-51), all draw our attention beyond the words of Jesus and beyond the eucharist itself to the person of Jesus who communicates his life-giving power through them.

John's account of the miracle is more Christ-centred than that of the Synoptics (Mk 6:31-44; 8:1-9 par.). For example, Jesus "sees" the crowd "coming to him" (v.5);

he takes the initiative in feeding them and he distributes the loaves and fish himself to the crowd (vv. 10-11). They, on their part, acclaim him as a prophet like Moses sent to feed his people and as the fulfilment of their hopes for a messianic king (vv. 14-15). He "takes" and "gives" (distributes) the bread, he "gives thanks" (vv. 11,23)—this is also the language of the liturgy and recalls the Last Supper accounts (Mk 14:22-25 par.; 1 Cor 11:23-26). Also, the gathering up of the fragments so that they are not "lost" (vv. 12-13) calls to mind the gathering up of the fragments at the end of the christian eucharist (*Didache* 9:3-4) and the imperishable life (v. 27) which christians share in the eucharist. The bread, then, is a sign of Jesus' eucharistic gift.

Furthermore, this scene looks to Israel of the past and to the eucharistic community of the future. First of all, Jesus is like Moses through whom God had provided the manna-food for his people Israel during the Exodus (Ex 16). Thus Jesus is the new prophet like Moses who, on a Passover feast, feeds his people with a new manna (vv. 4,14; Deut 18:15), which is his word since bread and manna are symbols of God's word or law (Wis 16:26). Moreover, this manna is also his eucharistic bread. Then the mention of Passover links the eucharist with the liberating and life-giving event of Jesus' death which is a new Exodus. Likewise, the Jewish Passover liturgy, with which the early christian eucharist had close links, gave an important place to the stories of the Exodus. Therefore, the point of this scene is that Jesus is the Moses-like prophet and Messiah who feeds his people with a new manna, a new bread. This new food or manna, then, is Jesus' word of revelation or wisdom received in faith (6:35) as well as his eucharistic bread. Faith and eucharist —these are the two themes of Jesus' discourse. But the crowd do not grasp the meaning of the person of Jesus that lies behind the miracle because their hopes for a Messiah are tainted by politics and power and they do not see the spiritual nature of his messianic kingship (v. 15).

JESUS WALKS ON THE WATERS.
6:16-21. — *'I am he'*

> [16]When evening came, his disciples went down to the sea, [17]got into a boat, and started across the sea to Capernaum. It was now dark, and Jesus had not yet come to them. [18]The sea rose because a strong wind was blowing. [19]When they had rowed about three or four miles, they saw Jesus walking on the sea and drawing near to the boat. They were frightened, [20]but he said to them, "It is I; do not be afraid." [21]Then they were glad to take him into the boat, and immediately the boat was at the land to which they were going.

Jesus will later describe himself as a divine revealer who comes down from heaven bringing God's life and saving power to the world (6:33). Therefore this scene shows the power of Jesus and illustrates that he is a transcendent revealer who comes from God, strengthens the faith of disciples and who brings the saving life of God. The darkness, on the other hand, suggests the sense of absence experienced by disciples without Jesus (v.17). Jesus "comes" just as Yahweh came to his people, manifesting his divine power and consoling them by his presence: "I am he": this phrase, which expresses God's transcendent, saving power (Deut 32:39; Is 41:4;43:10,13,25; Ezek chs. 36-37) is applied to Jesus throughout the gospel to describe him as God's divine and saving revealer (4:26;8:24,28; 13:19;18:5,8). In addition, the scene recalls another Exodus theme, which may have formed part of the Passover liturgy: as the people crossed the Red Sea, God showed his power over the wind and the waves (Ex 14; Pss 77:19;78:13,24). Similarly, Jesus now manifests his power to disciples.

SEEKING JESUS.
6:22-24.

> [22]On the next day the people who remained on the other side of the sea saw that there had been only one boat there, and that Jesus had not entered the boat with his disciples, but that his disciples had gone away alone. [23]However, boats from Tiberias came near the

place where they ate the bread after the Lord had given thanks. ²⁴So when the people saw that Jesus was not there, nor his disciples, they themselves got into the boats and went to Capernaum, seeking Jesus.

This transitional scene, which brings Jesus back to the crowds who "seek" him, prepares us for the meaning of the miracle for we are reminded not only of the miracle itself but also of the eucharist as Jesus "gave thanks" (v.23), and the "loaves" (vv.11,13) are now "the bread" because Jesus will soon speak of himself as "the bread of life" (v.35).

BREAD FROM HEAVEN.
6:25-34.

²⁵When they found him on the other side of the sea, they said to him, "Rabbi, when did you come here?" ²⁶Jesus answered them, "Truly, truly, I say to you, you seek me, not because you saw signs, but because you ate your fill of the loaves. ²⁷Do not labor for the food which perishes, but for the food which endures to eternal life, which the Son of man will give to you; for on him has God the Father set his seal." ²⁸Then they said to him, "What must we do, to be doing the works of God?" ²⁹Jesus answered them, "This is the work of God, that you believe in him whom he has sent." ³⁰So they said to him, "Then what sign do you do, that we may see, and believe you? What work do you perform? ³¹Our fathers ate the manna in the wilderness; as it is written, 'He gave them bread from heaven to eat.'" ³²Jesus then said to them, "Truly, truly, I say to you, it was not Moses who gave you the bread from heaven; my Father gives you the true bread from heaven. ³³For the bread of God is that which comes down from heaven, and gives life to the world." ³⁴They said to him, "Lord, give us this bread always."

The extended discourse of Jesus moves in typically johannine style: Jesus makes statements which are misunderstood by the crowd and then further clarified by him (vv.28,30,41,52). The first part deals directly with faith in Jesus: Jesus is the bread of life because through faith the believer enters into a life-giving relationship with him (vv.25-51). But the faith-response of the crowd is deficient as they "seek" him for the wrong reasons (v.26). Fascinated by what he had done for them, they were caught up by the thrill of unexpected wonders and failed to "see" the deeper meaning of his miracle. But Jesus now asks them to look beyond the bread which man can eat and earn by the work of his hands to the mystery and meaning of his person and to seek him in the true sense. "Seeking" Jesus means turning towards him in faith as the transcendent one, approved by God and endowed with the power of God for he brings the ever-sustaining life of the Father to those who believe in him (v.27). Such faith in Jesus is not something they can achieve or work for because it is the work of God in the heart of the believer (vv.28-29).

But their faith still remains limited to a longing for signs and wonders (v. 30; cf. 4:48), for a sign even greater than the one he had already given them, since they hope for a new and more enriching manna than that which Moses had given them (Ex 16:4, 15; Ps 78:24; Wis 16:20). The central points of the Scripture they quoted will be developed throughout what follows: Jesus "gives," he gives "bread from heaven" and he gives them this bread to "eat." Jesus not only gives them himself through his life-giving word of revelation but he is also the Father's gift to them since he is sent by the Father on a life-giving mission to those who believe in him (v. 33). Like the Samaritan woman, the crowd respond by asking Jesus for this gift without understanding what they are really asking for (4:15). The whole discourse from vv. 32-51 is a development of the biblical quotation of v. 31 according to a Jewish homiletic technique (midrash).

COMING TO JESUS FOR LIFE.
6:35-40.

> 35 Jesus said to them, "I am the bread of life; he who comes to me shall not hunger, and he who believes in me

shall never thirst. [36]But I said to you that you have seen me and yet do not believe. [37]All that the Father gives me will come to me; and him who comes to me I will not cast out. [38]For I have come down from heaven, not to do my own will, but the will of him who sent me; [39]and this is the will of him who sent me, that I should lose nothing of all that he has given me, but raise it up at the last day. [40]For this is the will of my Father, that every one who sees the Son and believes in him should have eternal life; and I will raise him up at the last day."

Jesus now spells out the need of faith in himself, a faith which is a "coming" to him and an active movement of attachment to him. Besides, it is the will of his Father that man should have life through faith in Jesus. The Jews believed that God's greatest gift was his law, his word of wisdom which satisfies man's deepest longings (Sir 24:21; Prov 9:5) and now Jesus identifies himself with this revealed wisdom of God. He is a source of life ("the bread of life") for those who believe in him, accept his message or "come to" him (v.35); but his listeners refuse to do so. Besides, faith in Jesus is a work of God the Father who "gives" disciples to Jesus. Yet it is his Father's will that men should come to receive divine life through faith in Jesus. Thus, it is the Incarnate Jesus who mediates this divine life to believers and through whom we enter into a life-giving communion with God now and in eternity (vv.38-40).

LIFE FROM HEAVEN.
6:41-51.

[41]The Jews then murmured at him, because he said, "I am the bread which came down from heaven." [42]They said, "Is not this Jesus, the son of Joseph, whose father and mother we know? How does he now say, 'I have come down from heaven'?" [43]Jesus answered them,

"Do not murmur among yourselves. ⁴⁴No one can come to me unless the Father who sent me draws him; and I will raise him up at the last day. ⁴⁵It is written in the prophets, 'And they shall all be taught by God.' Every one who has heard and learned from the Father comes to me. ⁴⁶Not that any one has seen the Father except him who is from God; he has seen the Father. ⁴⁷Truly, truly, I say to you, he who believes has eternal life. ⁴⁸I am the bread of life. ⁴⁹Your fathers ate the manna in the wilderness, and they died. ⁵⁰This is the bread which comes down from heaven, that a man may eat of it and not die. ⁵¹I am the living bread which came down from heaven; if any one eats of this bread, he will live for ever; and the bread which I shall give for the life of the world is my flesh."

Like the people in the desert who refused to believe Moses, God's spokesman, the crowd, too, reject, "murmur against" the bread from heaven, that is, Jesus himself who is God's heavenly revealer (vv.41-42; Ex 16:2,7,12). But Jesus does not let their lack of faith pass without comment and then he goes on to speak positively about faith (v.43). "Coming to" Jesus in faith is not only the will of the Father (v.38) but it is also his work, for the Father draws believers to faith in Jesus (v.44). Consequently, to believe in Jesus is to be open to God. Moreover, the prophets had spoken of a new covenant when God would "teach" his people through a new law which would be more than an external message. It would also affect them interiorly and now this time has arrived in Jesus who is "from heaven," that is, from God (cf. v.41; Is 54:10; Jer 31:33). In listening attentively to him, one hears the Father for he is the source of the teaching of Jesus. God the Father, then, draws believers to faith in Jesus in two ways: through the message of Jesus; and as an interior "teacher" (cf. v.45) himself, he makes the message of Jesus an interior law of the heart through the power of his Spirit (14:17,26). Finally, Jesus, who knows the Father (v.46), is "bread from heaven" because he is a revealer coming from God bringing to those who are receptive to God a life which is eternal, that is, indestructible since it is the very life of God (vv.49-50). Jesus is also called "living bread" for he is endowed with the fullness of life which he shares with those who believe in him (v.51).

Although this part of Jesus' discourse primarily refers to that living communion with Jesus through faith, there are some indirect reminders of the eucharist, for example, "bread of life," "living bread." "The bread which I shall give for the life of the world is my flesh"—these words are very similar to the Last Supper account: "This is my body which is given for you" (Lk 22:19). Here "flesh" not only refers to Jesus as the Incarnate Son who gave himself for the life of the world on the cross but it is also the person of Jesus who continues to give himself and to communicate his life in the eucharist. Hence, in the same glance John sees Jesus give himself on the cross and in the eucharist so that we may have a share in his life.

EUCHARISTIC LIFE.
6:52-59.

> 52The Jews then disputed among themselves, saying, "How can this man give us his flesh to eat?" 53So Jesus said to them, "Truly, truly, I say to you, unless you eat the flesh of the Son of man and drink his blood, you have no life in you; 54he who eats my flesh and drinks my blood has eternal life, and I will raise him up at the last day. 55For my flesh is food indeed, and my blood is drink indeed. 56He who eats my flesh and drinks my blood abides in me, and I in him. 57As the living Father sent me, and I live because of the Father, so he who eats me will live because of me. 58This is the bread which came down from heaven, not such as the fathers ate and died; he who eats this bread will live for ever." 59This he said in the synagogue, as he taught at Capernaum.

In this description of the eucharist as "eating flesh and drinking blood," "flesh and blood" is a Hebrew idiom for the whole *person* so that the sense is: sacramental communion is a personal communion (encounter) with Jesus who shares his life and the life of his Father with us (v.53). Eucharist is a mutual "abiding," a life of mutual presence of one person to another, a reciprocal indwelling which does not submerge the personality of another (v.56; cf. 15:4-6). Besides, in the eucharist Jesus continues that life-giving mission which he had received from his Father and he communicates the life he receives from the Father, who is the source of all "life" (v.57). Therefore, Jesus, the source and bread of life, who came down from heaven and gave his life for the world, becomes a sacramental bread of life (v.55; cf. v.51), and, now ascended, he continues to give his own person, his "flesh and blood," in the eucharist. Finally, the life-giving communion experienced in the eucharist is a pledge of and reaches its perfection in an eternal communion with Jesus and his Father (vv.54,58). Yet it is not a kind of food which gives instant and automatic claim to immortality, since its life-giving effect is assured only for the person of faith.

The two themes of this discourse, faith and the eucharist, cannot be separated for neither faith nor the eucharist are directly the focus of attention but rather both are unified in the person of Jesus who offers a living relationship through faith and sacrament. Therefore, the sacramental experience, instead of replacing faith in Jesus, expresses and confirms it, and since the whole discourse is Christ-centred, it moves from Jesus' Incarnation, mission and death towards the eucharist. For John eucharistic faith is to believe that the same, risen, Incarnate Jesus continues to give himself to believers in a personal communion and to exercise his life-giving mission.

WORDS OF LIFE.
6:60-71.

> ⁶⁰ Many of his disciples, when they heard it, said, "This is a hard saying; who can listen to it?" ⁶¹ But Jesus,

knowing in himself that his disciples murmured at it, said to them, "Do you take offense at this? [62]Then what if you were to see the Son of man ascending where he was before? [63]It is the spirit that gives life, the flesh is of no avail; the words that I have spoken to you are spirit and life. [64]But there are some of you that do not believe." For Jesus knew from the first who those were that did not believe, and who it was that would betray him. [65]And he said, "This is why I told you that no one can come to me unless it is granted him by the Father."

[66]After this many of his disciples drew back and no longer went about with him. [67]Jesus said to the twelve, "Do you also wish to go away?" [68]Simon Peter answered him, "Lord, to whom shall we go? You have the words of eternal life; [69]and we have believed, and have come to know, that you are the Holy One of God." [70]Jesus answered them, "Did I not choose you, the twelve, and one of you is a devil?" [71]He spoke of Judas the son of Simon Iscariot, for he, one of the twelve, was to betray him.

Among disciples there are two kinds of reaction to Jesus' words (vv.60-66;67-71; vv. 60-65 refer back to vv.43-47) and Jesus reflects first on the negative response he receives. That a man from Nazareth should claim that he is a life-giving revealer sent from God is "hard" to take (vv.60-61) and only faith can overcome the "offence" or stumbling-block of the Incarnation. But if his message is too hard for them to take, then a worse shock awaits them when they will see him raised on the cross and then it will be a real test of their faith to believe in his death and resurrection (v.62). However, eventually his words will make sense to them and will actually become life-giving through the power of the Holy Spirit whom disciples will receive after Jesus has passed to his Father. They do need such a Spirit for man ("flesh") is weak and cannot open himself in faith to Jesus without the help of the Spirit. It is he, then, who will make Jesus' words meaningful and life-giving for disciples as he gives enduring power to the words of Jesus so that they become effective, Spirit-filled and life-giving for believers, for those whom the Father invites to "come to" Jesus (v.63). On the other hand, lack of faith is the root cause why one of his intimate disciples betrays him (vv.64-65).

At this turning-point many of his followers refuse to stand by Jesus. However, the intimate group of twelve stay, even if one of them, Judas, is under the power of darkness and unbelief, and Simon confesses faith in Jesus on their behalf (cf. Mk 8:27-33 par). He takes up Jesus' claim that his words are spirit and life and confirms that Jesus, as revealer of God, does not speak "hard" or weak, human words, but words which lead to life and give life if accepted in faith (v.68; cf. v.63). Moreover, disciples have grown in their understanding of faith about Jesus and for them he is the Holy One of God, that is, he is the Messiah who is sent by God to reveal him and also to give life to believers through his self-revelation as Son of God (v.69; Acts 2:27).

A Sacramental Gospel

Christ's sacramental presence and action in his community of christian disciples are clearly called to mind in this chapter and in the dialogue with Nicodemus (vv.53-58;3:5). Sometimes, too, there are more subtle reminders of sacraments in symbolism that is veiled, obscure and sometimes subject to various interpretations. For example, the water and blood flowing from the pierced side of Jesus implies that his self-offering in death brings new life, which comes to us in baptism (water) and the eucharist (blood:19:34). Also, an Easter meal by the lakeside, where Jesus "takes" bread and "gives" it to disciples, evokes the presence of the risen Lord in the eucharist (21:13).

Sometimes it is difficult to determine the limits of John's interest in sacraments for his interest comes through, not as the primary meaning of the words of the gospel, but as a further meaning which christians after the resurrection of Jesus, in the light of their own sacramental experiences, can understand. Hence, there is a danger of evaluating the gospel symbolism through interpretations of a later age, of approaching the gospel with our dogmatic presuppositions. Therefore, sacramental implications of John's symbols have to be drawn from the text of John, from his own explanations, from the context of the whole gospel and of the New Testament, and even from Old Testament texts and images. Following these criteria, it is probable that there are also references either to baptism or the eucharist in the healing of the blind man (9:1-7), the footwashing (13:5-11) and the image of the vine (15:1-17). However, it is not clear whether the power to forgive sins (20:23) refers to baptism or to a sacrament of reconciliation. In fact, it may include both sacraments.

Though we may call his gospel the most sacramental of all the gospels, John's centre of attention is never the sacraments themselves or the cultic life of the community. Rather his interest centres on the mission and self-revelation of Jesus on earth. In the work and words of Jesus he sees signs and reminders that point to his continued presence among his people, and, besides, his vision of Jesus' work extends beyond his death and resurrection. Thus, Christ's mission on earth, his self-revelation and his communication of life are only fulfilled through his return to the Father, through the sending of the Spirit and, within the life of the church, through the word and sacramental action of Jesus.

Yet the gospel does express the sacramental faith of the community for which it was written. The various stages in the composition of the gospel show how the early christian community had reflected more and more on the meaning of their sacramental life in relation to the work and message of Jesus. Therefore, it is possible that some statements about sacraments are editorial additions at a later stage in the formation of the gospel (3:5—the mention of "water" and 6:51-58). These bring out more clearly the implications of Jesus' message for the sacramental life of the church.

In the light of our present understanding of sacraments, two points of johannine theology, in particular, are worth recalling. First, John shows how faith and sacrament cannot be separated (6:53-58). Secondly, sacraments are essentially Christ-centred so that sacramental communion is a personal communion with Christ. Just as Christ during his mission on earth invited people to faith and to personal communion with him, so also now this call continues to be realized in our personal communion with Christ through word and sacrament.

Controversy and Further Self-Revelation at the Temple. 7:1-10:42

JESUS AND HIS RELATIVES.
7:1-13

7 After this Jesus went about in Galilee; he would not go about in Judea, because the Jews sought to kill him. ²Now the Jews' feast of Tabernacles was at hand. ³So his brothers said to him, "Leave here and go to Judea, that your disciples may see the works you are doing. ⁴For no man works in secret if he seeks to be known openly. If you do these things, show yourself to the world." ⁵For even his brothers did not believe in him. ⁶Jesus said to them, "My time has not yet come, but your time is always here. ⁷The world cannot hate you, but it hates me because I testify of it that its works are evil. ⁸Go to the feast yourselves; I am not going up to this feast, for my time has not yet fully come." ⁹So saying, he remained in Galilee.

¹⁰But after his brothers had gone up to the feast, then he also went up, not publicly but in private. ¹¹The Jews were looking for him at the feast, and saying, "Where is he?" ¹²And there was much muttering about him among the people. While some said, "He is a good man," others said, "No, he is leading the people astray." ¹³Yet for fear of the Jews no one spoke openly of him.

The climax of Jesus' public ministry is centred around the temple in Jerusalem after his "work" of healing and the "sign" of the bread with their accompanying discourses (7:1-10:42). A series of argumentative, almost heated dialogues (chs. 7-8), follow the relatively calm and coherent discourses of Jesus (chs. 3,4,6) so that the atmosphere of conflict dominates this part of the gospel and prepares us for the final outcome of this conflict—his death leading to resurrection. There is controversy, hostility and division among his listeners and the air of conflict is heightened by repeated statements that Jesus is in danger of his life. Besides, attempts are made to put him under arrest or lynch him on the spot and we are explicitly reminded of his coming "hour"—his death and resurrection (7:6,8;8:20).

These chapters (7-10) reflect, even more stridently than chapter 5, the controversy between Jesus and the Jews during his lifetime and the controversy between the johannine community and the synagogue. The pivotal points of this controversy are the person of Jesus as Son of God and his authority which stands above the law. The charges brought against him are: he is a violator of the law, of the sabbath —a "sinner" (9:16, 24; cf. 5:1-18); he is a blasphemer (8:58; 10:24-38; cf. 5:17-18), a false teacher who leads the people astray (7:14-18, 45-49; 9:24-34; cf. 18:19-24; 19:7). Later he will be accused of being an enemy of the Jewish nation (11:47-53).

In this pervading atmosphere of conflict Jesus discloses his authority as Son of God and he also shows that messianic expectations concerning him are inadequate: he is the Christ because he is Son of God (7:26-30; 10:24-38). In fact, these chapters constitute the trial of Jesus. That conflict, which in the other gospels reaches its climax in the trial of Jesus before the sanhedrin (Mk 16:61-64), is anticipated already by John in the public ministry. He omits the trial of Jesus before the sanhedrin (cf. 18:19-24) because his trial has, in a way, taken place during his public ministry and his appearance before Annas and Pilate is just a ratification of the verdict passed on him by "the Jews" during his public life (compare Mk 16:61-64 with Jn 5:17-18; 10:24, 33-36; 19:7). This conflict between Jesus and the Jews during his public ministry, eventually leading to death, reflects the life-situation of the johannine community in conflict with the synagogue.

In addition, there is a solemnity about the events and the teaching of Jesus as he speaks and acts in the temple, the centre of Jewish religion and life, within the liturgical setting of the feast of Tabernacles (7:2,37). Even the questions and answers about the origin of the Messiah, his power of miracles, the various Exodus motifs are linked with the feast which celebrated the messianic hopes of the people (7:27-31,40-42). For example, "living waters," symbolizing the Holy Spirit, reflect the water ritual of the feast (vv.37-39) and Jesus proclaims himself "light of the world" during this feast which was also named the "feast of lights" and which recalled the Exodus when God guides his people with a pillar of light (Ex 13:21). Jesus, then, proclaims himself light for the world during the feast of lights when it was customary to have the whole temple illuminated.

These chapters (7-8) generally have less appeal than most in the whole gospel because, perhaps, they appear as a series of disjointed controversies which are sometimes repetitive. Yet they do contain some of the gospel's most important reflections on Christ, for example, on his origins, his transcendence, his relationship with his Father, his sinlessness (7:16-18,23-29,41-42,52;8:16-19,24-29,46,58), and also on the Holy Spirit (7:37-39) and christian living, for example, on "seeking and finding" Jesus, the christian life of freedom (7:33-34;8:21,31-47). However, a key to help readers move more easily through these chapters is that the dialogue often develops in typically johannine style, by means of questions and answers. Thus, Jesus makes a statement that is not grasped and is actually misunderstood and then further clarified by him (e.g. 7:34-35; 8:33).

The discussions are introduced with the opening question of Jesus' going up to Jerusalem. Judea, (which includes Jerusalem) is for Jesus a place where he faces the forces of unbelief represented by the Jerusalem authorities, called "the Jews" (v.1; cf. vv.13,32,47-48). Thus the stage is set and the time is the feast of the Tabernacles which was an autumn feast lasting eight days. Originally a harvest festival, its liturgy celebrated Israel's dwelling under God's protection in the desert and the people's hopes for a coming Messiah. Jesus' "brothers"—the word can cover masculine relatives of varying degrees, brothers, half-brothers, cousins, brothers-in-law (2:12)—show a false attitude towards Jesus' mission and they lack true faith in him, since they are interested only in family prestige. While they acknowledge he can do great "works," such as his healing "work" (ch. 5), they want him to produce sensational results and achieve worldly publicity. Thus their attitude is "worldly" in the sense that it is inspired by the evil one or by the forces of unbelief, and manifests itself in negative responses of unbelief which are called "evil works" (v.7). These are not actions which are morally wrong but they reflect the attitude of forces called "the world" which hate Christ and close themselves to the light. Here the attitude of Jesus' relatives is radically different from that of Jesus. As regards Jesus himself, the time of his "going up" to his Father, the "hour" of his death and resurrection is not determined by himself but by his Father (v.6). However, he secretly goes up to the city where his very presence is a source of tension and awakens a variety of responses, and where the religious authorities, "the Jews" (v.11), seek him only to silence him. But some admire him while others believe that he is leading the people away from the faith of their fathers.

TAUGHT BY MY FATHER.
7:14-24.

[14]About the middle of the feast Jesus went up into the temple and taught. [15]The Jews marveled at it, saying, "How is it that this man has learning, when he has never studied?" [16]So Jesus answered them, "My teaching is not mine, but his who sent me; [17]if any man's will is to do his will, he shall know whether the teaching is from God or whether I am speaking on my own authority. [18]He who speaks on his own authority seeks his own glory; but he who seeks the glory of him who sent him is true, and in him there is no falsehood. [19]Did not Moses give you the law? Yet none of you keeps the law. Why do you seek to kill me?" [20]The people answered, "You have a demon! Who is seeking to kill you?" [21]Jesus answered them, "I did one deed, and you all marvel at it. [22]Moses gave you circumcision (not that it is from Moses, but from the fathers), and you circumcise a man upon the sabbath. [23]If on the sabbath a man receives circumcision, so that the law of Moses may not be broken, are you angry with me because on the sabbath I made a man's whole body well? [24]Do not judge by appearances, but judge with right judgment."

The first controversy is about Jesus' right to teach, his power over the sabbath and his origins (7:14-36). Throughout these controversies there is a double stage: while Jesus is arguing with the crowd in the foreground, in the background the authorities are planning his arrest. Questioned about his right to teach without having had any formal training under a recognised teacher, such as a rabbi received, Jesus speaks about his relationship with his Father (v.16). The person of faith, namely, one who responds to God in Jesus, will easily recognize that he does not speak independently of his Father's will, for his teaching comes from his Father and he is his Father's voice (v.17). Far from being an approved teacher who looks to his own advancement, Jesus is in harmony with and dependent on his Father, seeking only his advancement, and he teaches nothing against his Father's will, since he is a true revealer who speaks no falsehood.

And still people want to kill somebody who is sent by God because he violated the sabbath law of Moses in healing a paralytic (5:18,45-47). In this they are going against the very author of the Mosaic law, God himself, whom Jesus represents. Besides, there is something very hypocritical about their attitude to the law. For example, circumcision, which took place eight days after birth, was allowed on the sabbath but why, then, is it not permissable to perform an act of healing which affects the whole person? Hence, they should judge more fairly and not look on his action of healing just as a violation of the sabbath.

WHERE DOES HE COME FROM?
7:25-36.

> [25]Some of the people of Jerusalem therefore said, "Is not this the man whom they seek to kill? [26]And here he is, speaking openly, and they say nothing to him! Can it be that the authorities really know that this is the Christ? [27]Yet we know where this man comes from; and when the Christ appears, no one will know where he comes from." [28]So Jesus proclaimed, as he taught in the temple, "You know me, and you know where I come from? But I have not come of my own accord; he who sent me is true, and him you do not know. [29]I know him, for I come from him, and he sent me." [30]So they sought to arrest him; but no one laid hands on him, because his hour had not yet come. [31]Yet many of the people believed in him; they said, "When the Christ appears, will he do more signs than this man has done?"
>
> [32]The Pharisees heard the crowd thus muttering about him, and the chief priests and Pharisees sent officers to

arrest him. [33]Jesus then said, "I shall be with you a little longer, and then I go to him who sent me; [34]you will seek me and you will not find me; where I am you cannot come." [35]The Jews said to one another, "Where does this man intend to go that we shall not find him? Does he intend to go to the Dispersion among the Greeks and teach the Greeks? [36]What does he mean by saying, 'You will seek me and you will not find me,' and, 'Where I am you cannot come'?"

Once again (cf. 5:15-19) the discussion moves from the question of the sabbath to the mystery of the person of Jesus, to his origin from and his return to his Father. Since his person and his claims are always a sensitive matter for the authorities (cf. 5:18), hostility mounts and the first attempt to arrest Jesus is recorded. Besides, positive responses from the crowd to Jesus not only become fewer; they also manifest ignorance about the mystery of who Jesus really is.

First of all, the question whether he is Messiah, which is a prominent theme in this chapter (vv. 31, 40-42, 52), is raised by a group from Jerusalem who are more positive towards Jesus than the authorities (cf. v.32). Their difficulty is this: they know that Jesus comes from Nazareth but there was also a current of thought according to which the Messiah's presence on earth would be hidden and then he would suddenly appear and manifest himself in great power to the people (v.27). Certainly, Jesus' origin is a mystery and though his audience may know his "geographical" origins, they do not know that he comes from the Father. Because the Father sent him his life is one of continual dependence on and communion with the Father who is the real source guaranteeing the apostolic mission of Jesus. Thus, the Father is "true," he truly communicates and reveals himself in Jesus (v.28). As the one sent by the Father, Jesus has a unique and special knowledge of the Father, in contrast to the ignorance of his listeners, for he comes "from (the side of)," that is from the intimacy of his Father (vv.28-29).

But these claims lead to another clash between the revealer and unbelief. However, even the plan to arrest him is subject to Jesus' sovereign power and, therefore, when his "hour" comes no one can lay a hand on Jesus till he permits it (cf. 18:6-8). Then a questioning but positive reaction indirectly suggests that Jesus is a Messiah who does "signs" that lead people to faith. Besides, the move to arrest him leads Jesus to speak of his return to his Father, which is his way to glory (v.32). Now the conflict with the forces of unbelief is coming to a head because Jesus will be with his people only for a "little while" more (v.33). These themes of the "little while," which can refer to his coming death or to his return after death (cf. 13:33;14:19; 16:16) and "seeking and finding" Jesus (8:21) reappear in the gospel. Here, to seek and to find Jesus is a call to accept him now in faith because soon it will be too late, he will have gone to his death, and the person who lacks faith cannot "find" Jesus, that is, he cannot enter into a life of personal communion with Jesus and be united with Jesus now (and also in the future). In other words, he cannot be "where I am" (v.34; cf. 12:26;14:3;17:24).

The words of Jesus about "going away" are misunderstood (7:35). But the question about his going to the Jewish Diaspora to work among the gentiles is open to two answers: on one level, his going away is not a journey abroad in the sense the crowd take it, for Jesus is going to his Father through death and resurrection (13:1). On another level, it is through his death that Jesus will have drawn "all" and will have influenced the gentile world by the time the gospel is composed (12:21-24,32).

RIVERS OF LIVING WATER.
7:37-44.

> [37]On the last day of the feast, the great day, Jesus stood up and proclaimed, "If any one thirst, let him come to me and drink. [38]He who believes in me, as the scripture has said, 'Out of his heart shall flow rivers of living

water.'" [39] Now this he said about the Spirit, which those who believed in him were to receive; for as yet the Spirit had not been given, because Jesus was not yet glorified.

[40] When they heard these words, some of the people said, "This is really the prophet." [41] Others said, "This is the Christ." But some said, "Is the Christ to come from Galilee? [42] Has not the scripture said that the Christ is descended from David, and comes from Bethlehem, the village where David was?" [43] So there was a division among the people over him. [44] Some of them wanted to arrest him, but no one laid hands on him.

On the last day of the feast of Tabernacles, a second discourse of Jesus, punctuated by controversy (7:37-8:59) opens with a solemn promise of the Holy Spirit (vv.37-39) to which the crowd reacts (vv.40-44), and we have a picture of the Sanhedrin authorities frustrated and helpless when faced with the problem of "this man" Jesus (vv.45-52). Here Jesus' statement (vv.37-38) is better construed as: "If anyone thirst, let him come to me and let him who believes in me drink. As the Scripture has said: 'Out of his heart shall flow rivers of living water'". Thus Jesus promises "living water" to the believer, and in quoting from "Scripture" he combines two traditions: first, in the days of the Messiah there will be a purification of man, symbolized by water flowing out of the temple (Ezek 47:1-12; Zech 14:8). Secondly, during the wanderings of Israel water was given to the people from a rock in the desert through Moses (Ex 17:6; Ps 78; 1 Cor 10:4). Besides, in the liturgy of the feast of Tabernacles, on the seventh day, water was brought in solemn procession from the pool of Siloam and poured on the altar. (Jn 9:7).

Jesus has been speaking about himself as a Messiah (vv.25-31) and now in his promise of living water he is claiming to be the end-time prophet-like Moses and Messiah who brings these new, living waters, waters which flow from under the temple (cf. 4:10-14). "Out of his (Jesus') heart" these waters come, in other words, he, as the risen Lord, is a new temple and also the source of the Holy Spirit who is given after his death and resurrection (2:13-22). Thus Jesus is a Messiah and Servant of God who baptizes with, communicates the Spirit, since the Holy Spirit is active in the words of Jesus, which become living, life-giving words through the power of the Spirit (3:34; 6:63; cf. 1:32-33). Consequently, his words are life-giving (water) within the believer when they are Spirit-filled (4:16). The sense, then, of Jesus' promise is that the Holy Spirit, who deepens the faith of believers, will come after the death and resurrection of Jesus who will then give, "baptize with" this Spirit.

His hearers understand from his words that he is the promised prophet-like Moses or Messiah who possesses the Spirit but some doubt whether he is really the Messiah because they know only his Galilean origins (v.41; cf. 1:46; 6:14; Deut 18:15) and they do not know that he comes from Bethlehem (Mic 5:1). However, we cannot conclude that the evangelist was ignorant of Jesus' birth at Bethlehem because for him the geographical origins of Jesus, whether from Bethlehem or Galilee, are irrelevant. Thus the discussions end in division and the desire of some to arrest him remains ineffectual.

DIVISION
7:45-52.

> [45] The officers then went back to the chief priests and Pharisees, who said to them, "Why did you not bring him?" [46] The officers answered, "No man ever spoke like this man!" [47] The Pharisees answered them, "Are you led astray, you also? [48] Have any of the authorities or of the Pharisees believed in him? [49] But this crowd, who do not know the law, are accursed." [50] Nicodemus, who had gone to him before, and who was one of them, said to them, [51] "Does our law judge a man without first giving him a hearing and learning what he does?" [52] They replied, "Are you from Galilee too? Search and you will see that no prophet is to rise from Galilee."

In addition to the divided responses in the crowd, there is also division and frustration among the authorities opposed to Jesus when the officers sent to arrest him come back impressed (cf. v.43). Besides, Nicodemus, the Pharisee, takes a stand in favour of Jesus and it is ironical that the Pharisees, who denounce the crowd for believing in Jesus on the grounds that they do not know or conform to the law, have to be pulled up themselves and reminded about the law concerning a fair hearing (Ex 23:1; Deut 1:16). Ultimately, sarcasm is the only refuge of the authorities as they scoff at Jesus' Galilean origins (v.52). For Nathanael, too, the Galilean origins of Jesus had posed problems but at least he was more open, for he came, saw for himself and found faith (1:46).

THE ADULTERESS.
7:53-8:11— *'Neither do I condemn you.'*

8 ⁵³They went each to his own house, ¹but Jesus went to the Mount of Olives. ²Early in the morning he came again to the temple; all the people came to him, and he sat down and taught them. ³The scribes and the Pharisees brought a woman who had been caught in adultery, and placing her in the midst ⁴they said to him, "Teacher, this woman has been caught in the act of adultery. ⁵Now in the law Moses commanded us to stone such. What do you say about her?" ⁶This they said to test him, that they might have some charge to bring against him. Jesus bent down and wrote with his finger on the ground. ⁷And as they continued to ask him, he stood up and said to them, "Let him who is without sin among you be the first to throw a stone at her." ⁸And once more he bent down and wrote with his finger on the ground. ⁹But when they heard it, they went away, one by one, beginning with the eldest, and Jesus was left alone with the woman standing before him. ¹⁰Jesus looked up and said to her, "Woman, where are they? Has no one condemned you?" ¹¹She said, "No one, Lord." And Jesus said, "Neither do I condemn you; go, and do not sin again."

This story does not belong to the Fourth Gospel as it was originally composed but was inserted later, perhaps in the third and fourth century, into this part of the gospel, presumably because it seemed to be a good link between these chapters: it breaks up a long sequence of discourse; Jesus is teaching in the temple (7:14,28;8:2); he warns about judging people externally (7:21;8:7,15); the authority of the law is in question here and throughout these chapters and Jesus has a confrontation with the Pharisees. However, the delicate expression of Jesus' mercy is more typical of Luke (hence some manuscripts place the scene after Lk 21:38) and yet "the portrayal of Jesus as the serene judge has all the majesty that one would expect of John" (Brown). However, tradition has accepted the account as authentic and inspired Scripture.

Jesus' words carry authority and draw the crowds as he "sits" and teaches in the temple (8:2) and whereas God exercises mercy to sinners through him, scribes and Pharisees show no mercy. In this they are unreasonable since they, too, are sinners. But, in fact, they look on this woman as an instrument whereby they can bring a charge against a man respected by the people as a rabbi and so they put him in a tight spot and try to trap him. If he pardoned her, he would be accused of encouraging the people to break the law of Moses which prescribed death by stoning (Lev 20:10; Ezek 16:38-40;23:45-48; Deut 13:9-10; Dan 13). If he agreed that she should be stoned to death, he would lose his name for mercy. Jesus' writing on the ground, however, remains a mystery - perhaps he may have been acting out symbolically the words of Jeremiah about the deep-rooted nature of Israel's sin in rejecting God: "Those who turn away from you shall be written in the earth" (17:13). However, his action may have been a studied refusal to pronounce judgment. In any case we are no wiser about what Jesus wrote in the sand than we are about what Nathanael was doing under the fig-tree (1:48).

6:20). "Who are you?" - after all his explanations of himself this question evokes a reply which expresses his frustration (v.25). Besides, he could assert many things in judgment about them but he keeps within his Father's mandate, that is, to reveal what his Father, who is reliable and truthful, has communicated to him.

Though his hearers do not understand, Jesus points forward to the cross which will be a clear demonstration to those willing to believe. There he is a triumphant king, a transcendent Son of Man in communion with his Father who manifests his love and offers the gift of saving life to the world (v.28;3:14-15). Moreover, Jesus can be sure that God will not desert him, for he always does his Father's will, and, above all, he will not be deserted during his "hour" of suffering when he will reveal his love for his Father and his saving intentions as regards the whole world (v.29;16:32). The concluding positive response at this stage of the controversy may seem surprising, but its purpose is to prepare for the description of true discipleship which follows (vv. 30-31).

CHRISTIAN FREEDOM.
8:31-47.

[31]Jesus then said to the Jews who had believed in him, "If you continue in my word, you are truly my disciples, [32]and you will know the truth, and the truth will make you free." [33]They answered him, "We are descendants of Abraham, and have never been in bondage to any one. How is it that you say, 'You will be made free'?"

[34]Jesus answered them, "Truly, truly, I say to you, every one who commits sin is a slave to sin. [35]The slave does not continue in the house for ever; the son continues for ever. [36]So if the Son makes you free, you will be free indeed. [37]I know that you are descendants of Abraham; yet you seek to kill me, because my word finds no place in you. [38]I speak of what I have seen with my Father, and you do what you have heard from your father."

³⁹They answered him, "Abraham is our father." Jesus said to them, "If you were Abraham's children, you would do what Abraham did, ⁴⁰but now you seek to kill me, a man who has told you the truth which I heard from God; this is not what Abraham did. ⁴¹You do what your father did." They said to him, "We were not born of fornication; we have one Father, even God." ⁴²Jesus said to them, "If God were your Father, you would love me, for I proceeded and came forth from God; I came not of my own accord, but he sent me. ⁴³Why do you not understand what I say? It is because you cannot bear to hear my word. ⁴⁴You are of your father the devil, and your will is to do your father's desires. He was a murderer from the beginning, and has nothing to do with the truth, because there is no truth in him. When he lies, he speaks according to his own nature, for he is a liar and the father of lies. ⁴⁵But, because I tell the truth, you do not believe me. ⁴⁶Which of you convicts me of sin? If I tell the truth, why do you not believe me? ⁴⁷He who is of God hears the words of God; the reason why you do not hear them is that you are not of God."

After his comments on the lack of faith which he experiences from his audience, Jesus continues the discussion on a positive note, by showing how the life of believing disciples is a life of freedom which consists in being free from sin and, more positively, living as children of God (vv.30-31).

Through "the truth" the christian grows in freedom from sin which is contrasted with slavery to sin (vv.32,34). To "commit sin" is to let oneself be dominated by the diabolic power that sets itself against the will of God (cf. v.44). But fundamentally and concretely sin is the rejection of Christ, whereas by accepting him who is the truth, because he reveals God through his word, the christian is liberated from sin, that is, from unbelief (vv.32-33). Consequently, he grows in freedom the more he allows the word of Jesus to penetrate the heart and become part of living through the help of the Holy Spirit, who is the Spirit of truth (16:13; 6:63).

Since freedom is related to life as children of God, Jesus now speaks about his own Sonship (vv.35,38,40,42,46) and the life of disciples as children of God (vv.36,47), while at the same time he contrasts them with "diabolic" sonship, which is the life of unbelief (vv.37,40,41,44,47). But his audience insist they are free already (v.33), for as descendants of Abraham, as the people of the covenant, they are not subject to other nations for Yahweh alone is their Lord and they belong to that people who are called "the son(s) of God" (Ex 4:22-23; Deut 14:1; Hos 11:1). Thus their freedom as children (sons) of God consisted in serving God and in submitting to his law, his word.

However, Jesus challenges their claims since they cannot be true children of God if they do not believe in him, and he shows that true freedom is the life of faith in Jesus himself, acceptance of his truth, submission to his word (vv.40, 43). Therefore, christians become free and are God's children when they submit themselves to God and to Christ, by interiorizing the self-revelation and the word of Jesus. Just as the freedom of Jesus consists in being a "son" who "continues in the house forever," that is, who is always in communion with his Father, so also christians live as free "sons" in the house by remaining in communion with Jesus and his Father through faith, by accepting the word of Jesus. Freedom, therefore, to be "of God," that is, to live under God's influence through the word received in faith from Jesus (vv.42,47). Freedom of the children of God is a life lived in docility towards the word, the "truth" of Jesus; in other words, it is to be a disciple of Jesus, the Son of God, in contrast to living as a child of "the devil," who is the author of unbelief in man's heart (v.44).

This freedom, then, is a continued and progressive life of discipleship and those people are free who are true children of God in so far as they live a life of communion through faith and love with Jesus and the Father. But in what sense can we call this human freedom? Human freedom is the power to become what one should be, to be oneself in fullness, as the Italian philosopher, M. Sciacca, says: "Man is only free when he is fully prisoner of the truth." Likewise, according to Jesus, christian freedom is the life of children of God, lived fully in faith and love and through which we realize ourselves in realizing our christian faith. Such a life of freedom is submission to the "truth," that is, to Jesus as the revealer of God in his person, words and example.

This freedom is the opposite of "diabolic" sonship, which is the life of unbelief dominated by the power of evil (v.44) and so now Jesus accuses those who refuse to believe in him that they cannot claim God is their Father. Because of their unbelief they are acting under the influence of the evil one and they cannot, therefore, be "of God"; in other words, they do not lead a life of communion with Jesus and the Father through faith (vv.41,44). Jesus is contrasted with the devil who is a "murderer" because he kills faith and, consequently, love, in the hearts of believers (v.44; 1 Jn 3:12). Besides, there is no "truth" in him since he is opposed to the truth which is Jesus himself as the self-revelation of God. But Jesus, as the Incarnate Son of God is sinless (v.46) for he is entirely docile to the word of the Father and he mediates perfectly the truth he receives from him. Thus in his mission he lives fully in the light of the Father and obeys him perfectly.

GREATER THAN ABRAHAM.
8:48-59.

> [48]The Jews answered him, "Are we not right in saying that you are a Samaritan and have a demon?" [49]Jesus answered, "I have not a demon; but I honor my Father, and you dishonor me. [50]Yet I do not seek my own glory; there is One who seeks it and he will be the judge. [51]Truly, truly, I say to you, if any one keeps my word, he will never see death." [52]The Jews said to him, "Now we know that

you have a demon. Abraham died, as did the prophets; and you say, 'If any one keeps my word, he will never taste death.' [53]Are you greater than our father Abraham, who died? And the prophets died! Who do you claim to be?" [54]Jesus answered, "If I glorify myself, my glory is nothing; it is my Father who glorifies me, of whom you say that he is your God. [55]But you have not known him; I know him. If I said, I do not know him, I should be a liar like you; but I do know him and I keep his word. [56]Your father Abraham rejoiced that he was to see my day; he saw it and was glad." [57]The Jews then said to him, "You are not yet fifty years old, and have you seen Abraham?" [58]Jesus said to them, "Truly, truly, I say to you, before Abraham was, I am." [59]So they took up stones to throw at him; but Jesus hid himself, and went out of the temple.

In spite of strong negative reactions Jesus continues to reveal himself as he speaks about his life of communion with the Father and his preeminence over their father Abraham, who has already featured in the controversy (cf. vv.31-47), and some themes of the previous chapter are also resumed. Because of their unbelief, Jesus had accused his audience that their father was the devil to which they retort by accusing him of being possessed (cf. 7:20). For the Jews, to be a Samaritan was identical with being possessed, perhaps because their false worship was considered to be inspired by the forces of evil or because they were associated with an esteem for magical powers (Acts 8:9). But Jesus is not inspired by any force of evil because in his mission he is dedicated to and fully honours his Father; they, however, dishonour God by rejecting Jesus (v.49;7:18;5:41-44). However, the Father will honour or vindicate ("judge") Jesus in the "hour" of his triumph and those who accept Jesus will receive the gift of true life (vv.50-51).

But the power of Jesus to confer life through his word is taken on a purely physical level as a claim to have special power over death and, therefore, to be greater than Abraham or the prophets, for even they were subject to death. But the claims of Jesus are confirmed by his Father who is their God and who manifests himself in Jesus, especially in his death and resurrection (v.54). They are, in fact, rejecting their own God in rejecting Jesus, who is in communion with him, and they are liars since they openly express their unbelief with regard to Jesus, who is the truth. But the root cause of their unbelief is the evil one in whom there is no truth for he is opposed to Jesus who is the truth. It is the evil one who inspires their unbelief as he speaks to them inwardly and sows unbelief in their hearts (vv.55,44).

Jesus rebuts their appeal to Abraham who was a forerunner to Jesus and who looked forward to the day of Jesus (vv.56,53). Besides, Abraham's experience of seeing God's promise of blessings to his people, initially realized in the birth of Isaac, includes within itself the prospect of a coming Messiah and an awareness of God's long-term plan for his people (Gen 17:17;21:6). Thus later traditions held that Abraham saw the whole history of his descendants in a vision. Jesus, therefore, is the true fulfilment of their history that began with the promise to Abraham and along these lines he gives a partial response to their question (v.53;4:12).

However, after another misunderstanding—as if Abraham's vision meant that he saw Jesus and that Jesus saw him on earth—there comes the climax of Jesus' revelations about himself: "Before Abraham was, I am" (cf. 8:24,28). Thus Jesus, who existed before Abraham, is greater than one born out of human life alone, for he is the transcendent one in whom God is present, revealing and offering God's salvation to man: "I am (he)." Jesus identifies himself, too, with the name of Yahweh: "I am who am" (Ex 3:14), which expresses the nature of God as well as his saving action for his people. Consequently Jesus stresses both his closeness to God and his mission for the salvation of mankind. But this claim to divinity provokes a reaction equivalent to punishment for blasphemy (Lev 24:16), so that Jesus has to "hide" himself, not only physically, but he withdraws his presence and refuses to reveal himself to them any further. This withdrawal closes the whole section (chs. 7-8) which had begun with Jesus going up to the temple "in secret" (7:10).

Sent by the Father

In these controversies (chs. 7-8) and throughout the gospel (especially in chs. 5 and 17) Jesus frequently calls his Father "he who sent me." This recurring phrase expresses that all his life and work are a response to a mission the Father has given him. Therefore, the johannine Christ is essentially a person on mission to the world which God loves so much (3:16-17). What gives drive and meaning to his life is the constant awareness of a mission to accomplish in the world on behalf of his Father.

To "send" always implies two sides of a mission: one is sent by somebody (the internal aspect of a mission) and for some purpose (external aspect). The gospel stresses both of these inseparable aspects in the mission of Jesus: he is "sent," he "comes," "descends from heaven," he "comes out of" or "proceeds from" the Father in order to accomplish a mission which is twofold: to reveal what God is like and what we can become and also to communicate the life of God to man (10:10; ch. 6). This works of Jesus as revealer is described in terms of "light" (8:12;9:5) and as a "witnessing to the truth" (18:37).

The relationship of Jesus with his Father is the internal aspect and basis of his mission which is thoroughly dominated by that very personal relationship with the Father on account of which he seeks "not my own will but the will of him who sent me" (5:30;6:38-39). No other New Testament writer emphasizes so much the mystery of Jesus' relationship with his Father (chs. 5:10,17). There is a unity of action, will and love between himself and the Father (5:30;8:29;15:9-10) but the sending motif is to be understood in the light of Jesus' oneness with his Father, since he is also a "Son" (ch. 5), to whom the Father communicates the fullness of his own life. Besides, the Father loves his Son with his whole being so that they are totally one, united in work, life and love. This Father-Son relationship is one of the most significant features of johannine theology. "The relation of Father and Son is an eternal relation . . . The human career of Jesus is . . . a projection of this eternal relation . . . upon the field of time" (Dodd, *Interpretation*, p. 262).

Furthermore, the gospel contains an extensive theology of mission, for not only Jesus but also the Holy Spirit, John the Baptist and disciples are "sent." But the Father is the source of all missions as the unsent sender. Yet all other missions revolve around that of Jesus. Thus the Holy Spirit is sent by the Father along with the Son (14:26) and his mission, which is described in terms similar to that of Jesus, is to reveal Jesus as Son and to communicate his life through his inner action in the hearts of believers (6:63;16:14). As a Paraclete and Spirit of truth he gives interior witness, strengthens faith in Jesus and leads believers into an ever deepening communion of faith with him (15:26;16:13).

John the Baptist is also "sent" from God to witness to Jesus and thus draw people to faith in him (1:6-8,33) and Jesus "sends" disciples who share in and continue the mission Jesus himself received from his Father (17:18;20:21-23). Their mission is to reveal, to witness to Jesus and to bring others through faith to share in his life (4:36-38;15:27). Moreover, there is a clear unity of thought and vocabulary about the way John describes these four missions (of Jesus, the Holy Spirit, John the Baptist, disciples). Generally speaking, mission means that God the Father or his Son or both send representatives into the world to help in the divine, saving work of revealing and communicating life. While every mission revolves around that of Jesus, the Father is the "mission centre," the source from which all missions derive. Finally, as regards the purpose and meaning of mission in the Fourth Gospel, to have a mission is to make others, through faith, sharers in the inner life of God.

The Healing of the Blind Man.
9:1-41.

THE LIGHT OF FAITH.
9:1-7.

> **9** As he passed by, he saw a man blind from his birth. ²And his disciples asked him, "Rabbi, who sinned, this man or his parents, that he was born blind?" ³Jesus answered, "It was not that this man sinned, or his parents, but that the works of God might be made manifest in him. ⁴We must work the works of him who sent me, while it is day; night comes, when no one can work. ⁵As long as I am in the world, I am the light of the world." ⁶As he said this, he spat on the ground and made clay of the spittle and anointed the man's eyes with the clay, ⁷saying to him, "Go, wash in the pool of Siloam" (which means Sent). So he went and washed and came back seeing.

On the feast of "lights" (Tabernacles), while confronting the darkness of unbelief, Jesus had proclaimed that he was the light of the world, that is, he is the revealer of the life and love of God (8:12). Now he shows in what sense he is "the light" by healing a man who was born blind (9:5), for the opening of the eyes of the blind man is a "sign," a miraculous work which reveals who Jesus is (9:16;10:41). While on one level we are witnessing the physical healing of a blind man by Jesus, on a deeper level the opening of his eyes to the light of day is a sign that eyes of faith are opened by him and to him who is the "light of the world," the one "sent" to reveal the Father (vv.5,7).

Therefore, Jesus not only opens the eyes of this beggar by his touch to see the light of day for the first time. The blind man is also gradually led along by Jesus to "see" him in faith, to believe in him and to worship him (vv.37-38). Consistently this level of meaning is driven home and seven times the catch-phrase "opening eyes" occurs in order to stress that Jesus opens the man's eyes physically and in faith (vv.10,14,17,21,26,30,32). In the Old Testament, too, "opening the eyes" of the blind also refers to faith in God (Is 42:7). In addition, the washing in the waters of Siloam, the emphasis on sin (vv.2-3,40-41) and the mention of light suggest a symbolism of baptism which removes sin. This is confirmed by the fact that in the First Letter of John (1:5-10), which is strongly influenced by the baptismal liturgy, "light" is connected with baptism in so far as it means the instruction received through the teaching of the gospel and necessary for initiation into the christian community.

The account of the healing (vv.1-7) explains the meaning of Jesus' action. First of all, Jesus "saw" this blind man, and sometimes in the gospel when Jesus "sees" people it is also implied that he sees their possibilities for faith or that he sees some special meaning in what is going to happen to them (1:47-48,50;5:6;19:26). Then the question of the disciples about sin (v.2) suggests two possibilities: it was a view that the sins of parents were punished in their children (Deut 5:9; Job 3:3-4), and also some teachers at the time held that there could be a "prenatal" sin! If a woman, for example, worshipped in a pagan temple, the child in the womb also committed a sin of idolatry. However, the disciple did not have all this in mind and they merely ask Jesus in a rather vague way. But man's physical blindness is not due to any sin of his or of his parents. Rather the fundamental sin is deliberate blindness with regard to Jesus, the light (vv.39-41) and, therefore, those who will harrass the blind man, in this case the religious authorities, and who reject Jesus, these are the guilty and sinful ones.

The opening of the eyes of the blind man is not only a sign but it is also a work of God which Jesus does and must do before his "hour" comes ("I must work" rather than "*we* must work":v.4). Because he is the light, the revealer of God, he will give not only physical light but also the light of faith, which is a "work" of God, to this man (6:29). The blind man, in turn, will see the light of day and he will also see in faith that Jesus is the light, the transcendent revealer of God. Even the waters of Siloam are drawn into the symbolism of the scene, as the name reminds the evangelist of a similar word in Hebrew, which means "send." Thus Jesus is the one sent by the Father to be the light of the world (v.7).

COMING TO THE LIGHT.
9:8-17.

⁸The neighbors and those who had seen him before as a beggar, said, "Is not this the man who used to sit and beg?" ⁹Some said, "It is he"; others said, "No, but he is like him." He said, "I am the man." ¹⁰They said to him, "Then how were your eyes opened?" ¹¹He answered, "The man called Jesus made clay and anointed my eyes and said to me, 'Go to Siloam and wash'; so I went and washed and received my sight." ¹²They said to him, "Where is he?" He said, "I do not know."

¹³They brought to the Pharisees the man who had formerly been blind. ¹⁴Now it was a sabbath day when Jesus made the clay and opened his eyes. ¹⁵The Pharisees again asked him how he had received his sight. And he said to them, "He put clay on my eyes, and I washed, and I see." ¹⁶Some of the Pharisees said, "This man is not from God, for he does not keep the sabbath." But others said, "How can a man who is a sinner do such signs?" There was a division among them. ¹⁷So they again said to the blind man, "What do you say about him, since he has opened your eyes?" He said, "He is a prophet."

The atmosphere of hostility, controversy and division (v.16) throughout this story belongs to the struggle between the light, and the blindness or darkness of unbelief. What follows (vv.8-38) describes the controversy over

Jesus' healing of the blind man on the sabbath. This grows gradually in intensity: at first the neighbors are perplexed (vv.8-12), then the parents of the blind man are interrogated (vv.18-23) and he himself is subjected to two interrogations (vv.13-18a,24-34). Whereas the climax of the blind man's coming to the light of faith in Jesus is reached in his confession of faith (vv.35-38), the climax of the struggle between light and the darkness of unbelief is the confrontation between Jesus and the Pharisees (vv.39-41). Besides, the blind man who comes to faith in Jesus, the light, is contrasted with those who reject the light and become blind to Jesus, namely, the Pharisees.

Jesus progressively reveals himself as he takes the initiative and invites this man to open his eyes in faith to who he is. The blind man, too, progressively discovers the light and his first response is to call Jesus a "man," a man such as he had never experienced before, one who "opened" his eyes (v.11). Next he goes on to accept Jesus as a "prophet," one who, because of his words and healing action, shows that he has a special mission from God.

'LET HIM SPEAK FOR HIMSELF.'
9:18-23.

> [18]The Jews did not believe that he had been blind and had received his sight, until they called the parents of the man who had received his sight, [19]and asked them, "Is this your son, who you say was born blind? How then does he now see?" [20]His parents answered, "We know that this is our son, and that he was born blind; [21]but how he now sees we do not know, nor do we know who opened his eyes. Ask him; he is of age, he will speak for himself." [22]His parents said this because they feared the Jews, for the Jews had already agreed that if any one should confess him to be Christ, he was to be put out of the synagogue. [23]Therefore his parents said, "He is of age, ask him."

The parents of the blind man are uncooperative because they are afraid that if they acknowledge Jesus as the healer of their son they might be expelled from the worshipping community. Here the evangelist is also reflecting on the contemporary situation of conflict, when confessing faith in Jesus as the Messiah resulted in expulsion from the social and political community of Israel (v.22;12:42;16:2). As regards the attitude of the blind man's parents, E. Hoskyns comments: "A father is always ready to receive all the honour and advantage he can from the talents of an understanding son, when the world applauds. But he is the first who draws back when the use of those talents is likely to bring him into any trouble with the great" (*The Fourth Gospel,* ad. loc.).

BLIND TO THE LIGHT.
9:24–34.

24So for the second time they called the man who had been blind, and said to him, "Give God the praise; we know that this man is a sinner." 25He answered, Whether he is a sinner, I do not know; one thing I know, that though I was blind, now I see." 26They said to him, "What did he do to you? How did he open your eyes?" 27He answered them, "I have told you already, and you would not listen. Why do you want to hear it again? Do you too want to become his disciples?" 28And they reviled him, saying, "You are his disciple, but we are disciples of Moses. 29We know that God has spoken to Moses, but as for this man, we do not know where he comes from." 30The man answered, "Why, this is a marvel! You do not know where he comes from, and yet he opened my eyes. 31We know that God does not listen to sinners, but if any one is a worshiper of God and does his will, God listens to him. 32Never since the world began has it been heard that any one opened the eyes of a man born blind. 33If this man were not from God, he could do nothing." 34They answered him, "You were born in utter sin, and would you teach us?" And they cast him out.

The blind man suffers for his belief in Jesus as the
Pharisees try to browbeat him into saying that Jesus did
not heal him. But because he is stubborn and persistent
in his attachment to Jesus, he progresses further in faith.
For him Jesus is more than a special "man" or "prophet"
and, far from being a sinner, Jesus is a true worshipper
of God who is in communion with and listened to by God
for he comes from God and he does the Father's will
(v.31;4:34;5:30; 1 Jn 5:14).

While the blind man opens gradually in faith to the
light, the Pharisees become blind, even though they see
physically (cf. v.40). For them the man who confesses
faith in Jesus is sinful and his physical infirmity is a sign
of his complete blindness in Judaism (v.33). Thus they
harden more and more in their refusal to believe while
their blindness or their lack of faith manifests itself in
sceptical questioning and in their claim that they "know":
"*How* were your eyes opened? . . . *How* can a man who
is a sinner do such signs? *How* then does he now see?"
(vv.16,26). Consequently, they have no need of further
light for they "know": "We know that this man is a sinner
. . . We know that God does not listen to sinners" (vv.24,
29,31). Thus their knowledge is blindness and they refuse
to accept Christ and to open their eyes to what mag-
nificently challenges their sight. Besides, they represent
all those who are deliberately closed to the light. What
they know about the law, that alone counts and what
they claim to know reveals their ignorance (v.24).

THE BLIND AND THOSE WHO SEE.
9:35-41.

> 35 Jesus heard that they had cast him out, and having
> found him he said, "Do you believe in the Son of man?"
> 36 He answered, "And who is he, sir, that I may believe
> in him?" 37 Jesus said to him, "You have seen him, and
> it is he who speaks to you." 38 He said, "Lord, I believe";
> and he worshiped him. 39 Jesus said, "For judgment I

came into this world, that those who do not see may see, and that those who see may become blind." [40]Some of the Pharisees near him heard this, and they said to him, "Are we also blind?" [41]Jesus said to them, "If you were blind, you would have no guilt; but now that you say, 'We see,' your guilt remains."

In this pedagogy of faith Jesus takes the initiative once more as he "finds," that is, deliberately seeks out the blind man in order to lead him to deeper faith (v.35; cf. 1:41, 43,45). Now the blind man comes into the full light of faith as he responds to the transcendent Messiah and Son of Man with a confession of his faith (vv.35-37).

Finally, in confrontation with the Pharisees (vv.39-41) Jesus speaks about a "division" (a discrimination, judgment: v.39) which his presence provokes, that is: his presence among men evokes a double response: some believe in ("see") him, others reject him ("become blind"). On the other hand, the blind man represents those who accept Jesus, the light, since he is one of those people who does not "see," that is, he has a limited understanding of the law or the divine will but he is not closed or proud and, therefore, he is open to and comes to believe in Jesus. On the other hand, the Pharisees stand for those who "see" in so far as they have a better understanding of the law and they boast about this: "we know . . ." Thus before the fullness of the light they are incapable of going beyond the small light they have and they become even more blind during the confrontation with Christ. Finally, the story ends on the theme with which it began, namely, sin, as Jesus points out that sin really begins when one claims there is no need of further light, whereas there are some who remain ignorant of Christ through no fault of their own (v.41).

The Gospel of Light and Darkness

When Jesus claimed that he was the revealer of God, the "light of the world" (8:12;9:5), he was using an image that his audience would have associated with God himself. This image was taken from ordinary life and applied to God by the Hebrews for whom light was so essential to life that it was the first thing to be created by God (1:3-4). Besides, with the light of day begins the time of life, activity and happiness, for to "see the light" is to live (Ps 49:20). Thus light was closely associated with life itself.

Because he is the source of happiness and salvation, God is light and life: "For with you is the fountain of life; in your light do we see light" (Ps 36:9). Furthermore, the "light" of Yahweh's countenance is his favour and saving love (Ps 4:6) and, generally speaking, God is light because he reveals himself in word and power. Similarly, in the Fourth Gospel Jesus is called light because he reveals God, in particular, his life and his love. In addition, light and darkness denoted the opposition between moral good and evil (Is 5:20;59:9-10). Since in primitive conditions lack of light causes many accidents and since people stumble and fall in the dark, darkness means disaster, misfortune and sin. This contrast between light and darkness was even more polarized in the literature of Qumran where we find a "prince of lights" and an "angel of darkness" (Belial) locked in struggle for domination over mankind.

For the evangelist, darkness is sin and the rejection of Christ, who is the light; it is lostness without Christ (1:5;3:19-21). Thus to live without Christ, to reject him, who is the revealer of God, is to walk in the dark (8:12), to live one's life in that area of darkness, of deliberate unbelief which is dominated by the power of evil, Satan. On the other hand, to "walk in the light" (12:35) is to live according to the revelation of God communicated to us in Jesus. Besides, God himself is "light" (1 Jn 1:5) because he reveals himself to us in the person, words and example of Jesus. Finally, this light-darkness motif belongs to that series of contrasts (dualism) between opposite forces which is very typical of the gospel: truth-falsehood (8:44-45), to be saved—to perish (3:16-17).

Jesus the Shepherd.
10:1-21.

PERSONAL CALL AND RESPONSE.
10:1-6.

10 "Truly, truly, I say to you, he who does not enter the sheepfold by the door but climbs in by another way, that man is a thief and a robber; ²but he who enters by the door is the shepherd of the sheep. ³To him the gate-keeper opens; the sheep hear his voice, and he calls his own sheep by name and leads them out. ⁴When he has brought out all his own, he goes before them, and the sheep follow him, for they know his voice. ⁵A stranger they will not follow, but they will flee from him, for they do not know the voice of strangers." ⁶This figure Jesus used with them, but they did not understand what he was saying to them.

Still in an atmosphere of conflict, Jesus describes himself as a messianic leader of his people by means of an image which would have been very familiar to his audience: he is the messianic shepherd and a leader for christian disciples. The Old Testament often describes God's care for his people in images taken from pastoral life, with particular reference to their Exodus, to the protection and deliverance they experienced in their history (Pss 77:21; 78:52). Thus John describes Jesus as leading out and going before his people as a shepherd (10:4-5; Deut 1:30; Ex 3:10). The image often describes the guidance, care and companionship God offers not only to his people but also to the individual (e.g. Ps 23) and in Ezekiel condemns the leaders of Israel as false shepherds and promises he will look after his people by setting over them one shepherd, a Messiah (Ezek ch. 34: this closely resembles Jn 10:1-18). Besides, the image shepherd-sheep appears as well in the Synoptics but what distinguishes the johannine use from all others is the emphasis on the mutual relationship between Jesus and the individual disciple (Lk 12:32; 15:3-7; Mk 14:27; Mt 18:12-14).

First of all, the image presents Jesus as the expected leader of his people (vv.1-5) and we have the impression that some of the "sheep" (v.3) do not belong to the "flock" of Jesus, only those who follow him (v.4). Thus as the true leader of a new community of christian disciples (v.1) he is contrasted with false claimants who are probably to be identified as messianic, political revolutionaries rather than the religious leaders of the Jews. Consequently he "leads out" and "goes before" his sheep, the disciples, as their leader and liberator. Although he himself has been rejected by the religious leaders of Israel, he remains a leader who forms a new community of disciples, each of whom receives a personal invitation to "follow" him in faith. Moreover, each disciple he "calls by name" (v.3), that is, personally, so that the christian disciple recognizes the intimate and personal quality of his call to faith by Jesus. But disciples do not merely hear his voice, his words; they also listen to his message and live it.

THE WAY OF LIFE.
10:7-10.

> [7]So Jesus again said to them, "Truly, truly, I say to you, I am the door of the sheep. [8]All who came before me are thieves and robbers; but the sheep did not heed them. [9]I am the door; if any one enters by me, he will be saved, and will go in and out and find pasture. [10]The thief comes only to steal and kill and destroy; I came that they may have life, and have it abundantly."

The image of the shepherd is not only a parable, a figurative word-picture which needs further clarification by Jesus (v.6); it is also an enigmatic statement which has to be interpreted in the light of his death and resurrection

(cf. vv.11,15,17-18). Jesus takes two ideas from the image—
"door" (vv.7-10) and "shepherd" (v.2) and develops them
by showing how he is the "door" (vv.7-10) and also a "good
shepherd" (vv.11-18). First, he is the door for the sheep,
because in and through him alone disciples enter into the
sphere of salvation or divine life ("pasture"). Thus he
is the way to that abundant, divine life which he has in
fullness from the Father and which he communicates to
those who enter into a communion of faith in him (vv.9-10;
cf. 14:6) so that he is not only the way of access to life or
salvation, but in Jesus the goal of salvation is attained
through faith in him. Also the relationship he offers is
one of familiarity and freedom, for Jesus puts no obstacles
in the way of disciples who, having turned in faith to him,
can "go in and go out" as they please—this expression
means familiarity and free access in a relationship (Acts
1:21;9:28).

A "GOOD" SHEPHERD.
10:11-21.

> [11]"I am the good shepherd. The good shepherd lays
> down his life for the sheep. [12]He who is a hireling and
> not a shepherd, whose own the sheep are not, sees the
> wolf coming and leaves the sheep and flees; and the
> wolf snatches them and scatters them. [13]He flees because
> he is a hireling and cares nothing for the sheep. [14]I am
> the good shepherd; I know my own and my own know
> me, [15]as the Father knows me and I know the Father;
> and I lay down my life for the sheep. [16]And I have other
> sheep, that are not of this fold; I must bring them also,
> and they will heed my voice. So there shall be one flock,
> one shepherd. [17]For this reason the Father loves me,
> because I lay down my life, that I may take it again.
> [18]No one takes it from me, but I lay it down of my own
> accord. I have power to lay it down, and I have power
> to take it again; this charge I have received from my
> Father."

> [19]There was again a division among the Jews because of these words. [20]Many of them said, "He has a demon, and he is mad; why listen to him?" [21]Others said, "These are not the sayings of one who has a demon. Can a demon open the eyes of the blind?"

Jesus calls himself a "good" shepherd because, first, he lays down or freely gives his life out of love for his disciples and, secondly, because he offers them a life of special intimacy with him (vv.11,14), for disciples "know" him and he "knows" them. This knowledge is not a mere intellectual understanding of a relationship; for the Hebrews to "know" a person meant to experience him through knowledge and love. Therefore, this mutual "knowing" is the communion of life between Jesus and disciples through which they come to share in that very life Jesus receives from the Father (10:28;17:3). As the Son knows and receives life from his Father, so those who know the Son know the Father and share in the gift of their life (v.15). In addition, by offering disciples this communion of life and by laying down his life for them, he draws them together so that they become united through their faith in him, the one shepherd. Therefore, in the course of history the christian community of disciples will grow, and perhaps Jesus is referring to the gentiles who will come into the church. Thus the unity of christians will grow in proportion to believers' submission to Christ, their shepherd, in faith, so that there is a progressive development in the living unity of christians in one shepherd, Christ (v.16).

Besides, the Father loves his Son not only because he lays down his life in love for disciples and unites them as one community, but also because Jesus communicates life to disciples through his resurrection by "taking" his life again (v.17). In fact, all of Jesus' shepherd-task of guiding, caring for and uniting disciples together is the will of a Father and also the loving response of a Son. All this Jesus freely undertook out of love for mankind, since laying down his life was not imposed on him by any human being or power. This was the way he expressed his "pastoral care" for disciples and it was also a loving response of a shepherd-Son to his Father (v. 18).

The reaction to the parable had been a failure to understand (vv. 1-5) and now the reaction to its explanation (vv. 7-18) is division (vv. 19-21).

A SHEPHERD SON.
10:22-30.

> ²²It was the feast of the Dedication at Jerusalem; ²³it was winter, and Jesus was walking in the temple, in the portico of Solomon. ²⁴So the Jews gathered round him and said to him, "How long will you keep us in suspense? If you are the Christ, tell us plainly." ²⁵Jesus answered them, "I told you, and you do not believe. The works that I do in my Father's name, they bear witness to me; ²⁶but you do not believe, because you do not belong to my sheep. ²⁷My sheep hear my voice, and I know them, and they follow me; ²⁸and I give them eternal life, and they shall never perish, and no one shall snatch them out of my hand. ²⁹My Father, who has given them to me, is greater than all, and no one is able to snatch them out of the Father's hand. ³⁰I and the Father are one."

When Jesus' claim to be the messianic shepherd of his people is challenged, he pursues further the subject of his messianic work and his relationship with his Father, even though there is an interruption (vv. 23-24). But the feast of Dedication was closely linked with the feast of Tabernacles and it celebrated the reconstruction of the altar and the temple (cf. v. 36: Jesus is "consecrated" or sanctified). Also, Jesus is still in the temple precincts and with the winter his public self-revelation is coming to an end, too.

This discourse of Jesus (vv.25-30;34-38) hinges around two pointed assertions: "I and the Father are one" (v.30); "the Father is in me and I am in the Father" (v.38). As the hostile "gathering" around Jesus (v.24) provokes him to answer unambiguously whether he is the Messiah or not, the trend of his reply is that he is the Messiah precisely because of his relationship to his Father as Son of God. His life-giving words and actions, his "works," which he does in communion with his Father, point to the mystery of who he is, for they issue from and reveal a Father-Son relationship (v.25). But his unreceptive hearers refuse to recognize him as their shepherd, whereas those who believe receive the gift of indefectible life and protection from himself and his Father (v.28). Consequently, they are the "sheep of his hands" (Ps 97:7) and also of the protective hand of his Father (v.29). Thus he carries out his mission as shepherd in close communion with his Father and the Father's role as shepherd is realized in his shepherd Son in such a way that they are equal in power and share life together (v.30).

THE "GOOD" WORKS OF FATHER AND SON. 10:31-42.

31The Jews took up stones again to stone him. 32 Jesus answered them, "I have shown you many good works from the Father; for which of these do you stone me?" 33The Jews answered him, "It is not for a good work that we stone you but for blasphemy; because you, being a man, make yourself God." 34Jesus answered them, "Is it not written in your law, 'I said, you are gods'? 35If he called them gods to whom the word of God came (and scripture cannot be broken), 36do you say of him whom the Father consecrated and sent into the world, 'You are blaspheming,' because I said, 'I am the Son of God'? 37If I am not doing the works of my Father, then do not believe me; 38but if I do them, even though you do not believe me, believe the works, that you may know and understand

that the Father is in me and I am in the Father." [39]Again
they tried to arrest him, but he escaped from their hands.

[40]He went away again across the Jordan to the place
where John at first baptized, and there he remained.
[41]And many came to him; and they said, "John did no
sign, but everything that John said about this man was
true." [42]And many believed in him there.

But hostility intensifies as Jesus defends his mission of
revealing and giving life, that is, he defends his "works."
To these he appeals as evidence that he is Son of God and
Messiah, for they are "good," that is, they are beyond
reproach and they also invite the admiration of faith because they are the works of a "good" shepherd and because
they come from God (v.32). However, his claim is taken
as blasphemy. But if Scripture considered it legitimate to
call the people of Israel "gods" or "sons of the Most High,"
because they had received from God the special gift of his
word or law (Ps 82:6), all the more reason, then, why he
could call himself a Son of God (vv.33-35). As the Incarnate
Son sent by his Father, he is sanctified or consecrated in
his humanity for he is a divine Word made flesh and he
possesses the fullness of the Holy Spirit (1:32-33). In addition, the effect of this sanctification by God is that Jesus
lived out fully his life of Sonship during his mission and
belonged fully to his Father, especially in his death which
was the most supreme expression of his life as a loving Son
of his Father.

Then Jesus makes a final appeal for faith as he requests
his hearers to look to his works: through them they will
come to believe and appreciate more and more that he and
the Father not only share the same works but also the same
life. If he really does not do works which belong to the
Father, then they should not accept his claims (vv.37-38).

This public revelation of Jesus ends on a note of hostility
(v.39) and Jesus is forced to get away from this hostility
(vv.40-42) to where he began his ministry (1:28) and where
believers confirm the first positive testimony about him,

namely, that of John the Baptist. Here the mention of "signs" and "many" believers prepares the reader for the last great "sign" of his public life, which will evoke widespread faith (11:45), namely, the raising of Lazarus.

The "works" of Jesus

Jesus frequently summarizes all his activity, his mission as a "work" or "works" (especially in chs. 5 and 10) - a theme which recalls the "works" of God in the Old Testament. These are God's works in creation and in the direction of the world as well as his saving deeds in the history of his people (Gen 2:2; Ps 28:5; Ex 34:10; Deut 11:2-7). In addition, these "works" reveal God and they are related to his saving activity.

In the Fourth Gospel, too, they are linked with the revelatory and saving activity of Jesus. In fact, they describe the whole activity of Jesus in so far as he reveals the Father and communicates his life either in its totality as a "work" (4:34;17:4) or in its parts as "works." But these works include his words (14:10) and his miracles (5:20;7:21;9:4) both of which reveal him and the Father and also aim at conferring life on those who believe in Jesus.

By means of "works" attention is drawn to two central realities in the gospel: revelation-faith and communion. For example, Jesus never speaks of "my works" for they are his Father's even though he himself does them. Therefore, what is stressed about the works of Jesus is that they reveal the communion between himself and the Father and they result from this communion (10:25,38).

Not only Jesus and the Father do "works" together but also disciples do "works" precisely through their communion with Jesus who works in them (14:12). Thus faith is a "work" of God in the believer (6:29). As regards Jesus, then, his works reveal and result from his communion with his Father, and as regards the believer, the various manifestations of faith in Jesus are also "works" (3:19;14:12) which result from the believer's communion with Jesus and the Father and which are his response to God revealing himself in Jesus.

D. PREPARING FOR THE "HOUR"
11:1-12:36

The Raising of Lazarus
11:1-54.

FRIENDS AT BETHANY
11:1-6.

> **11** Now a certain man was ill, Lazarus of Bethany, the village of Mary and her sister Martha. ²It was Mary who anointed the Lord with ointment and wiped his feet with her hair, whose brother Lazarus was ill. ³So the sisters sent to him, saying, "Lord, he whom you love is ill." ⁴But when Jesus heard it he said, "This illness is not unto death; it is for the glory of God, so that the Son of God may be glorified by means of it."
> ⁵Now Jesus loved Martha and her sister and Lazarus. ⁶So when he heard that he was ill, he stayed two days longer in the place where he was.

NOWHERE IN THE GOSPEL do so many features of the johannine Christ appear all at once as in the account of the raising of Lazarus. For example, he is "Lord," "Son of God," "the Christ," "teacher," "rabbi" and one who reveals the power and life of God as he calls Lazarus from the tomb "with a loud voice" (v.43). Then, he not only prays as a Son about his communion with his Father (vv.41-42) but he is also the human Christ who consoles Mary and Martha. We can suppose that it was at the home of these friends at

Bethany that he frequently stayed (Mk 11:11;14:3; Lk 10:38). Moreover, he weeps and is troubled at the tomb (vv.33-36) and we feel the touch of Jesus' humanity in this story more than in any other gospel, particularly in his love for Mary, Martha and Lazarus (vv.5,36).

The events of this chapter (and ch. 12) prepare for and prefigure the "hour" of Jesus' death and resurrection so that the raising of Lazarus (vv.1-44) with its sequel (vv.45-54) is a paradox: Jesus gives a man life; men are condemning Jesus to death. For the evangelist this miracle of "sign" is the direct cause of Jesus' death for it provokes a session of the Jewish supreme council (the Sanhedrin: v.47), which is intent on putting him to death. Throughout, the main point stressed is: Jesus is the resurrection and the life for he confers the gift of divine life through his self-giving death. Therefore, the physical raising of Lazarus from death is a "sign" that Jesus gives "life" to believers now and on "the last day" (11:23-26;12:18). Besides, the story not only prefigures Jesus' resurrection but also his death, since Jesus is going up to Jerusalem to raise Lazarus and also to die himself (vv.7-16); in fact, after the miracle he himself is condemned to die (v.53).

Therefore, Jesus who has passed from death to life gives the gift of divine life to believers. This death-rising to life motif runs through the whole story, for it is applied to Lazarus, to Jesus, to the individual christian (vv.16,23-26) and to the christian community (vv.50-52). Besides, this is the climax of the "signs" of Jesus' public ministry and it not only resembles (11:9-10;9:4-5) but it is explicitly related to the healing of the blind man (11:37). Previously, the theme of Jesus, the light, has been acted out in the healing of the blind man and now here the raising of Lazarus illustrates that he is "the life" (v.25). Both miracles, then, are signs of who Jesus is and what he brings to mankind. But in none of them does the sign more closely approach the reality, namely, life from God, than in the gift of physical life.

In this account, too, the struggle between faith and unbelief reaches a dramatic high-point as there is a great surge of faith because of the miracle (11:45). But the Jewish authorities vigorously oppose this enthusiasm and it even provokes them to plan the death of Jesus (11:45-48,53; 12:10-11,19). Consequently, at the moment when Jesus reveals his life-giving power as Son of God, unbelievers decide to annihilate him (v.4) so that unbelief, which consists in the rejection of Jesus, leads to his death. On the other hand, it is faith in Jesus which leads to life.

The meaning of the miracle is explained at the beginning (v.4), in the centre (vv.23-26) and towards the end of the account (v.40). First, the illness of Lazarus is not to end in death because Jesus will give life. Besides, like the sign of Cana (2:11), his action of giving life to Lazarus will reveal the "glory of God," i.e. the life-giving power he possesses as Son and his own filial communion of love with God by which he honours or glorifies his Father (vv.40-42). The miracle will also bring Jesus to his "glorification," that is, it will lead to his death and resurrection (vv.4,53).

Then in his conversation with Martha Jesus explains that he makes people "rise" again and communicates his divine life, not only on "the last day" but also in the present, to those who believe in him, since he possesses life in the fullness (v.25; cf. 5:21,26). Besides, he *is* the "resurrection," i.e. he is (he effects) the total victory of life over death. "I am the resurrection and the life" - this punch-line of the story is explained positively and negatively in terms of life and death: "He who believes . . . though he *die* . . . shall *live. Whoever lives* . . . shall never *die*." By this paradoxical mode of expression, the concepts of death and life are removed to another sphere for which human life and human death are only images and hints. While the believer may suffer an earthly death he has *life* in a higher sense and for the man who remains on in his earthly existence and is a believer, there is no death. Unlike our way of thinking, the evangelist does not separate the physical and spiritual aspects of life and death, because to "live" and to "die" include as their main content "spiritual" life or "spiritual" death (sin). Thus for him who believes in Jesus death scarcely exists because he "lives" fully. Then the opposite of life is not physical death but rather sin and the deliberate rejection of faith in Jesus - that is real death.

Consequently, the raising of Lazarus to physical life is a sign that Jesus gives life to the believer in the present and at the final resurrection. In his reply later to Martha Jesus stresses the condition for receiving this life from Jesus - faith (v.40). If she understands in faith the meaning of his miracle, then she will see in it the "glory of God," i.e. the life-giving power he possesses as Son and his own filial communion of love with his Father.

First, the introduction (vv.1-16) gives the setting (vv.1-6) and Jesus' dialogue with his disciples about going up to Jerusalem (vv.7-16). Here, the main characters are the sisters, Mary (distinguished by the evangelist from Mary Magdalene) and Martha and their brother Lazarus, who is "loved" by Jesus (vv.3,36). He also represents all christians who are friends, the "beloved" of Jesus (3 Jn 15). As Jesus gives physical life to his beloved Lazarus, so too he will give life to his beloved christians who believe in him. Besides, there are reminders of Jesus' death and resurrection: the mention of Mary who anoints Jesus for burial (v. 1; 12:1-8) and the title "Lord," which is used for the risen Jesus in the resurrection accounts. Throughout, the sisters address Jesus as "Lord" and Jesus calls himself "Son of God" (only here and in 5:25) as he explains the meaning of the sign to come. The insistence at the outset on Jesus' love for Lazarus (vv.5-6) shows that his failure to go to Lazarus does not mean that he does not care. Rather, out of love he does not go to help the sick for he will be of more help to Lazarus when he is dead! Perhaps the reason why he "stays" away from Bethany is that he was to await the will of his Father (vv.41-42).

THE WAY TO LIFE AND DEATH.
11:7-16.

> [7]Then after this he said to the disciples, "Let us go into Judea again." [8]The disciples said to him, "Rabbi, the Jews

were but now seeking to stone you, and are you going there again?" [9]Jesus answered, "Are there not twelve hours in the day? If any one walks in the day, he does not stumble, because he sees the light of this world. [10]But if any one walks in the night, he stumbles, because the light is not in him." [11]Thus he spoke, and then he said to them, "Our friend Lazarus has fallen asleep, but I go to awake him out of sleep." [12]The disciples said to him, "Lord, if he has fallen asleep, he will recover." [13]Now Jesus had spoken of his death, but they thought that he meant taking rest in sleep. [14]Then Jesus told them plainly, "Lazarus is dead; [15]and for your sake I am glad that I was not there, so that you may believe. But let us go to him." [16]Thomas, called the Twin, said to his fellow disciples, "Let us also go, that we may die with him."

Even the discussion whether Jesus should go up to Judea highlights the main point of the story, namely, the death-life motif, for Jesus is going up to Jerusalem not only to die (vv. 7-10, 16) but also in order to raise Lazarus to life (vv. 11-15). Thus his journey is a way to his "hour," a way to his death and a way to life or resurrection for Lazarus and himself. Now the critical time, his "hour" is near for Jesus, and this journey is his last "lap" before his hour. Yet it is still an important moment of activity (vv. 9-10) and the time for a last great "sign" which falls within God's plan and providence. In fact, his going up to Judea is a call to continue to carry out God's works (cf. 9:4-5). Thus, a law of human life is applied to Jesus and also to the christian: people journey securely for the twelve hours of day when the sun shines but stumble during the night when the light goes. So the work of Jesus must be accomplished in the allotted time and he must continue openly and freely to do the will of the Father.

For the christian, the "light" is Jesus and if he believes he "sees" him who is the revealer of God for his life and he walks safely in the light of faith. But when one does not receive Christ in faith, one is plunged into the darkness of sin and unbelief. Here the miracle, which is to take place,

is a promise of "life" because Jesus explains that he is going
to "awaken" Lazarus from "sleep." However, the disciples
misunderstand him: "he will recover" (lit. "will be saved").
But expressions such as "awakening," "sleeping" and
"recovering" (1 Cor 7:39; Mt 27:52) on a second level of
meaning explain that Jesus will raise Lazarus and raises
believers also to eternal life from death. Therefore, this
event should have for them a special meaning: it is a sign
that leads them to faith in Jesus and strengthens their faith
in him, especially now before his "hour." Through this sign,
then, they should come to believe in him as one who overcomes his own death, who gives life and victory to believers
through his death and resurrection.

But the disciples do not understand this meaning, as is
clear from the comment of Thomas: "If he wishes to go, let
us go with him and we will have the same fate as Lazarus,
i.e. death." Obviously he does not pick up Jesus' invitation
to faith in him through the coming sign (vv.15-16) and yet
he shows a positive willingness to "follow" Jesus and to "die
with him." Thus unconsciously his remark is also a statement about christian discipleship as a life of dying and
living with Christ (Rom 6:8). Hence the disciple is like a
grain of wheat for he dies and rises with Jesus (12:24) and his
life of following Jesus is one of faith and self-giving after
his example. In addition, the believer shares now in his
life through faith and is also promised a life of eternal communion with Christ.

JESUS AND MARTHA.
11:17-27.

[17]Now when Jesus came. he found that Lazarus had
already been in the tomb four days. [18]Bethany was near
Jerusalem, about two miles off, [19]and many of the Jews
had come to Martha and Mary to console them concerning their brother. [20]When Martha heard that Jesus was
coming, she went and met him, while Mary sat in the
house. [21]Martha said to Jesus, "Lord, if you had been

here, my brother would not have died. [22]And even now I know that whatever you ask from God, God will give you." [23]Jesus said to her, "Your brother will rise again." [24]Martha said to him, "I know that he will rise again in the resurrection at the last day." [25]Jesus said to her, "I am the resurrection and the life; he who believes in me, though he die, yet shall he live, [26]and whoever lives and believes in me shall never die. Do you believe this?" [27]She said to him, "Yes, Lord; I believe that you are the Christ, the Son of God, he who is coming into the world."

The main part of the story (vv.17-44) first describes the coming of Jesus to Bethany (vv.17-19), where he is met by Martha (vv.20-27) and Mary (vv.28-32) and then his raising of Lazarus (vv.33-44). That Lazarus has been in the tomb for four days places beyond doubt that he is well dead (vv. 17,39). Here "the Jews," who come to console the sisters, are no longer the hostile authorities but the ordinary people of Judea and Jerusalem, who are often receptive to Jesus (vv.31,33,36,45). But the theological centre of the story is the dialogue of Jesus with Martha (vv.20-27). Generally, the two sisters are true to the picture Luke gives of them (10:38-42): in his account Martha is busily serving at table, while Mary "sat at the Lord's feet and listened to his teaching." In John's account Martha rushes out to meet Jesus, while Mary sits quietly at home (vv.29,31). But when Mary hears that the "teacher" has come, she hurries out and "fell at his feet" (v.32).

Martha "believes" in Jesus, but her faith is inadequate for, while she is a woman of faith and trust, she does not yet believe in his power to give life (vv.21-24,27,39). Though the christian confession of faith is on her lips (11:27;20:31), she does not grasp that he is a life-giving Messiah and Son of God or that he is "life" itself (v.25). However, she regards Jesus as an intermediary who is heard by God (v.22). Then the climax of her dialogue with Jesus explains the "sign": Jesus is victorious over death and gives life to the believer now and on "the last day" (vv.23-26).

JESUS AND MARY.
11:28-32.

> 28When she had said this, she went and called her sister Mary, saying quietly, "The Teacher is here and is calling for you." 29And when she heard it, she rose quickly and went to him. 30Now Jesus had not yet come to the village, but was still in the place where Martha had met him. 31When the Jews who were with her in the house, consoling her, saw Mary rise quickly and go out, they followed her, supposing that she was going to the tomb to weep there. 23Then Mary, when she came where Jesus was and saw him, fell at his feet, saying to him, "Lord, if you had been here, my brother would not have died."

The scene of the meeting between Jesus and Mary does not advance the action, for the only difference between her greeting (v.32) and that of Martha (v.21) is that Mary "fell at his feet." This is an expression of her grief and also of her reverence for Jesus. Besides, Mary of Bethany is always pictured at "Jesus' feet" as she is one who laments the death of Lazarus and of Jesus (Lk 10:39; Jn 11:2,32;12:3). Also, her behaviour at the tomb of Lazarus is like that of Mary Magdalene at the tomb of Jesus, who laments her dead and absent Lord (20:11-15). "The teacher calls you" (v.28): perhaps this is an invitation for the reader to come with Mary to Jesus in faith and listen to his word. Similarly, Luke describes her as listening to Jesus' "teaching" (Lk 10:39).

JESUS CONFRONTS DEATH.
11:33-40.

> 33When Jesus saw her weeping, and the Jews who came with her also weeping, he was deeply moved in spirit and troubled; 34and he said, "Where have you laid him?" They said to him, "Lord, come and see." 35Jesus wept. 36So the Jews said, "See how he loved him!" 37But some of them said, "Could not he who opened the eyes of the blind man have kept this man from dying?"

³⁸Then Jesus, deeply moved again, came to the tomb; it was a cave, and a stone lay upon it. ³⁹Jesus said, "Take away the stone." Martha, the sister of the dead man, said to him, "Lord, by this time there will be an odor, for he has been dead four days." ⁴⁰Jesus said to her, "Did I not tell you that if you would believe you would see the glory of God?"

The account focuses on the reactions of Jesus, as he prepares to accomplish the sign, and on the reactions of those who stand around the tomb. In facing the reality of human death, Jesus shows how closely identified he is with man and man's distress as he weeps and is "troubled," not primarily because of the loss of a loved friend, as the by-standers interpret his tears, since he is going to raise him to life. On one level, his grief manifests the concern and love of God so that the Jews could truly say: "see how he loved him." But the "troubled" state of Jesus means that he is touched by the darkness of the fate of human death. Frequently the sadness and darkness of our world, the situation of distress and persecution evoke tears in the New Testament and here the distress of the tomb is not by-passed; rather it is overcome in faith (vv. 25,39; Heb 5:7; Acts 20:19; Rev 7:17;21:4).

Thus the evangelist does not gloss over the harshness of physical death and for him the grief of Jesus is a sad prelude to his effective prayer to his Father (v.41), just as his "troubled" state facing his own death is followed by a prayer to his Father (12:27-28). Consequently, the christianity of this gospel is aware of the darkness of human death ending life on earth, and in this knowledge directs the believing glance to the never-ending future and indestructible quality of the life given in and through Jesus (8:51;12:25). In addition, for the person who understands in faith, the miracle is an experience of "the glory of God" (v.40; cf. above p. 153).

Surprisingly, the reaction of Jesus is also one of anger, for this is the meaning of the phrase "deeply moved in spirit" (vv.33,38). He is angry either because he finds himself face to face with the realm of Satan, which is linked with the powers of death (13:27-30;14:30) or because of the by-standers' lack of faith and understanding, as they do not understand Jesus' troubled state in the face of death and his concern to banish the darkness of death. Martha, for example, stresses only the definitiveness and reality of her brother's death (v.39). Moreover, this scene is closely linked with the healing of the blind man and in the unfavourable comment of the bystanders, who complain that Jesus did not avert the death of Lazarus, the evangelist conveys that Jesus is not only the light but also the life of the world (v.37).

'COME FORTH.'
11:41-44.

> [41]So they took away the stone. And Jesus lifted up his eyes and said, "Father, I thank thee that thou has heard me. [42]I knew that thou hearest me always, but I have said this on account of the people standing by, that they may believe that thou didst send me." [43]When he had said this, he cried with a loud voice, "Lazarus, come out." [44]The dead man came out, his hands and feet bound with bandages, and his face wrapped with a cloth. Jesus said to them, "Unbind him, and let him go."

The evangelist does not dwell on the details of the miracle but rather on Jesus' prayer of communion to his Father. Here the Incarnate Son lifts human eyes to his transcendent ("heaven") Father (v.41;17:1) in a prayer in which petition and answer dovetail, for Jesus' prayer before the actual miracle is one of *thanksgiving* rather than a petition, which we would normally expect in this situation. Also, the ad-dress, "Father," expresses the note of communion and intimacy between himself and his Father. "You have heard me": here Jesus does not ask anything because he has absolute confidence in his Father and as a Son, who is in constant communion with his Father, he always does what is "pleasing" to him (8:29). In fact, he knows that whatever

he asks is in accordance with his Father's will and is therefore heard (1 Jn 3:21-22; 5:14). Thus, in a way, there is no
specific moment of actual petition in mind here because
Jesus is in constant communion with his Father, who
always "hears," even the unspoken thoughts of his heart.
Therefore, he has already "heard" his petition for Lazarus.

Similarly, his own prayer facing death is a proclamation
of communion with his Father (12:28) and is the request of
one who stands in perfect unity with his Father. Thus
Jesus continually stands before God as the asker and, therefore, as the receiver without needing to petition his Father,
because his Father has placed all in his hands (3:35-36; 13:3;
17:2). In reality, he had no need to petition him because all
his life is in accordance with his Father's will and in this
sense his whole life is a prayer. Consequently, the sympathy
in work and thought between Father and Son is always
perfect and uninterrupted and now revealed in action (5:19).
Prayer, then, as regards Jesus, is the conscious realization of
the divine will and not a petition for what is contingent
(1 Jn 3:22) or for any uncertain or unexpected gift. This is
the deeper sense of Martha's comment (v.22).

The thanksgiving and joy of Jesus, because the hearing
of his prayer will lead the crowd to believe, is not self-
centred, for his only wish is that they will come to know the
Father who sent him (v.42). Because the prayer is heard they
will see a miracle which is the work of the Father. Through
the exercise of the life-giving power of the Father ("the glory
of God": v.40), they will come to know the Father in faith
and receive "life" (vv.25-26) through faith themselves.
Clearly, Jesus does not want to gain anything for himself.

The words and actions of Jesus at the tomb also convey
the meaning of Lazarus' restoration to life as a sign, not only
of the eternal life which believers receive through faith; it is
also a promise that on the last day Jesus will raise believers
to eternal life. In fact, the scene at the tomb acts out in a
dramatic fashion what Jesus has already promised (ch. 5).
The text speaks for itself: "All who are in the *tombs* will
hear his *voice* (i.e. of the Son of Man) . . . and *come forth* . . .

to the *resurrection of life*" (5:28-29). "Lazarus had already been in the *tomb* . . . I am the *resurrection* and the *life* . . . He cried with a loud *voice* . . . 'Lazarus, *come forth*'" (11:17,25, 43). This "loud voice," a way of expressing the power of Jesus, is the voice of the Son of Man, the transcendent Jesus who will summon believers "who have done good" (5:29) to a final resurrection of life "on the last day" (11:24).

ONE MAN DIES FOR THE PEOPLE.
11:45-53.

> [45]Many of the Jews therefore, who had come with Mary and had seen what he did, believed in him; [46]but some of them went to the Pharisees and told them what Jesus had done. [47]So the chief priests and the Pharisees gathered the council, and said, "What are we to do? For this man performs many signs. [48]If we let him go on thus, every one will believe in him, and the Romans will come and destroy both our holy place and our nation." [49]But one of them, Caiaphas, who was high priest that year, said to them, "You know nothing at all; [50]you do not understand that it is expedient for you that one man should die for the people, and that the whole nation should not perish." [51]He did not say this of his own accord, but being high priest that year he prophesied that Jesus should die for the nation, [52]and not for the nation only, but to gather into one the children of God who are scattered abroad. [53]So from that day on they took counsel how to put him to death.

The end of the account, which describes the effects of Jesus' sign (vv.45-54) drives home the paradox: Jesus' gift of life leads to his own death. Therefore, the statement of the high priest (v.50) gets special comment. But the effect of the miracle is divisive: on the one hand, the hesitating crowd of Jerusalem grows strong in their faith in Jesus because of the sign and they will acclaim him king because of it (v.45;12:9,17). On the other hand, this ground-swell threatens the leaders and leaves them helpless. Narrowness, ambition, and desire for power lurk beneath the seemingly religious tone of their excuses (vv.47-48). They claim to defend the religious freedom of their people: because of this revolutionary, Jesus, the Romans will come and destroy their temple and their nation. But the irony is that the policy followed by the leaders brought about in the end the precise result it was designed to avoid, for by the time the gospel was written, the Romans had come, destroyed their temple and scattered the Jewish people (v.52).

While the leaders "gathered" to kill Jesus (v.47), the christian community, God's dispersed children, are "gathered" into one (v.52), having become children of God through Jesus' death. In this crucial moment of history, in "that famous year" (18:13), Caiaphas, who, as the high-priest would have been considered to have the gift of prophecy, gives voice to a maxim of political expediency which reveals his craft and cynicism: one person should die for the people. While accusing others of ignorance, he reveals his own great ignorance by his unconscious prophecy. Clearly he is anxious to get rid of this man Jesus for fear he might, as one more in a series of troublemakers, provoke the Romans to action. Therefore, it would be necessary to put Jesus to death for the safety and security of the people (v.50). But the high-priest is God's instrument for proclaiming a deeper meaning: Jesus dies on behalf of a new people, the christian community. Thus by his death the children of God, the community of believers, are gathered into one (v.52) and it is through the death of Jesus that they are made children of God. Again the death-life motif appears: the giving birth to the new people of God takes place through the imparting of divine life. Therefore, a family unity of all the children of God results from the divine life imparted to them through the death of Jesus and also through their response of faith (vv.45,48). Thus Jesus dies for the life of the world (6:51) and through his death and their response of faith, he gathers into one community a scattered group - the Church.

PRESSURE TACTICS.
11:54-57.

> [54]Jesus therefore no longer went about openly among the Jews, but went from there to the country near the wilderness, to a town called Ephraim; and there he stayed with the disciples.
> [55]Now the Passover of the Jews was at hand, and many went up from the country to Jerusalem before the Passover, to purify themselves. [56]They were looking for Jesus and saying to one another as they stood in the temple, "What do you think? That he will not come to the feast?" [57]Now the chief priests and the Pharisees had given orders that if any one knew where he was, he should let them know, so that they might arrest him.

After this "sign" the atmosphere in and around Jerusalem becomes more explosive so that Jesus withdraws again and now only disciples are with him (cf. 10:40). As the conflict between faith and unbelief continues, the mention of Passover suggests that Jesus' death is near and, whereas some seek Jesus in good will, the leaders of the people try to isolate him even more by employing pressure tactics on the crowd (v.57; 12:10,42).

ANOINTING FOR BURIAL.
12:1-8.

> **12** Six days before the Passover, Jesus came to Bethany, where Lazarus was, whom Jesus had raised from the dead. [2]There they made him a supper; Martha served, and Lazarus was one of those at table with him. [3]Mary took a pound of costly ointment of pure nard and anointed the feet of Jesus and wiped his feet with her hair; and the house was filled with the fragrance of the ointment. [4]But Judas Iscariot, one of his disciples (he who was to betray him), said, [5]"Why was this ointment not sold for three hundred denarii and given to the poor?"

⁶This he said, not that he cared for the poor but because he was a thief, and as he had the money box he used to take what was put into it. ⁷Jesus said, "Let her alone, let her keep it for the day of my burial. ⁸The poor you always have with you, but you do not always have me."

The anointing of Jesus at Bethany and his entry into the city as king prefigure and prepare for the events of his "hour," for his death and resurrection. First of all, Mary of Bethany, who "fell at the feet" of Jesus (11:32) now anoints his feet with expensive perfume and then wipes them with her hair. This action of Mary and Jesus' comment on it in his reply to Judas (vv.3,7) are the distinctive focus of John's account (cf. Mk 14:3-9; Mt 26:6-13; Lk 7:36-38).

Whereas one might anoint the feet of a dead person in preparation for burial, it was not the custom to anoint the feet of a living person. Here the gesture of Mary, which anticipates Jesus' burial after his death (19:39-40), takes its meaning from Jesus' words: "Leave her alone; she kept this perfume until now to prepare me for burial" (v.7). Thus Mary's action constitutes an anointing of his body for burial and unconsciously she was performing a prophetic action. While the Sanhedrin were plotting Jesus' death (11:53), Mary's action is preparing him for death. Besides, Jesus' gift of life to Lazarus meets with two reactions: on the one hand, the "gathering" of the Sanhedrin (11:47) is the supreme refusal to believe; on the other hand, the anointing by Mary, one of the family loved by Jesus (11:5), is a culminating expression of loving faith. Already, Caiaphas had unconsciously prophesied the death of Jesus and its effects (11:50) and likewise Mary, by her action, unconsciously gives a preview of his burial.

The costly perfume and the scent which filled the whole house (v.3), accent the dignity of Jesus, who rightly receives this token of respect and thus they prefigure the honourable interment after his death (19:39-40). Thus she gives witness to deep faith in Jesus, which he, in defending her action, acknowledges: "You do not always have me" (v.8): those present will not have Jesus always among them because he goes to his death and burial (12:35-36). But Mary has recognized the dignity and greatness of his presence and by her gesture of loving faith she has reminded those present who it is they have in their midst. The emphasis, then, is not on the first part of his statement: "The poor you have always with you," for the point is not that the deprivation of poverty is an inevitable social condition for all time (cf. Deut 15:11) but rather that the death of Jesus will leave disciples deprived of his presence.

Therefore, Mary is bearing witness unconsciously to Jesus' dignity and glory in death and burial by her deed which is a testimony of loving faith and a call to faith in the glory and dignity of Jesus who passes through death and burial to his Father. In contrast to her faith, the forces of unbelief are at work in Judas, who will reject Jesus through betrayal. Not only is he the agent of the prince of darkness (6:70;13:2,27); also this trusted "financier" of the small community, who had a place of honour beside Jesus (v.6; 13:27-29), turns thief as well as traitor. Thus the scene as a whole expresses the moments of grief, sadness, unbelief, betrayal and glory which the "hour" of Jesus will bring. It means, too, that Jesus, though physically absent, remains for believers, even in his death, the hidden, glorified one to whom honour and worship is due.

A KING'S WELCOME.
12:9-19.

> [9]When the great crowd of the Jews learned that he was there, they came, not only on account of Jesus but also to see Lazarus, whom he had raised from the dead. [10]So the chief priests planned to put Lazarus also to death, [11]because on account of him many of the Jews were going away and believing in Jesus.
>
> [12]The next day a great crowd who had come to the feast heard that Jesus was coming to Jerusalem. [13]So they took branches of palm trees and went out to meet him,

crying, "Hosanna! Blessed is he who comes in the name of the Lord, even the King of Israel!" [14]And Jesus found a young ass and sat upon it; as it is written,
[15]"Fear not, daughter of Zion;
    behold, your king is coming,
    sitting on an ass's colt!"
[16]His disciples did not understand this at first; but when Jesus was glorified, then they remembered that this had been written of him and had been done to him. [17]The crowd that had been with him when he called Lazarus out of the tomb and raised him from the dead bore witness. [18]The reason why the crowd went to meet him was that they heard he had done this sign. [19]The Pharisees then said to one another, "You see that you can do nothing; look, the world has gone after him."

As the crowds become more involved in Christ and faith in him becomes more widespread, the authorities plan to eliminate not only this faith but also its source—Lazarus himself, whose raising from the dead by Jesus had been the "sign" leading many to faith (vv.9-11). In this atmosphere of conflict between faith and unbelief, Jesus enters the city of his death as messianic king (vv.12-19). Just as the anointing at Bethany prefigures his burial in death, so also his entry into the city and his acclamation by the crowd as king look ahead to his enthronement or exaltation as king on the cross where he manifests God's love which draws believers to Jesus (3:14-16; 12:32). Thus through his death he becomes the king or the Lord of life for all believers (18:37). Besides, it is only later after his resurrection that disciples, through the light of the Holy Spirit, grasp this deeper meaning of Jesus' action and the crowd's response.

First of all, the crowd take palm branches and go out to welcome Jesus, as if he were a victorious king, with the words of the psalm, which originally referred to the entry of the king into the temple to give thanks for victory (v.13; Ps 118:15; Mk 11:7-10 par.). In the life of the people this had become a joyful prayer of expectancy for their Messiah-Saviour, one "who comes in the name of the Lord," i.e. as

Yahweh's representative, the longed-for leader who brings redemption that ends enslavement once and for all. Therefore, Jesus is "coming" to Jerusalem and he, the messianic king, whose coming has been awaited by his people, is on his way. Thus with shouts of praise and joy ("hosanna") they wish God's blessings on Jesus, the Saviour and true messianic king of God's people, Israel (1:49).

Jesus is seated on a donkey, not as a political or warlike leader but as king of a universal, definitive kingdom which begins in Sion and spreads throughout the world (v.15; Zech 9:9-10). But his kingship is not of "this world" (18:37) for this is not the temporal domination of a king but the power of a master who welcomes disciples and wishes to see all, "the world" (v.19), come to him. Also his kingship begins with his enthronement or exaltation on the cross where he manifests God's love and "draws" people to believe in him. Now, mounted on a donkey in solemn procession, Jesus, the expected king, God's true representative, is among his people (v.13), who are not to be "afraid" because he is the manifestation of God, God's own king in their midst (Zeph 3:16-17). But the crowd unwittingly, without realizing the full implications, proclaim him as the king or Lord of life for all believers (11:25), as God's self-manifestation among them. Even the Pharisees in their frustration are also unconscious prophets of the universal kingship of Jesus, the one who offers life to all "the world" who follow or "go after" him (12:19).

The Meaning of the "Hour" of Jesus.
12:20-36.

THE GRAIN OF WHEAT.
12:20-26

20Now among those who went up to worship at the feast were some Greeks. 21So these came to Philip, who was from Bethsaida in Galilee, and said to him, "Sir, we wish to see Jesus." ²²Philip went and told Andrew; Andrew went with Philip and they told Jesus. ²³And Jesus answered them, "The hour has come for the Son of man to be glorified. ²⁴Truly, truly, I say to you, unless a grain of wheat falls into the earth and dies, it remains alone; but if it dies, it bears much fruit. ²⁵He who loves his life loses it, and he who hates his life in this world will keep it for eternal life. ²⁶If any one serves me, he must follow me; and where I am, there shall my servant be also; if any one serves me, the Father will honor him."

After these two events which look forward to his "hour," Jesus now explains the meaning of this "hour" (vv. 20-36): it is a time when he is "glorified" and "lifted up"; it is also a time of victory and "judgment." This explanation is occasioned by the arrival of some Greeks who want to see him and the discourse ends with Jesus going into hiding in the face of more hostility and unbelief which his words provoke (v. 36). Again, as often happens throughout the gospel, his words of self-revelation (vv. 23-28, 31-32, 35-36) alternate with reactions of incomprehension from the crowd (vv. 29, 34).

Already the Pharisees had unconsciously proclaimed the universal scope of his kingship and the "whole world" which "has gone after him" (v. 19) is immediately mirrored in the gentiles who come to "see" him. But their coming points to the future, worldwide effect of Jesus' death and resurrection, the "much fruit" (v. 24) and "all" those whom Jesus "draws" to "see" him in faith and "follow" him (vv. 20, 24, 26, 32). Consequently, these gentiles are the vanguard of mankind coming to Jesus in faith.

The "hour" of Jesus, which embraces death and resurrection, begins with the arrival of these Greeks and this points to the universal effect of his death which "draws" to faith. Also, the hour is a time which initiates a new era in salvation history. Though it is the hour of Jesus (2:4), it is not controlled by himself or mankind, for it is determined by his Father (7:6,8;8:20). Moreover, it is an hour of anguish and suffering when he is "troubled," as he faces his struggle against the forces of evil and unbelief (v.27;11:33;13:21).

But it is also a time of triumph, because the fruits of his death are all those people who are "drawn" by his self-giving love on the cross to believe (v.32). Then, as the "Son of Man," a title which emphasizes his saving work achieved through death and resurrection, he is "glorified" (v.23), just like the Suffering Servant, who was himself exalted and glorified (Is 52:13). Therefore, the passion is the "hour" of glory and leads to, receives light and meaning from, the resurrection. Indeed, the evangelist cannot contemplate the suffering of Jesus without seeing at the same glance the effects, through the resurrection, of Jesus' saving work and love, which reach their climax on the cross. The passion, then, is already a "glorification" of Jesus.

In the Old Testament "glory" and "glorification" in relation to God mean that he reveals himself in the exercise of his power and his love and that people respond by "honouring" and "glorifying" him in some positive manner. Similarly, Jesus on the cross leading to resurrection, reveals God's saving life and love while disciples respond by following Jesus and through faith in him they receive the saving life of God (17:1-2). Then this saving work and power of Jesus (glorification) are described in the image of a wheat-grain, which dies and bears much fruit. In other words, the death of Jesus leads to life for many, since through faith believers come to share in his divine life. Thus Jesus, the Son of Man, is glorified by the fecundity of a death which leads to the birth of a new people. These will have been drawn to him in faith, a faith which contemplates God's love in the crucified, exalted Lord (12:32;3:14-16).

But the law of death and life is true for disciples as well as for Jesus. Therefore, in order to enter into a communion of life with Jesus now and in the after-life, there is need to "hate" one's life (v.25), that is, through self-giving in following and serving Jesus, believers come to "live" in the true sense (v.25;11:16). Thus the call to follow Jesus is an invitation to be "with him" and to share in his life. But being with Christ and sharing in his life is also a gift of the Father and his way of honouring all those who believe in his Son (v.26).

THE GLORY OF FATHER AND SON.
12:27-36.

> [27]"Now is my soul troubled. And what shall I say? 'Father, save me from this hour'? No, for this purpose I have come to this hour. [28]Father, glorify thy name." Then a voice came from heaven, "I have glorified it, and I will glorify it again." [29]The crowd standing by heard it and said that it had thundered. Others said, "An angel has spoken to him." [30]Jesus answered, "This voice has come for your sake, not for mine. [31]Now is the judgment of this world, now shall the ruler of this world be cast out; [32]and I, when I am lifted up from the earth, will draw all men to myself." [33]He said this to show by what death he was to die. [34]The crowd answered him, "We have heard from the law that the Christ remains for ever. How can you say that the Son of man must be lifted up? Who is this Son of man?" [35]Jesus said to them, "The light is with you for a little longer. Walk while you have the light, lest the darkness overtake you; he who walks in the darkness does not know where he goes. [36]While you have the light, believe in the light, that you may become sons of light."
>
> When Jesus had said this, he departed and hid himself from them.

The prayer of Jesus to his Father as he faces death and the Father's response, expressed in the "voice from heaven" (vv.27-28) show that not only Jesus but also his Father are "glorified" in the "hour." Surprisingly, Jesus does not pray to be spared the suffering, but rather the heart of his prayer is: "Father, glorify your name" (v.27). He wishes that the saving life and love of God ("name") may be manifested in his own suffering and also that people may come to acknowledge God as the loving Father of Jesus and as their own Father because of what he has done for them in and through Jesus. Thus his petition is also a prayer of revelation and communion, for it reveals the perfect harmony and communion of will and love between Jesus and his Father in this "hour" (cf. 11:41-42).

This glorification of Jesus is also the glorification of his Father, for Jesus accepts and faces death in loving response to his Father, knowing that he is revealing the Father's saving life and love for man. In comparison with the Synoptics' account of the prayer of Jesus in the garden, this scene stresses more the revelatory quality of Jesus' suffering, which for John is a manifestation of divine love and of the communion between Jesus and his Father (Mk 14:32-42 par.). Matthew and Mark, in contrast with John do not mention an answer of the Father to the prayer of Jesus in the garden. Luke, however, by introducing an "angel," who comes to strengthen Jesus, implies that God responds with his supportive presence (22:43).

But in this account the "voice," which reveals the communion between Jesus and his Father, is a response from the Father to Jesus in prayer and in this respect it differs from that "voice from heaven" in the baptism and transfiguration of Jesus (Mk 1:11 par.; 9:7 par.). In addition, this voice is "from heaven," that is, it is a divine, authoritative revelation of the Father which confirms and grants the request of Jesus. Therefore, it is a twofold 'Amen' of the Father to his Son's prayer: it has been so and it will be so, i.e. the Father's name has been glorified and will be glorified.

But the response of the Father also implies that the Son, too, has been glorified and will be glorified, for, significantly, the "name" of the Father is not repeated: lit. "I have glorified and I will glorify again." This response expresses that just as the Father revealed and offered his life and love to man on earth through Jesus, who, in turn, revealed or "glorified" his Father, so now this revelation will continue throughout the passion, resurrection of Jesus and even afterwards. Therefore, the saving work of the Father and of

Jesus continues in the life of the christian community. This happens through the Holy Spirit who "glorifies" or manifests down through history both Jesus and his Father in the hearts of believers (16:13-15).

This "voice from heaven" is not only a divine "Amen" to the prayer of Jesus and a revelation of the Father on behalf of his Son. It is also an invitation to the crowd to believe in his Son for the "hour" has come when the believer can see the supreme revelation of divine love for man and the loving communion between Jesus and his Father in the work of redeeming mankind (12:32;3:14-16). But the two different reactions of the crowd show they do not understand or believe (v.29). Besides, this "voice from heaven" conveys that the era of salvation and judgment has begun with the "hour" of Jesus' death leading to resurrection. This image of the "voice from heaven" is sometimes found in Jewish apocalyptic literature where it is related to a prayer and also a divine response which consists of a revelation about coming days of salvation and judgment (Henoch 65:2-4; Apoc of Baruch 22:1;4 Esdras 6:11-28).

The "hour" is a time of "judgment" and victory (v.31), for the passion of Jesus in the gospel marks the climax of a confrontation between Jesus and the power of evil or unbelief at work in those who deliberately reject and condemn Jesus (19:13-15). Now at the end before his death, a final assault is made on Jesus by Judas, who acts under the influence of the powers of darkness, the "ruler of this world" (v.31;13:2,27) and all those who will reject Jesus, will have "judged" or condemned themselves (3:18). But the "hour" is not only associated with the climax of this confrontation with the powers of darkness. It is also a moment of victory when Jesus defeats the "ruler of this world" by drawing so many believers to himself from the cross which is his throne (12:31-32;14:30). Therefore, he is the victor since, lifted up and enthroned like a king on the cross from where he reveals God's love, he invites and draws those who are receptive to this supreme expression of a loving Father and a loving Son.

However, the crowd do not grasp the meaning of Jesus' work and destiny as a Son of Man lifted up on the cross, as they hope for a messianic king whose rule would be eternal (Ps 89:37) and therefore they cannot accept that the Son of Man and Messiah should die. Consequently, Jesus does not enter into further debate but urgently exhorts them to believe, for the time is short. Rather let them accept him who is the light, the revealer of God, make him and his message the guide and norm for their lives, and avoid the darkness of unbelief (vv. 35-36). Then, illustrating dramatically his words about the passing of the "light," Jesus hides himself and withdraws in the face of increasing hostility.

E. CONCLUSION AND SUMMARY OF JESUS' PUBLIC MINISTRY. 12:37-50.

THE MYSTERY OF REJECTION.
12:37-43.

³⁷Though he had done so many signs before them, yet they did not believe in him; ³⁸it was that the word spoken by the prophet Isaiah might be fulfilled:

"Lord, who has believed our report, and to whom has the arm of the Lord been revealed?

³⁹Therefore they could not believe. For Isaiah again said,
⁴⁰"He has blinded their eyes and hardened their heart,
lest they should see with their eyes and perceive with their heart,
and turn for me to heal them."

⁴¹Isaiah said this because he saw his glory and spoke of him. ⁴²Nevertheless many even of the authorities believed in him, but for fear of the Pharisees they did not confess it, lest they should be put out of the synagogue; ⁴³for they loved the praise of men more than the praise of God.

The first part of the gospel (chs. 1-12) ends with a reflection on the response of people to Jesus (vv.37-43) and a solemn proclamation of Jesus recapitulating some leading ideas already developed in the gospel (vv.44-50). That lack of response which Jesus encountered in spite of his many "signs" (v.37: cf. 1:11), is also an invitation to the reader to believe in him, and the destiny of Jesus, which is already reflected in the rejected Servant of God (Is 53:1) is part of God's plan for his Son. Thus Jesus relived the experience of a prophet like Isaiah to whom God revealed that his message would fall on deaf ears and that no matter what he did or said he would go unrecognized by wilfully blind eyes (v.40; Is 6:10). But this rejection of Jesus does not disprove his claims in any way; rather it confirms them and invites people to accept him.

Reflecting on the mission of Isaiah, the evangelist conceives him as getting a preview of the glory and life of God made manifest in Jesus, and the prophet is contrasted with the blindness of unbelievers, of people who actually lived in the time of Christ and who were yet unable to recognize this "glory" in Jesus (1:14). There were, in fact, many influential people who accepted Jesus, but through fear and human respect would not acknowledge their faith in him (5:44).

EPILOGUE.
12:44-50.

44And Jesus cried out and said, "He who believes in me, believes not in me but in him who sent me. 45And he who sees me sees him who sent me. 46I have come as light into the world, that whoever believes in me may not remain in darkness. 47If any one hears my sayings and does not keep them, I do not judge him; for I did not come to judge the world but to save the world. 48He who rejects me and does not receive my sayings has a judge; the word that I have spoken will be his judge on the last day. 49For I have not spoken on my own authority; the Father who sent me has himself given me commandment what to say and what to speak. 50And I know that his commandment is eternal life. What I say, therefore, I say as the Father has bidden me."

The last public message of Jesus is a summary of his mission and a summons to faith. This faith, however, reaches beyond the person of Jesus, for its goal is the Father who manifests himself in Jesus. Also, Jesus himself carries out his mission always in the awareness that he represents his Father and, therefore, to contemplate Jesus in faith is to recognize him as the revealer of the Father, the "light." Moreover, to believe in him is to be liberated from darkness, from the sphere of unbelief, sin, of estrangement from God (v.46), whereas to reject him and his word is to condemn oneself and to become alienated from God. Jesus only saves and it is man alone who condemns or judges himself (v.48).

Finally, Jesus owes his whole mission and message to the Father. Formerly the words of God, which are communicated by Moses to the covenant people, had been the basis of a human life lived in harmony with God and man (Deut 8:3;18:18-19;32:45-47). But Jesus is greater than Moses, for he speaks the Father's very words and those who accept him come to share in the life of Jesus and his Father. Therefore, Jesus has, he is, the Word of life (v.50; 1 Jn 1:1-3).

Part III.
THE "HOUR" OF JESUS.
13-21.

THE COMPOSITION OF CHAPTERS 13-17

Jesus' final message to his disciples (13:31-17:26) is preceded by a meal scene in which Jesus performs a prophetic action in washing the feet of his disciples and then makes a verbal prophecy about his betrayal (13:2-20). The evangelist probably knew of an independent tradition that Jesus had washed the disciples' feet and he frames that scene with traditions about the betrayal. He expands this with dialogue and traditional material about discipleship in order to link the footwashing with the death of Jesus. The duplicate interpretation of Jesus' prophetic action (vv. 2-11, 12-20) probably reflects two originally separate accounts that have now been combined by the evangelist.

The most striking aspect of this Last Supper scene is that there is no mention of the institution of the eucharist as in the Synoptics. John divorces the eucharist from the Last Supper context and interprets it as the food and drink that gives eternal life (6:51-58). Just as water baptism is a new birth or begetting which gives eternal life (3:3-8) so also eating the flesh and blood of Jesus nourishes that life. He shapes a distinctive view of sacraments according to which visible elements are signs communicating life through communion with Jesus.

Though there are similarities between the Last Supper accounts of the Synoptics and the discourse of Jesus on the bread of life (Lk 22:19; Jn 6:51) this does not explain satisfactorily why he omits the institution of the eucharist from his Last Supper account. Many explanations have been offered among which the following are selected as the most plausible:

(a) John understood the eucharist as a key sign of Jesus' messiahship and drew on the traditional early christian association of the bread with manna to link his eucharistic teaching and the miracle of the loaves in ch. 6.

(b) John's view of sacraments as communicating life through personal communion with Christ finds a more suitable context in the discourse on the bread of life where, in typically johannine fashion, the focus is on Jesus as the bread of life. From the beginning of ch. 13, however, the focus is on the "hour" of Jesus when he manifests his love to the full for his own through the most supreme expression of his love (cf. 19:30; 13:1 is a caption for all that is to come). This love is expressed most effectively *during* the Last Supper in the symbolic action of footwashing. Since it is very probable that the evangelist did know that the institution of the eucharist took place at the Last Supper, instead of simply removing it, he interprets it for the worshipping community, as Paul also did for the Corinthians (1 Cor 11:17-34). The footwashing, therefore, is an explanation of what the eucharist is really all about. It is a commentary on the deeper meaning of the eucharist: it reveals Jesus as the servant who gives his life out of love for, in the service of, others. Where the Synoptics narrate the institution of the eucharist, John narrates its fulfillment and realization and thus links worship with service of the community. Not that the footwashing is a symbol of the eucharist but it is a help for those participating in the eucharist to understand its meaning. It symbolizes the self-giving of Jesus out of love which the eucharist represents and celebrates. It has also been suggested that the gospel is based on homilies preached at the eucharist assembly and that John's account of the footwashing is a homily with the words of institution omitted because they are not relevant to the theme of the homily.

13:31—17:26

These chapters are not always united because the final words of ch. 14 (vv. 30-31) indicate the end of a discourse and Jesus' departure from the table. Yet Jesus still continues to speak for three more chapters and only in 18:1 does the departure take place. An earlier written form of the gospel probably contained a last discourse consisting of an introduction (13:31-38) and a final address of Jesus, substantially the same as what is now ch. 14. This is mainly his message of comfort and consolation for disciples, distressed over his words about going away. Then more discourses were tacked on to what was already part of the gospel, the longest addition being chs. 15-16. The central theme of these chapters is the life of the disciples and their encounter with the "world" after Jesus' departure.

There are three main sections in these chapters which are closely linked:

15:1-17: some motifs, such as requests in prayer, union with Christ, love, have been mentioned already in 13:31—14:31. The central theme is that love should unite the disciples with Jesus and with one another.

15:18—16:4a: this deals with the contrasting theme of "hatred". These two sections do not touch the theme of Jesus' departure so prominent in 13:31—14:31. They focus rather on the position of the community, moving from the positive images of union, fruitfulness and love which characterize the community to the hostility and rejection that it will experience in the "world." There is a striking similarity between ch. 15 and ch. 10.

16:4b-33: here many motifs of 13:31—14:31 are duplicated: Jesus' imminent departure; the question about where Jesus is going; the sorrow of disciples; Paraclete sayings; disciples will see Jesus again; the Father loves the disciples; requests in prayer; disciples will desert Jesus.

The prayer of ch. 17 was probably not part of the Farewell Discourse in the earlier edition of the gospel, where ch. 14 was directly followed by ch. 18. It seems to stand apart from chs. 15-16, for it is a tightly knit whole welding material together more smoothly than any other parts of the previous sections. As Jesus' prayer of "the hour," it provides a perfect climax to the discourse as a whole. It may have been an independent composition added at the same time as chs. 15-16, though it links well with ch. 16 since it also envisages the situation of disciples in the "world" (16:20, 28, 32; 17:1, 13-15).

The first discourse, then, (13:31—14:31) belongs to an earlier stage in the composition of the gospel, when it probably contained a last discourse consisting of an introduction (13:31-38) and a final address (ch. 14). The gospel at this stage has been the work of an "evangelist," some dominant preacher and theologian, who had given shape to the material and who may have edited his work more than once. Probably a redactor, a disciple of the evangelist, and belonging to the "johannine school," is responsible for the addition of chs. 15-17. However, he probably drew heavily on material that came from the evangelist for 15:1—16:4a and for ch. 17.

A. THE LAST SUPPER.

13:1-30
JESUS WASHES THE FEET OF DISCIPLES: A SIGN OF LOVE AND DEATH.
13:1-11.

13 Now before the feast of the Passover, when Jesus knew that his hour had come to depart out of this world to the Father, having loved his own who were in the world, he loved them to the end. ²And during supper, when the devil had already put it into the heart of Judas Iscariot, Simon's son, to betray him, ³Jesus, knowing that the Father had given all things into his hands, and that he had come from God and was going to God, ⁴rose from supper, laid aside his garments, and girded himself with a towel. ⁵Then he poured water into a basin, and began to wash the disciples' feet, and to wipe them with the towel with which he was girded. ⁶He came to Simon Peter; and Peter said to him, "Lord, do you wash my feet?" ⁷Jesus answered him, "What I am doing you do not know now, but afterward you will understand." ⁸Peter said to him, "You shall never wash my feet." Jesus answered him, "If I do not wash you, you have no part in me." ⁹Simon Peter said to him, "Lord, not my feet only but also my hands and my head!" ¹⁰Jesus said to him, "He who has bathed does not need to wash, except for his feet, but he is clean all over; and you are clean, but not every one of you." ¹¹For he knew who was to betray him; that was why he said, "You are not all clean."

UNTIL NOW Jesus had addressed his message to a wider
audience and had prompted a double reaction: some accepted, others rejected him. At this point his self-revelation
to the world is closed (18:20) and in the second part of the
gospel (chs. 13-20) he reveals himself only to a small group
of believing disciples. While on occasions he had referred
to the coming hour of his death and resurrection and the
meaning of his "glorification," now the actual events of the
"hour" are described. They are preceded, however, by a
long discourse (13:31-17:26) which interprets them much
in the same way as discourses in the first part of the gospel
explain the "signs" of Jesus (cf. ch. 6). Also, these "signs"
of his public life are now over and that is why some call the
first part of the gospel "the book of signs," the second part
"the book of glory," although resurrection appearances
are also referred to as "signs" (20:30-31).

The opening words (v. 1) are a caption for all that is to
come (chs. 13-19), for they describe the motivating force
which leads Jesus to wash the feet of disciples and to lay
down his life in love for them. His death, therefore, expresses the completeness of his love and this love is now
dramatically symbolized in the footwashing. But his death is
also a victory since it is a return to his Father. Besides, death
comes at Passover time when Jesus dies as a Passover Lamb
and brings forgiveness (1:29; 19:14,36). However, the
Synoptics and the Fourth Gospel differ as to whether
Jesus died on the eve of Passover or on the feastday itself.
In any case, Jesus faces death as master of the situation and
fully aware of what was ahead, although this Last Supper
atmosphere is also tense with hope and tragedy. Now the
forces of darkness which lead Jesus to his death are set in
motion and are at work in Judas (vv. 2,18,27). Yet they are
opposed by Jesus who has received all power from his
Father, in particular, the power to save by his self-giving
death, which is symbolized by the footwashing, and also the
power to break the power of evil at work in Judas (vv. 2-3).

This gesture of washing the feet of his disciples is given
two interpretations by Jesus. First, it is a kind of prophetic

action which represents his death, expressing symbolically what was the essential of the life and suffering of Jesus, namely, that love which undertakes the most humble service in order to save mankind (vv.2-11). Thus Jesus acts out beforehand his humble self-giving in death just as Mary of Bethany acted out the anointing of his body for burial (12: 1-7). Secondly, the gesture is an example of self-giving and humble service to be imitated by disciples (vv.12-20). Therefore, it is both a prophetic action pointing to his death out of love and a moral example.

The action in itself, too, is an expression of humble service and love. As sandalled feet tended to get dusty on unpaved roads, the usual hospitality consisted of providing water for a guest to wash his own feet. But the washing of the master's feet was not required of a slave; rather it was a service occasionally offered by disciples to a teacher or rabbi out of devotion (cf. v.14). Now Jesus, God's Son on his way back to his Father, performs a gesture which would express the spirit of loving and humble service. Thus Jesus manifests in a symbolic action the spirit of humble and self-giving love with which he lays down his life for his friends (15:13). Also, through his death, disciples are drawn into a communion of life with Jesus, through which they "have a part" with him (v.8) and, therefore, they must have their feet washed in order to express symbolically that they are brought into a communion of life with Jesus through his death, which is an act of self-giving and humble service to mankind. Thus Peter has to learn that it is not the act of washing which matters most but rather what it means—the death of Jesus out of love (v.10: omitting "except for his feet"). It is only after his death and resurrection that disciples will see the connection between his death and this gesture of Jesus in washing their feet (v.7). Also, this fellowship with Jesus "cleanses" disciples from sin, except the one who is preparing to betray him (vv.8,10,11). Moreover, for christian readers the washing with water and the "cleansing" would have been a reminder of the baptismal liturgy (Acts 22:16; Titus 3:5; 1 Cor 6:11).

"I HAVE GIVEN YOU AN EXAMPLE."
13:12-20.

> [12]When he had washed their feet, and taken his gar-
> ments, and resumed his place, he said to them, "Do you
> know what I have done to you? [13]You call me Teacher
> and Lord; and you are right, for so I am. [14]If I then, your
> Lord and Teacher, have washed your feet, you also ought
> to wash one another's feet. [15]For I have given you an
> example, that you also should do as I have done to you.
> [16]Truly, truly, I say to you, a servant is not greater than
> his master; nor is he who is sent greater than he who sent
> him. [17]If you know these things, blessed are you if you
> do them. [18]I am not speaking of you all; I know whom I
> have chosen; it is that the scripture may be fulfilled, 'He
> who ate my bread has lifted his heel against me.' [19]I tell
> you this now, before it takes place, that when it does take
> place you may believe that I am he. [20]Truly, truly, I say
> to you, he who receives any one whom I send receives me;
> and he who receives me receives him who sent me."

This gesture is also a symbol for christian living, for
disciples and all christians not only share, "have a part"
(cf. v.8) in the life which comes through the death of Jesus;
they must also imitate the spirit behind this action and the
spirit of love which leads Jesus to death. Thus the "master"
(v.16) has done something which expresses the kind of self-
giving and humble service disciples should offer one
another. "I have given you an example, that you also should
do as I have done to you": the similarity between these
words and the "new commandment" (v.34) shows that the
love and self-giving service which were typical of his life,
and especially of his death, are to be the measure of disciples'
service in mutual humility and love. Thus disciples who
continue the mission of Jesus are not only privileged to be
associated with him in his dignity as their Lord and teacher;
they also share in his life of self-giving and humble service
of others (vv.14,16,20). This lesson about love and service

retains the association with the death of Jesus, which has been symbolized by the footwashing (vv. 2-11) and disciples are implicitly asked to carry love to the point of laying down their life for others (vv. 16-17).

Once more, as happens throughout this Last Supper scene, there intrudes the thought of a close friend who betrays, as the problem of Judas, who has remained untouched by what Jesus said (v. 11), is raised: how could someone so specially chosen and trusted by Christ betray him? The explanation given is that his betrayal did not come as a complete surprise to the disciples because Jesus had forewarned them, so this very fact should strengthen and help them to believe that he is a transcendent revealer of God, even if they see him humiliated in death (vv. 18-19). This betrayal belongs, also, to God's plan as reflected in Scripture (Ps 41:9), no matter how shocking it may appear: a chosen friend who was sharing his table "lifts his heel" against Jesus; in the Near East to "life one's heel," which means literally to show the bottom of one's foot to someone, was a gesture of contempt. Thus Judas turns informer against Jesus and hands him over to a violent death.

THE BETRAYER AND THE BELOVED DISCIPLE. 13:21-30.

> 21When Jesus had thus spoken, he was troubled in spirit, and testified, "Truly, truly, I say to you, one of you will betray me." 32The disciples looked at one another, uncertain of whom he spoke. 23One of his disciples, whom Jesus loved, was lying close to the breast of Jesus; 24so Simon Peter beckoned to him and said, "Tell us who it is of whom he speaks." 25So lying thus, close to the breast of Jesus, he said to him, "Lord, who is it?" 26Jesus answered, "It is he to whom I shall give this morsel when I have dipped it." So when he had dipped the morsel, he gave it to Judas, the son of Simon Iscariot. 27Then after the morsel, Satan entered into him. Jesus said to him, "What you are going to do, do quickly. 28Now no one at

the table knew why he said this to him. [29]Some thought that, because Judas had the money box, Jesus was telling him, "Buy what we need for the feast"; or, that he should give something to the poor. [30]So, after receiving the morsel, he immediately went out; and it was night.

The attention now shifts from the symbolic action of Jesus to relationships and to the exchanges between Jesus, Judas, the Beloved Disciple and Peter. On the one hand, Jesus is master of the situation, for he takes the initiative, and speaks about his future betrayal; he not only knows what is in Judas' heart, but he even sets in motion his own betrayal by offering him a morsel (vv.21,26,27). Yet he is "troubled" by the shadow of his coming betrayal since he is confronted by the power of unbelief and evil which is at work in Judas and which eventually sets him on his way to betray him (v.21; cf. 11:53;12:27). In response to an inquiry of the Beloved Disciple and prompted by Peter, Jesus gives Judas a morsel. This basic gesture of oriental hospitality was a token of intimacy, for the host usually invited a guest to dip with him for food in a common dish. Perhaps, also, Jesus is extending to Judas (cf. 12:6) a special gesture of esteem whereby the host singles out a guest whom he wishes to honour and picks for him a choice morsel of food (usually bread) from the common plate. But even this sign of affection, a final grace, is rejected. Meanwhile, the other disciples, except perhaps Peter and the Beloved Disciple (cf. vv.23-25), do not grasp the situation, but the evangelist stresses the importance of this moment with the crisp and loaded comment: "and it was night." He not only draws our attention to the time of the event but also to the darkness of evil and betrayal which possessed Judas.

Furthermore, the scene presents the good and bad extremes in the spectrum of discipleship. The Beloved Disciple also experiences a special gesture of affection, for he rests on Jesus' breast and experiences his love and thus enjoys an intimate communion with Jesus in a way similar to Jesus himself who is nearest to the Father's heart, "turned towards the bosom of the Father" (1:18). It is only after and because of this gesture of intimacy that the gospel calls him the "Beloved Disciple." While Judas is an individual disciple of flesh and blood, he also represents the powers of darkness and unbelief opposed to Jesus (v.27). Similarly, the Beloved Disciple stands for all faithful disciples, beloved by Jesus, even if he is also an individual, whose authority stands behind the Fourth Gospel (cf. 21:24), and, therefore, of paramount importance in the community for which the gospel was written. Thus he appears in a special position of intimacy with Jesus; not that Peter, his friend (v.23) is downgraded for he, too, is a man of authority and in a trusted position as regards Jesus (cf. ch.21). However, the gospel does not make clear the identity of the Beloved Disciple.

B. THE PARTING MESSAGE OF JESUS.

13:31-17:26.
JESUS DEPARTS: DISCIPLES FOLLOW.
13:31-38.

³¹When he had gone out, Jesus said, "Now is the Son of man glorified, and in him God is glorified; ³²if God is glorified in him, God will also glorify him in himself, and glorify him at once. ³³Little children, yet a little while I am with you. You will seek me; and as I said to the Jews so now I say to you, 'Where I am going you cannot come. ³⁴A new commandment I give to you, that you love one another; even as I have loved you, that you also love one another. ³⁵By this all men will know that you are my disciples, if you have love for one another."

³⁶Simon Peter said to him, "Lord, where are you going?" Jesus answered, "Where I am going you cannot follow me now; but you shall follow afterward." ³⁷Peter said to him, "Lord, why cannot I follow you now? I will lay down my life for you." ³⁸Jesus answered, "Will you lay down your life for me? Truly, truly, I say to you, the cock will not crow, till you have denied me three times."

IN THE PRESENCE of his closest friends Jesus now commences to speak his final message (13:31-17:26). This is a farewell speech like that of a great man who gathers together his followers on the eve of his death in order to give them instruction to help them when he is gone. Already in washing their feet Jesus had acted out his death, a death which "cleanses" disciples and gives them a heritage and communion with him. But now he assured them that his death is not an end but a going away to his Father. Furthermore, this last discourse precedes what it explains, since it interprets the glorification of Jesus through his death and resurrection. Here Jesus repeatedly promises that he will return to his disciples through his resurrection, through indwelling and the gift of the Spirit; sometimes, too, he hints at a final coming. Above all, this return will bring them peace and joy and it will enable disciples to dwell in fellowship with him in a communion similar to that which exists between himself and his Father (15:1-17;17:21). Thus while he is on his way to his Father and about to enter into glory and communion with his Father, Jesus promises his disciples that they, too, will enter into communion in this life with him through the Spirit, who is the gift of the dying and risen Jesus.

These ideas develop in a style quite different from what we are accustomed to in modern literature, for the thought moves "spirally," that is: an idea appears, recedes, appears again later with more clarity, sometimes by means of a literary technique typical of the discourses throughout the gospel: Jesus makes a statement which is misunderstood; he then clarifies this by a further revelation (13:31-14:24). In spite of a certain unevenness and repetitiveness, for example, chs. 15-16 were added to and take up some themes of 13:31-14:31, the "Farewell Discourse" is "one of the greatest compositions in religious literature" (Brown). Although those who hear Jesus are his disciples, his words are directed to christians of all times and Jesus speaks as one who is on his way to his Father, since he is passing to glory through his death and resurrection. This is not a message of a dead man who can speak no more for it reflects the community's understanding of the living, risen Jesus in the light of the Spirit who continues to make it a living word for all christians.

Whereas Judas has gone off into the darkness (13:30), Jesus is on his way to the glory of his Father (vv. 31-32) and they cannot follow him. His "glorification" is precisely this departure of Jesus from his disciples and his return to be with his Father in glory. Already the coming of the Greeks (12:20-23), and the situation created by Judas' departure ("now"), herald the beginning of his "hour," of his "glorification": he has *begun* to be glorified (the tense in Greek indicates a beginning, referring to the passion) and he *will* ("at once") continue to be glorified, because the whole process, death, resurrection, his work as the risen Lord, is now being set in motion and is viewed as one continuous process stretching into the future. Also, during all this process the Father manifests himself and his life-giving power (his "glory"—cf. 17:1-2) in and through Jesus, while he, in loving obedience to his Father, reveals him and continues his work of salvation and so he honours or "glorifies" the Father.

Since Jesus, then, is on his way to his Father, he will not be with his disciples much longer (v. 33; cf. 7:33-36; 8:21). But even if he departs and they cannot "follow" him, still they can be "followers" of Jesus and they can keep his spirit alive among themselves through the command he gives them, as they continue their life in the world (vv. 34-35; cf. vv. 15-16). Indeed, as long as christian love is in the world, the world still encounters Jesus and thus, living out his "new commandment" is a response given, in view of Jesus' physical departure, by those who wish to continue his love, his presence in the world.

Jesus, then, defines the spirit of the new covenant community. Formerly, God had commanded the people of Israel to love God and their neighbour (Lev 19:18; Deut 6:5). But that command to love only concerned the Israelite neighbour. Now all disciples of Jesus are to be loved on the basis of faith in Jesus and love is no longer determined by blood or nationality. But this new commandment belongs to a new covenant or friendship effected by Jesus. Moreover, it is new because Christ is new and because he founds a new community of those beloved by Christ, a society of loving men and women who "love one another" (cf. 15:12-17). However, more fundamentally, the essence of the commandment as new is: "*as* I have loved you," that is: "love one another after my example and with that same gift of love with which I love you" (15:9-10). Besides, this fraternal love is to be a constant, and clearly unmistakeable sign that christians are disciples of Christ: "you *are* my disciples, if you *have* love" (v.35; cf. 1 5:16-17). As in Jewish life a "disciple" lived with his master (rabbi) and took on his way of life and religious faith, so also a christian disciple witnesses to Christ by a life-style of *agape* (love). Therefore, he not only recalls Jesus' own life of love but he also continues and prolongs this love of Christ himself.

At the end of this scene Peter comes more into the limelight (vv.36-38; cf. v.24) as we see him misunderstand Jesus and rely on his own false enthusiasm in his "following" of Jesus. While he wants to be like the true shepherd who lays down his life (10:11;21:15-19), he is overconfident about it and he does not estimate properly his own weakness or the difficulty in following Jesus. Later he will manifest this same lack of understanding and misguided enthusiasm in his following of Jesus (18:10-11). Only when Jesus has overcome death and the force of evil can others follow him. But Jesus' words, which contain both a warning of failure and a promise about following Jesus, will be realized in subsequent events (18:10-18,25-27;21:15-19), for what Peter promises to do, even in his misguided enthusiasm and ignorance, he will finally achieve having learned through failure, denial and reconciliation (21:15-19).

WORDS OF CONSOLATION:
THE WAY TO A PLACE WITH THE FATHER.
14:1-6.

14 "Let not your hearts be troubled; believe in God, believe also in me. ²In my Father's house are many rooms; if it were not so, would I have told you that I go to prepare

a place for you? [3]And when I go and prepare a place for
you, I will come again and will take you to myself, that
where I am you may be also. [4]And you know the way
where I am going." [5]Thomas said to him, "Lord, we do
not know where you are going; how can we know the
way?" [6]Jesus said to him, "I am the way, and the truth,
and the life; no one comes to the Father, but by me."

This chapter is Jesus' message of comfort and consolation
for disciples who are distressed over his words about going
away (13:33-36). But he assures them that his going to the
Father is more gain than loss for them, for he will become
closer to them after his resurrection and they will enter into
a deeper communion of life with himself and the Father.
In due course he explains how this is to happen. Therefore,
they should not be "troubled" by the prospect of a certain
loneliness in the world, exposed as they will be to hostile
forces of unbelief (cf. 16:33), without their friend. Rather
they should trust him and look on his departure as a victorious passing over to the Father in glory (v.1). He goes
on to speak of a "place" where he welcomes ("takes") disciples, of "many dwelling places" in his "Father's house" -
these are all images for that "area" of communion of life with
himself and his Father. Thus disciples will be where Jesus
himself is (cf. 12:26;17:24), in the Father's house, that is, they
will, with the help of the Spirit, enter through faith in this
life into a close relationship with himself and his Father.
Also, this special relationship is a gift of Jesus (vv.2-3) and
of his Father (v.23).

The many dwelling-places or "mansions" are not different
degrees of perfection or lower and higher grades in heaven
but the meaning is rather that the Father's love and life,
present in Jesus, are so immense that there is room for all
disciples in that communion which he offers. In fact, all the
expressions, "place," "dwelling-places" (cf. 14:23), "my
Father's house" (cf. 2:16) refer to Jesus himself, who is the
new temple (2:19;4:21-24;7:38-39) because in him and
through him believers enjoy communion with God.

In using another image, that of the "way," for the same
reality of communion with himself and the Father, Jesus

applies an Exodus theme to himself: he goes before disciples to seek out a place, to lead them to a new, promised land, that is, to a new, life-giving relationship through faith with God: "The Lord your God went before you in the *way* to seek out a *place* to pitch your *tents (dwelling-places)*, in fire by night, to show you by what *way* you should go . . ." (Deut 1:33). Thus the only way a christian disciple can "go" to the Father is through a fellowship of faith and communion of life with Jesus, who leads us, who is the way of the Father because he is the truth and the life. If, therefore, we accept Jesus, who is the truth, the self-revelation of God, we receive his life, for as the Incarnate Son he is the perfect revealer and mediator of God and the life he shares with his Father he also shares with believing disciples. Consequently, because he is Incarnate he can mediate God to human beings, and because he is the Son always near the Father's heart (1:18), he can share the life of God with us.

THE LIFE OF COMMUNION.
14:7-14.

> [7]"If you had known me, you would have known my Father also; henceforth you know him and have seen him."
>
> [8]Philip said to him, "Lord, show us the Father, and we shall be satisfied." [9]Jesus said to him, "Have I been with you so long, and yet you do not know me, Philip? He who has seen me has seen the Father; how can you say, 'Show us the Father'? [10]Do you not believe that I am in the Father and the Father in me? The words that I say to you I do not speak on my own authority; but the Father who dwells in me does his works. [11]Believe me that I am in the Father and the Father in me; or else believe me for the sake of the works themselves.
>
> [12]"Truly, truly, I say to you, he who believes in me will also do the works that I do; and greater works than these will he do, because I go to the Father. [13]Whatever you ask in my name, I will do it, that the Father may be glorified in the Son; [14]if you ask anything in my name, I will do it."

Jesus first explains that he is the "way" to the Father because he is in communion with him (vv. 7-11) and then he turns to the subject of communion between himself and disciples (vv. 12-14). In fact, to contemplate Jesus with the eyes of faith is to see the Father, for they live together in intimate communion (v. 7). Because he and the Father work and share life together, his words are the Father's voice and his whole activity of revealing and giving life ("works") are the power of the Father. Therefore, the person who looks closely at these "works" of Jesus with the eyes of faith will see that they are the works of someone who lives in intimate communion with God (vv. 10-11).

The christian life of communion with Jesus and the Father has two important consequences for disciples. Just as he himself is closely united with his Father in being and action (vv. 11-12), so also disciples are in close communion with Jesus as their risen Lord and they can do "greater works" than Jesus did in his public ministry! Though they are not specified here, these works are the various effects and manifestations in word and action of the disciples' faith in Jesus (3:21;6:29) and they result from this new communion with Jesus. Because Jesus has left behind the limitations of time and space imposed on him by the Incarnation, he can now act more freely and he does "works" through believers in and through his Spirit. In this way the faith and love of christian disciples make visible the invisible presence of the glorified Lord.

The second consequence of this communion with Jesus and the Father is that christians who pray with the Spirit of Christ know what to ask the Father and their requests are granted (vv. 13-14). Since they pray out a living communion of faith in Jesus, they pray trustingly and unselfishly. Thus a petition made "in the name of" Jesus is a prayer inspired by this communion with him and is offered under the impulse of a deep faith in Jesus. This prayer is all the more perfect the more it is "in the name of" Jesus, that is, based on communion with him through faith.

The disciple, then, who prays in the "name" of Jesus will take on, with the help of the Spirit, who interiorizes the message of Jesus, the sentiments of his Lord and will submit his will to that of Jesus and thus become one with him in thought and desire. Thus his prayer becomes a participation in Jesus' own prayer of communion with his Father, completely penetrated by the Spirit, free from egoism. Consequently, a prayer "in the name of" Jesus goes much deeper than a mere invocation of the name "Jesus" and the more one's life is penetrated by the teaching and example of Jesus, under the inspiration of the Spirit (vv. 16-17), the more unselfish, free, and assured does our prayer become. In short, the prayer in the name of Jesus, animated by the Spirit, makes us think and wish like him (15:7,16; 16:23-26; 1 Jn 3:22).

THE INDWELLING OF FATHER, SON AND SPIRIT. 14:15-24.

15"If you love me, you will keep my commandments. 16And I will pray the Father, and he will give you another Counselor, to be with you for ever, 17even the Spirit of truth, whom the world cannot receive, because it neither sees him nor knows him; you know him, for he dwells with you, and will be in you.

18"I will not leave you desolate; I will come to you. 19Yet a little while, and the world will see me no more, but you will see me; because I live, you will live also. 20In that day you will know that I am in my Father, and you in me, and I in you. 21He who has my commandments and keeps them, he it is who loves me; and he who loves me will be loved by my Father, and I will love him and manifest myself to him" 22Judas (not Iscariot) said to him, "Lord, how is it that you will manifest yourself to us, and not to the world?" 23Jesus answered him, "If a man loves me, he will keep my words, and my Father will love him, and we will come to him and make our home with him. 24He who does not love me does not keep my words; and the word which you hear is not mine but the Father's who sent me."

As the departure of Jesus to his Father means that he "comes" again, Jesus now explains further the nature of this "coming to you" (vv.18,23,28). Now this departure of Jesus to his Father profoundly affects not only the life of Jesus, for then he will be glorified; but, more important, his going is good news for all disciples. The reason is: the "coming" or new presence of Jesus, which primarily refers to the time of the church, of the Spirit, without, however, excluding a "coming" in resurrection appearances and on the "last day," involves three forms of *indwelling* for disciples. Jesus comes through the Spirit who is "in you" (vv.16-17) and he comes himself: "I in you" (vv.18-21); besides, his Father comes along with him and they "make our home with" disciples (vv.23-24). What, then, is the nature of this "indwelling" of Father, Son and Spirit?

Jesus' passing to the Father leads to a new situation that is characterized by "keeping my commandments," i.e. by living according to his word (cf. 15:10). This relationship between Jesus and disciples has already been explained in terms of faith (v.12), but now Jesus speaks of a loving relationship based on active docility to his word. This desire of Jesus to be loved is perfectly at home in the covenant atmosphere of the Last Discourse and Supper (cf. 13:34-35). Just as the covenant God of Sinai desired to be loved exclusively by his people (Deut 6:5), Jesus now calls for exclusive love because he is God's visible presence among disciples, establishing a new covenant of friendship with them.

Jesus had been a "paraclete," that is, someone called in to give assistance (RSV:"counsellor"), because he had helped disciples as their teacher and had been on familiar terms with them, assisting them in their faith. But now he has to go and instead a new "helper" will come, who will continue Jesus' work among them and through him disciples will come to understand the person and message of Jesus on a deeper level, for he will reveal Jesus, who is the truth (14:6). Besides, the Spirit will come to disciples as a gift from the Father at the request of Jesus. The same

Spirit was present among disciples in Jesus during his ministry and he was already known to them through the eyes of faith, since he had enabled Jesus to carry out his mission (cf. 1:32-33). But when Jesus is gone the Spirit will be "with" disciples as a dynamic power strengthening their relationship of faith in Jesus. He will also be "in them," enabling them to make the words of Jesus part and parcel of their lives. But the person who is closed to the Spirit is incapable, through lack of faith, to welcome him (v. 17).

Therefore, the "coming" of Jesus is related to the presence of the Spirit and yet the Spirit remains distinct from Jesus, while at the same time it is he who makes Jesus more present to christians. Thus the essence of his mission is to strengthen their faith-relationship with Jesus and help them make his word and message a living reality. Therefore, the Spirit works "in," is "with" disciples, so as to make Jesus more present to them, and it is through the Spirit, who is the gift of the Father, that Jesus "comes" to disciples.

Here for the first time in the gospel the Holy Spirit is named "Paraclete" (RSV:Counsellor) and "Spirit of truth." As regards the name "Paraclete," this belongs to the gospel vocabulary of the law-court and denotes anyone who comes to the help of another, as assistant, defender or advocate. For example, in Jewish literature, "paracletes" are all those who intercede in man's favour before God's "tribunal": the angels, the law, man's good works and merits. In another text, the risen Jesus is a "paraclete" because he intercedes for us in heaven with the Father (1 Jn 2:1).

But in the Fourth Gospel the Paraclete-Spirit (14:16, 26;15:26;16:7) is not an intercessor, for he carries out his mission on earth among disciples in that vast lawsuit or struggle between Jesus and the forces of unbelief, the "world" (in its negative sense), between light and darkness. Disciples, too, are part of this struggle, for the message of Jesus is communicated in a milieu of contestation and incredulity and, therefore, they need the Spirit-Paraclete, an assistant who strengthens faith in Jesus. Thus, in times of pressure from without he reinforces the attachment of disciples to Jesus.

This image from the law-court expresses the reality of revelation and faith. Besides, the title underlines the strengthening force of the Spirit regarding the future of disciples when their faith will be subjected to pressures. As Paraclete the Spirit has a function in the time of the Church, marked by conflict and opposition to the word, when Jesus is "absent." Then the Spirit will strengthen disciples so that they can bear witness to Jesus by their faith (15:26-27). Moreover, he is a Paraclete-accuser who gives testimony against those hostile to Christ by giving disciples the certainty that these are wrong and sinful (16:7-11). Therefore, he is "another Paraclete" because his mission is similar to and continues that of Jesus. Furthermore, his personal character is suggested by the fact that he is "another"—someone, quite distinct from Jesus, who will come after Jesus has gone to his Father.

After identifying himself as "the truth" (14:6), Jesus now promises a "Spirit of truth" (14:17;15:26;16:13). The Paraclete is also a Spirit of truth because he helps disciples grow in the "truth," which is the self-revelation of Jesus in his person, words and works. These two titles of the Spirit appear in the gospel only in Jesus' Farewell Discourse within the five so-called "promises of the Paraclete" (14:16-17;14:26;15:26;16:7-11;16:13-15: the second promise corresponds to the fifth and the third to the fourth). The reason why this second title is given to the Spirit is because it is he who reveals the truth, who is Jesus, to believers. Moreover, he leads believers to a deeper grasp and appropriation of the meaning and message of Jesus for life, and this work he accomplishes within them through his characteristically inward action.

In addition, because all his activity is directed towards the acceptance of the "truth," the self-revelation, the message of Jesus, the Holy Spirit is actually identified with this truth: "The Spirit is the truth" (1 Jn 5:6), just as the

Spirit is identified with the word in a dynamic, working unity: "The words that I have spoken to you are Spirit and life" (6:63). Therefore, the Spirit works in and through the word and the self-revelation (the truth) of Jesus so that they become living truth and living words, an inner possession and source of christian living.

The five promises of the Paraclete-Spirit seem to appear suddenly out of context and yet they are well integrated into the flow of thought in the discourse of Jesus, for they describe the relation of the Spirit to the Father, to the Son, and to disciples. First of all, he is related to the Father and Son as one sent to those who send and yet Jesus is only a mediator in sending him, for only of the Father is it said that he "gives" the Paraclete, since he is the ultimate source of all divine gifts (14:16,26;15:26). Secondly, there is much more said about his relation to the Son and thus he is to be seen above all in his relation to Jesus. For example, his mission is described as parallel to that of Jesus and in similar terms: he teaches (14:26;7:14), reveals (16:13-15;4:25), he is sent(14:26, cf. pp. 133-134)and given by the Father (14:16;3:16). Besides, disciples are the object of his mission. But the first promise (14:16-17) says little enough about the characteristic activity of the Spirit-Paraclete and it is only in the subsequent promises that we see how the Spirit is a Paraclete and a Spirit of truth in so far as he interiorly supports and deepens the attachment of christian disciples to the person of Jesus.

Jesus, then, does not desert his disciples. In fact, they, in contrast to those who reject Jesus, will be enabled through the Spirit to "see" him more clearly in faith and by "seeing" him in faith they will come to share in Jesus' own life (v.19). Moreover, after his death and resurrection, through the gift of the Spirit, they will come to realize that Jesus lives in intimate communion with God the Father as his Son and that they themselves, through faith, will come to share in their divine life (v.20). But this communion with Jesus depends on their own loving, active response to his word. It is also a communion of love by which they are drawn into the Father's love as loving disciples of his Son, and Jesus will disclose himself more and more to that disciple who responds to him in love by living his word (v.21). But this self-disclosure of Jesus is not a kind of dramatic theophany (Ex 33:13,18) such as Judas imagines (v.22). Rather it is an inner manifestation of love, an indwelling by which the Father and Son enter into a loving relationship with the disciple who loves Jesus by living out his word in action.

The departure of Jesus to his Father means, then, that the Father himself and the Son "come," offering a loving relationship (v.23) to the loving disciple. Resuming the earlier imagery (vv.2-3) Jesus describes this relationship as the Father and Son making their "dwelling-place" with the disciple. Now disciples are where Jesus is (v.30), that is, in the sphere of God's love, or "in my Father's house" which becomes the dwelling-place for the Father, the Son and the believer. This implies again that the risen Jesus is the new temple, the dwelling-place for the Father, himself, and disciples in a loving relationship. Thus the emphasis has shifted from Jesus as the way, who leads disciples into communion with the Father (vv.2-3), to the Father himself whose love is the source of their communion with Jesus and whose word comes to them in Jesus (vv.23-24).

This dwelling of the Father and the Son flows, therefore, from the Father's love for the disciples of his Son and is a manifestation of the Father's love, just as the Incarnation, too, was a manifestation of his love (3:16). To summarize the theology of "indwelling" in these words of Jesus: indwelling, which results from Jesus' departure to his Father, is the presence of the Father and the Son in a loving and life-giving relationship. The Holy Spirit, too, is active within disciples, enabling them to listen to and to live out lovingly God's word and revelation, manifest in Jesus. But the risen Jesus is the centre of this indwelling because he is the new temple in so far as through him christian disciples enter into a life of communion with God.

FINAL WORDS OF CONSOLATION.
14:25-31—*Presence in Absence.*

²⁵"These things I have spoken to you, while I am still with you. ²⁶But the Counselor, the Holy Spirit, whom the Father will send in my name, he will teach you all things, and bring to your remembrance all that I have said to you. ²⁷Peace I leave with you; my peace I give to you; not as the world gives do I give to you. Let not your hearts be troubled, neither let them be afraid. ²⁸You heard me say to you, 'I go away, and I will come to you.' If you loved me, you would have rejoiced, because I go to the Father; for the Father is greater than I. ²⁰And now I have told you before it takes place, so that when it does take place, you may believe. ³⁰I will no longer talk much with you, for the ruler of this world is coming. He has no power over me; ³¹but I do as the Father has commanded me, so that the world may know that I love the Father. Rise, let us go hence.

Summarizing the meaning of his departure and return, Jesus promises that the Holy Spirit will continue his mission interiorly within the hearts of disciples (vv. 25-26), for he himself and the Father will send the Spirit, the "helper" in faith for disciples, in order to reveal to them the meaning of Jesus, his work and message. Thus he will strengthen their faith by "teaching" and helping them to "remember" all that Jesus has communicated to them. First of all, he is a teacher of mind and heart, for he teaches what Jesus taught but causes it to enter into men's hearts. Secondly, in "recalling" to disciples all that Jesus said he will not only remind them of a teaching they might have forgotten; he will also make them understand interiorly the words of Jesus so that they may grasp their importance for christian living (2:17,22;12:16).

On his way to the Father Jesus asks disciples to have peace and not to be troubled (v.27; cf. v.1). This peace, which is often promised by God in the Old Testament for messianic days, is not the absence of war but it is a divine gift, like joy or salvation. Here it is the abiding gift of Jesus for the time of his absence (16:33), that peace of his presence to which the world of unbelief is closed. But the disciples should not be afraid or troubled because his departure entails a struggle and a victory over the forces of unbelief. Rather, they should be glad (v.28) because he accomplishes his life's purpose in going to his Father (cf. vv.3-4), who is the source and origin of his mission and of all that he has. Ultimately, it is the Father who brings everything to fulfilment, even the glorification of Jesus and in this sense Jesus calls him "greater." Furthermore, Jesus assures disciples that after his resurrection and the coming of the Spirit they will be able to recognize that all that has happened to Jesus took place just as he had said. While he is aware of the conflict with the powers of darkness and death which lies ahead, Jesus is confident that he will overcome, for the Father is in control of all that is happening and he will prevent evil from gaining any hold over Jesus. In fact, he gives Jesus all power at this time, (v.30) so that even in the struggle and the victory of death and resurrection, Jesus is acting all the time in loving obedience towards his Father.

Jesus, the Truth

Since the Christ of the Fourth Gospel is constantly presented as a revealer of God, it is not surprising to find many terms which underline the theme of revelation, for example, witness, light, word and also "truth." The Old Testament often speaks of the "truth" or fidelity of God towards his people (Deut 7:9), whereas in later Jewish literature "truth" often came to mean the revealed mystery of God, his wisdom or his teaching (Dan 10:21; Wis 6:9).

In the gospel truth is not an abstract ideal or an object of intellectual research such as it is often understood in Greek literature, but it is closely associated with the person of Jesus (14:6;1:14). In fact, it is Jesus himself as he reveals

God in his word, actions and in his own person. By accepting him who is the truth, man receives the gift of life (14:6) and a christian is "of the truth" (18:37) if he accepts the self-revelation of God in Jesus and makes it part of living. Therefore, truth is also a principle of moral living and it sets believers free from sin (8:32). Besides, the Holy Spirit is the Spirit of truth because it is he who internalizes and grants a deeper understanding of the self-revelation of God, present in the person, words and example of Jesus (16:13).

The Vine and the Branches.
15:1-17.

THE VINE OF LOVE.
15:1-8.

15 "I am the true vine, and my Father is the vinedresser. [2]Every branch of mine that bears no fruit, he takes away, and every branch that does bear fruit he prunes, that it may bear more fruit. [3]You are already made clean by the word which I have spoken to you. [4]Abide in me, and I in you. As the branch cannot bear fruit by itself, unless it abides in the vine, neither can you, unless you abide in me. [5]I am the vine, you are the branches. He who abides in me, and I in him, he it is that bears much fruit, for apart from me you can do nothing. [6]If a man does not abide in me, he is cast forth as a branch and withers; and the branches are gathered, thrown into the fire and burned. [7]If you abide in me, and my words abide in you, ask whatever you will, and it shall be done for you. [8]By this my Father is glorified, that you bear much fruit, and so prove to be my disciples."

This image sketches a series of relationships of love *(agape)*, which is a bond uniting Father, Son, disciples, and disciples with one another. But the key relationship is that between Jesus (the vine) and disciples (branches). The image is first described (vv. 1-8): the vinedresser (the Father), the vine (Jesus), branches (disciples) and fruit, which is later explained in terms of fraternal love. Then the image is clarified in terms of love-relationships (vv. 9-17). Furthermore, love has its source in the Father, it is disclosed in Jesus and disciples share in this gift of love and manifest it in their relationships within the community.

The vine (or vineyard) was an Old Testament symbol for the people of Israel. For example, Isaiah (5:1-7; cf. Ezek chs. 15;17;19) pictures God's covenant love for his people as a vinedresser who tends his vineyard with loving care. Also, to "bear fruit," with reference to a vine or other plants, is to live according to God's commandments with emphasis on justice and love (Is 5:7; Deut 32:32; Jer 8:13; Mic 7:1-6). Here it is Jesus who is the "true vine" (v. 1), for he replaces all imperfect manifestations, even the vine which was the people of Israel. Besides, the image repeats and develops some themes already dominant in the Farewell Discourse: the communion of disciples with Jesus and the Father and the theme of love itself, including fraternal love (e.g. 13:34-35).

The key points of the image are: the vinedresser who is the Father, the vine (Jesus) and the branches (disciples) who "abide" in one another, and the fruit. At the beginning the Father is mentioned as the one who tends the vine with its branches, for he is the "director" who sees that the branches are cleared of anything that might prevent them from producing fruit (vv. 1-2). This "pruning" or refining, which enables disciples to enter into a communion of faith and love with Jesus, is effected by means of the Father's word communicated by Jesus (v. 3). The relationship which Jesus offers (vv. 4-5) is described as a mutual "abiding," which implies a permanent presence of one person to another, intimate indwelling and familiarity. Like two friends present to one another in listening, understanding and loving response, the disciple is present to Christ and Christ present to him. Even more vividly than the "Body of Christ" in Paul, this image expresses the closeness of communion with Jesus: "I am the vine, you are the branches": paradoxically Christ is the whole tree, including the branches, for he is not just the tree-trunk and this suggests that he is the source of life for those who remain in communion with him.

Unless the disciple produces fruit, which is later defined as fraternal love, there is no communion with Jesus (v.2) and vice-versa—outside communion with Jesus there is no fruit (v.6). Thus christian disciples either remain in communion with Jesus and produce fruit or they separate themselves from him. Moreover, it is by actively accepting the words of Jesus into their lives with the help of the Holy Spirit (v.7;6:63) that disciples enter more and more into communion with Jesus. Consequently, petitions in prayer that are prompted by a life lived in union with him will be echoes of his own desires and they will be in harmony with his Father's will and therefore granted (cf. 14:13-14). The Father is mentioned again at the end because he is the ultimate source of the disciples' faith and love (v.8).

LOVE AND FRIENDSHIP.
15:9-17.

> [9]"As the Father has loved me, so have I loved you; abide in my love. [10]If you keep my commandments, you will abide in my love, just as I have kept my Father's commandments and abide in his love. [11]These things I have spoken to you, that my joy may be in you, and that your joy may be full.
>
> [12]"This is my commandment, that you love one another as I have loved you. [13]Greater love has no man than this, that a man lay down his life for his friends. [14]You are my friends if you do what I command you. [15]No longer do I call you servants, for the servant does not know what his master is doing; but I have called you friends,

for all that I have heard from my Father I have made known to you. [16]You did not choose me, but I chose you and appointed you that you should go and bear fruit and that your fruit should abide; so that whatever you ask the Father in my name, he may give it to you. [17]This I command you, to love one another."

The image is now more sharply defined in the language of love and friendship. First (vv.9-11), Jesus invites disciples to "abide in my love," that is, "in my love for you and in your love for me." This love is a descending gift of the Father, a bond which holds together in an invisible net a series of relationships between Father, Son and disciples (v.9). But the model and source of Jesus' love for disciples is the Father's own love for his Son, so that the whole act of love lavished by Jesus on disciples and evident most of all in his death, is the actual communication of God's gift of love in and through his Son. Thus, Jesus loves disciples with that same gift of love with which the Father loves him (17:23-24).

Furthermore, disciples remain in that bond of love with Jesus by "keeping his commandments," that is, they listen and respond in loving obedience to his word with the same spirit of docility and promptitude as Jesus listens and responds to his Father's word and will (v.10). According to the gospel (14:15,21) and the First Letter of John (1 Jn 2:3,4;3:22,24;5:3) "keeping" commandments is an active attention, docility and promptitude and expresses the relationship of Jesus to his Father as well as that of disciples towards Jesus. Thus a "commandment" is not presented so much as an ethical precept as a word lived in action and, therefore, it is often linked with love (14:15,21). "Keeping commandments," which is a sympathetic obedience to the spirit of a command rather than a rigid carrying out of its letter, is the loving response to God of a disciple who wants to "do what pleases him" (1 Jn 3:22).

Jesus himself remains in a continued presence of familiarity with his Father which always gives him joy. For him this joy consists in being loved by the Father and in responding out of love to him. Besides, the message of Jesus about God's love brings joy to disciples which is a share in Christ's own joy and consists in a divine gift, like peace and salvation, arising out of the disciples' experience of being loved by and in lovingly responding to Jesus and to the Father.

The message which Jesus brings to man from the Father (cf. v. 15) is about friendship and fraternal love (vv. 12-17). But this friendship is due to the initiative of Jesus because he has chosen christian disciples to be his friends, he has given his life on their behalf and because he offers them intimacy by sharing with them the secret of his life of love with his Father. Furthermore, this life of friendship brings a loving response to their prayers, for if they lead a life of communion with Jesus by responding to his word, then they take on the sentiments of Christ himself. Consequently, a prayer that is based on this communion of love with him becomes Jesus' own prayer - a prayer according to God's will, which will be heard and granted (cf. 14:13-14). The other side of the friendship with Jesus consists in the disciple's response to his word, that is, "keeping his commandments," in particular his word about fraternal love, which is "my commandment," since living this word is distinctive of those who are his disciples. Here the whole message of Jesus is reduced to this one commandment (vv. 12,17), because fraternal love is a sign, a "fruit" which manifests in the life of the christian the presence of the divine gift of love in the life of the christian. Therefore, to love one another "as I have loved you" (cf. 13:34-35), after his example and with the divine gift of *agape*, is a visible sign by which people recognize followers of Christ.

This image, like that of the shepherd (10:1-18), stresses the disciple's individual relationship with Jesus. But the attachment to Jesus through faith (10:2-4) is completed by the mutual life of love in the image of the vine and the branches which makes it clear that faith and love of Jesus are externalized in fraternal love. Such faith and love, which embrace love of the brethren, are the basis of christian community, the life of the Church. Furthermore, with its emphasis on unity (cf. 1 Cor 10:17), on Jesus' self-offering in love, and the theme of "abiding," this image probably also calls the eucharist to mind (6:51,56).

The Theology of agape (love)

This image is the kernel of the gospel's theology of love, although the First Letter of John carries it further, especially in 1 Jn 4:7-5:3. Love is presented as a divine gift whose source is the Father and he expressed it in his Son. Also, it is communicated to christians who believe in Jesus as the beloved Son of the Father and the epiphany of God's own love (3:16-17). Moreover, love is a quality, a force which activates personal relationships: the mutual love of Father and Son, of Jesus and disciples, and disciples with one another.

God is called "Father" because he is, *par excellence*, the one who loves and gives (ch. 17). He is the source of love and he is the Father of Jesus because he loves him (3:35). Besides, love is a communication of life and the Father gives Jesus the fullness of his own life (3:16;5:26). Through him also the Father makes believers children of God, since they share in his divine life (1 Jn 5:11). Therefore, only the Father "is love" (1 Jn 4:8,16) since he is perfect self-communication, sharing from eternity his love and his life with his Son. Also, he is the first lover for he loved us first by sending his Son into the world that we might have life (3:16; 1 Jn 4:9) and it is only in contemplating Jesus in faith that we discover that God is love. The cross, however, is the greatest manifestation of this divine love in Jesus. Faith is the discovery of this love in Jesus and from believing in love disciples come to receive the gift of love (17:26; 1 Jn 4:16), through which they are enabled to reach out in love to the Father, to his Son and to one another.

However, the Fourth Gospel does not give those practical guides to loving such as we find in Paul's hymn to *agape* (1 Cor 13). But it does enter more deeply into the roots of love, that is, into the various relationships of love and their meaning in the life of the christian. Thus we might summarize John's idea of love as the sharing of life together in concern and understanding. As regards the Father and Son, they share their intimate life together in perfect concern and understanding and christian living holds as its ideal that sharing of life with one another in concern and understanding under the impulse of love. And why? Because Jesus shares his life and love with disciples to the point of death and beyond it.

THREATS TO FAITH IN JESUS.
15:18-16:4.

[18]"If the world hates you, know that it has hated me before it hated you. [19]If you were of the world, the world would love its own; but because you are not of the world, but I chose you out of the world, therefore the world hates you. [20]Remember the word that I said to you, 'A servant is not greater than his master.' If they persecuted me, they will persecute you; if they kept my word, they will keep yours also. [21]But all this they will do to you on my account, because they do not know him who sent me. [22]If I had not come and spoken to them, they would not have sin; but now they have no excuse for their sin. [23]He who hates me hates my Father also. [24]If I had not done among them the works which no one else did, they would not have sin; but now they have seen and hated both me and my Father. [25]It is to fulfil the word that is written in their law, 'They hated me without a cause.' [26]But when the Counselor comes, whom I shall send to you from the Father, even the Spirit of truth, who proceeds from the Father, he will bear witness to me; [27]and you also are witnesses, because you have been with me from the beginning.

16 "I have said all this to you to keep you from falling away. ²They will put you out of the synagogues; indeed, the hour is coming when whoever kills you will think he is offering service to God. ³And they will do this because they have not known the Father, nor me. ⁴But I have said these things to you, that when their hour comes you may remember that I told you of them."

Jesus passes from the subject of love to "hate," that is, to that rejection which he himself and disciples later in the life of the church experience. Just as love is founded on faith, so also unbelief is the basis of "hatred." But what is the reason for this hostility and how can disciples cope with it? First, Jesus, in his desire to give disciples courage for their preaching and witness, consoles and strengthens the disciples (vv.18-25) by reminding them that the forces of sin and unbelief ("the world") will be directed against them because they are directed against Jesus himself and the Father.

Because they have been chosen as his friends and brought to a life of faith and love from the sphere of unbelief ("the world") disciples are in the destiny of Jesus himself who encountered unbelief and hostility (v.20;13;16). The hatred Jesus describes is the expression of unbelief and it means rejecting the word. In the measure that Jesus found faith, so too they will find faith through the word they bring to others (v.20). Because they bear his name as "Christians" ("on my account"; or because people are hostile to the name of Christ) they will experience "hatred" or rejection. But this has its ultimate basis in the fact that those who "hate" them are rejecting God's own self-revelation in the person of Jesus. "Hatred" then, which is a form of atheism, is the fundamental sin and consists in the deliberate rejection of God communicating himself in the works and words of Jesus (vv.22-24). However, like his betrayal (13:38-39), the rejection of Jesus is part of God's plan as reflected in Scripture (Pss 35:19;69:4).

To confront these external pressures on their faith, the disciples will have a helper, a "Paraclete" who will strengthen their personal faith in Jesus (v.26). In this struggle between Jesus together with his followers and the forces of unbelief, which is depicted in legal imagery, the Spirit will give "witness" in the hearts of disciples in favour of Jesus. This inner strengthening of their faith in Jesus will then enable them to give external "witness" (v.27), that is, to lead others to faith in Jesus. Besides, they have been with Jesus himself from the beginning of his ministry and, therefore, with the help of the Spirit they will be able to reveal him to others.

Jesus harps on this negative aspect of love, on hatred and persecution (16:1-4) in order to strengthen disciples against these dangers to their life of faith and love, and so a reminder in time will prepare them in some way for these situations of conflict (v.4). Jesus then specifies various forms of "hatred" they will encounter — all of them are grounded in unbelief, in the rejection of Jesus and his Father.

THE CONVINCING SPIRIT OF TRUTH.
16:4-15.

> "I did not say these things to you from the beginning, because I was with you. [5]But now I am going to him who sent me; yet none of you asks me, 'Where are you going?' [6]But because I have said these things to you, sorrow has filled your hearts. [7]Nevertheless I tell you the truth: it is to your advantage that I go away, for if I do not go away, the Counselor will not come to you; but if I go, I will send him to you. [8]And when he comes, he will convince the world concerning sin and righteousness and judgment: [9]concerning sin, because they do not believe in me; [10]concerning righteousness, because I go to the Father, and you will see me no more; [11]concerning judgment, because the ruler of this world is judged.
>
> [12]"I have yet many things to say to you, but you cannot bear them now. [13]When the Spirit of truth comes, he will

> guide you into all the truth; for he will not speak on his
> own authority, but whatever he hears he will speak, and
> he will declare to you the things that are to come. [14]He
> will glorify me, for he will take what is mine and declare
> it to you. [15]All that the Father has is mine; therefore I said
> that he will take what is mine and declare it to you."

Jesus continues to encourage disciples about the future
by assuring them of support in faith when they will be under
pressure and by helping them to overcome the sorrow they
feel at his departure. They, however, do not realize the goal
and meaning of his going back to his Father and only faith
in his departure as a return to the Father can overcome
their situation of grief (vv.4-6). Besides, only when he is gone
will the helping Spirit come to strengthen their faith. His
mission is now described as an interior work of convicting,
convincing or clarifying (v.8).

Just as the witnessing of the Spirit to Jesus takes place
in the hearts of believers (15:26), so too the Spirit is a kind
of witness for the prosecution against "the world," for in
pointing out the guilt of the "world," of the forces of unbelief, he strengthens the faith of disciples interiorly. Thus
he gives them the certainty of faith that the truth is on
Jesus' side and at the same time he "convicts" the world of
unbelief interiorly within the hearts of believers. He does
this by "convincing" christian disciples that deliberate
unbelief in Jesus is the fundamental sin, that Jesus has
passed to glory with the Father from where he continues to
work, and that he has conquered death and the forces of evil
(vv.8-11). But before the hostility of unbelief Jesus' disciples
will be exposed to stumbling-blocks (cf. 16:1) and they will
be tempted to give up. Then the convincing or convicting
action of the Spirit will come to their aid and strengthen
their faith in Jesus. While, on a historical level, they may be
condemned by human tribunals, in the eyes of God and on
the level of faith, it is they who judge the forces of evil and
unbelief in their hearts under the guidance of the Spirit.

The Spirit is not only a helper who builds up the commitment of disciples to Jesus in the face of difficulties but also, for disciples who are lacking understanding of his person and message (v.12), he is a Spirit of truth. Thus he is like a knowledgeable guide who leads disciples into the heart of the truth which is the teaching, work and the whole person of Jesus. Yet he does not propose a new doctrine; rather he provides a deeper understanding of the mystery of Jesus, of his life, action and words and their meaning for living (v.12). Also, he will unravel in the light of human history the "things that are to come" - the new order of things that has come with the death and resurrection of Christ. In other words, he helps christian disciples to see every event, every era in the light of Jesus and his message. Therefore, his work cannot be divorced from the words and person of Jesus because he communicates to believers what Jesus means to them in life (v.14). Therefore, he is not an independent revealer but he shares with believers what he knows of and receives from the Father and Son. Furthermore, in deepening their faith in Jesus he also reveals the Father, because all that Jesus has and is he receives from his Father (vv.14-15). But all this work of the Spirit in the life of the christian is not just an intellectual communication of doctrine, for his mission is to lead disciples more and more into a life of personal communion with Christ, who is the truth. Consequently, he is a Spirit for christian living.

A TIME OF JOY AND CLOSENESS.
16:16-28.

> [16]"A little while, and you will see me no more; again a little while, and you will see me." [17]Some of his disciples said to one another, "What is this that he says to us, 'A little while, and you will not see me, and again a little while, and you will see me'; and, 'because I go to the Father'?" [18]They said, "What does he mean by 'a little while'? We do not know what he means." [19]Jesus knew

that they wanted to ask him; so he said to them, "Is this what you are asking yourselves, what I meant by saying, 'A little while, and you will not see me, and again a little while, and you will see me'? [20]Truly, truly, I say to you, you will weep and lament, but the world will rejoice; you will be sorrowful, but your sorrow will turn into joy. [21]When a woman is in travail she has sorrow, because her hour has come; but when she is delivered of the child, she no longer remembers the anguish, for joy that a child is born into the world. [22]So you have sorrow now, but I will see you again and your hearts will rejoice, and no one will take your joy from you. [23]In that day you will ask nothing of me. Truly, truly, I say to you, if you ask anything of the Father, he will give it to you in my name. [24]Hitherto you have asked nothing in my name; ask, and you will receive, that your joy may be full.

[25]"I have said this to you in figures; the hour is coming when I shall no longer speak to you in figures but tell you plainly of the Father. [26]In that day you will ask in my name; and I do not say to you that I shall pray the Father for you; [27]for the Father himself loves you, because you have loved me and have believed that I came from the Father. [28]I came from the Father and have come into the world; again, I am leaving the world and going to the Father."

Jesus explains further what his going to the Father means: he will return in "a little while" and the disciples will enjoy a more intimate closeness with him, which will bring them joy (vv.20-24) and a better understanding of faith about himself (vv.25-28). Here Jesus is speaking mainly about his presence in the community in the time of the church rather than during his appearance after the resurrection, or on the last day, though these are not excluded.

In one sense, when Jesus goes away the disciples will not see him but, on the other hand, they will see him in faith when he becomes more present to them through the gift of the Spirit (v.19). The time of his ministry is now contrasted with a new era ("in that day": vv.23,26), which is inaugurated through his death and resurrection. This is a time of joy, when the grief, the pain of loss at his going away yields to an enduring joy, born of faith, which arises from the awareness of his risen presence among christian disciples. However, it is the Holy Spirit who will help this awareness to grow (cf. 16:12-15). Such an experience of absence leading to the joy of Jesus' presence is expressed in a traditional biblical image of a woman giving birth: in and through the "hour" of Jesus a new era has come to birth (Is 26:16-17; 66:7-10). But at the final coming of Jesus, his presence among disciples will be fully revealed, for in this life there is tribulation because of unbelief and hostility (v.21) and only at the end will the joy of the christian be complete. This enduring joy of the christian that comes with faith in Jesus contrasts with the cruel joy of those who reject Jesus (v.20).

This coming era, the time of the Spirit of Jesus, will see sorrow yield to joy, and perplexity to a certain and deeper knowledge of faith. Then the questioning of disciples, which reflects their lack of understanding, will be replaced through the coming of the Spirit by a deeper faith, a closer communion with Jesus and the Father. This communion with Jesus will also affect their prayer, for when Jesus will draw disciples into a closer communion of faith and love with himself and his Father, requests made in the "name" of Jesus, that is, which spring from an intimate communion with him, will be heard. Thus disciples will now be directly in touch with the Father through their communion with Jesus (vv.23,26-27) and they will pray with the sentiments of Christ himself (cf. 14:13-14) and according to God's will. The Father will grant these requests because he, too, is in communion with his Son and lovingly communicates himself to christians as the friends of his Son (v.23). Therefore, the disciples should not be distressed because Jesus is now completing the full "circle" of his existence (v.28) - he has come "from the side of" his Father and he is returning to him. His return, then, is the source of great blessings for all disciples, for example, joy and the intimacy of communion with the Father and the Son in the time of the Holy Spirit.

VICTORY AND PEACE.
16:29-33.

> [29] His disciples said, "Ah, now you are speaking plainly, not in any figure! [30] Now we know that you know all things, and need none to question you; by this we believe that you came from God." [31] Jesus answered them, "Do you now believe? [32] The hour is coming, indeed it has come, when you will be scattered, every man to his home, and will leave me alone; yet I am not alone, for the Father is with me. [33] I have said this to you, that in me you may have peace. In the world you have tribulation; but be of good cheer, I have overcome the world."

In response to his encouragement and promises, the disciples express their faith in Jesus: he is one who comes from God and who has very special knowledge as his revealer. Therefore, he does not need anyone to question him, because he knows the questions even before he is asked (v.30)! Yet Jesus questions the degree of their faith, for they had shown a great lack of understanding in questions, and their lack of faith will appear at the time of testing. Thus when Jesus comes to his suffering, they will not really care for him and they will seek their own safety. Still, Jesus ends on a note of hope as he explains the source of his own confidence when the time of his loneliness comes and he gives confidence to his disciples. Though they, his friends, will desert him in his passion, he will have the supporting presence of his Father (v.32; cf. 8:16,29). They, too, and all christian disciples, will face tribulation because of hostility and unbelief when he goes away. But he assures them of peace (cf. 14:27), which is a gift similar to joy and arises from their communion of faith with Jesus, from a faith which believes that Jesus has overcome the powers of evil through his death and resurrection (v.33).

They should "have courage," then, because through their faith and through his risen presence in the christian community they share in that peace and victory which the resurrection of Jesus has brought to humanity. However, this is not acquired effortlessly for it comes to disciples only through growth in faith in Jesus and through victory over sin (1 Jn 5:4-5).

The Prayer of Jesus
17:1-26.

A PRAYER FOR GLORY.
17:1-8.

> **17** When Jesus had spoken these words, he lifted up his eyes to heaven and said, "Father, the hour has come; glorify thy Son that the Son may glorify thee, ²since thou hast given him power over all flesh, to give eternal life to all whom thou hast given him. ³And this is eternal life, that they know thee the only true God, and Jesus Christ whom thou hast sent. ⁴I glorified thee on earth, having accomplished the work which thou gavest me to do; ⁵and now, Father, glorify thou me in thy own presence with the glory which I had with thee before the world was made.
>
> ⁶"I have manifested thy name to the men whom thou gavest me out of the world; thine they were, and thou gavest them to me, and they have kept thy word. ⁷Now they know that everything that thou hast given me is from thee; ⁸for I have given them the words which thou gavest me, and they have received them and know in truth that I came from thee; and they have believed that thou didst send me."

This chapter, which is the most prolonged prayer of Jesus in the gospels, is not only a kind of theological synthesis reflecting the content and direction of the whole gospel, but it also has distinctive features that make it a prayer. Since prayer takes up the whole person, christians pray as human beings and as people who are called to be children of God. Likewise, the johannine Christ, man and divine Son, in a solemn attitude of prayer, raises human eyes to "heaven" (v.1), that "space" in which he as Incarnate Son experiences communion with his Father (11:41). Prayer is also a relationship, a discovery of a centre in life, a longing for intimacy, for communion with God. Jesus, too, dis-closes here the nerve-centre of his life, which is a communion and intimacy with his Father and which finds expression in the repeated name "Father" (vv.1,5,11,21,24,25). Besides, with prayer there comes a heightened awareness of being loved by God and here Jesus is aware that he is loved by his Father (vv.23-24,26).

For John, to "give" is an expression of love and repeatedly the Father is described as one who "gives" to his Son—his words, his name, his glory, life-giving power, his mission, even disciples. Thus, while everything is the Father's gift to him (vv.7,10), Jesus, in turn, gives to disciples what he received out of the fullness of his Father's love (vv.8,14,22). Furthermore, in prayer the christian reflects on life, on his mission in life; similarly, Jesus reflects on his mission (vv.4,6-8) or on the "work" which the Father had given him to bring to perfect completion (v.4;4:34;5:36). This work means revealing the Father's name, that is, the person of God in so far as he manifests himself (v.6), and commu-nicating his life. This work, by which he glorifies or re-veals his Father, he brought to perfect completion on the cross in loving obedience to his Father (v.4;19:30). To disciples, in particular, Jesus manifested the Father and communicated his word while they accepted his message and came to believe and understand in faith the mystery of Jesus, that he is sent by the Father, that he has received all that he has from his Father.

Just as christians express to God in prayer their central preoccupations and deepest longings for themselves and others, Jesus, too, voices his concerns: his Father's glorification and the welfare of his disciples and all believers (v.20). Moreover, he looks forward to a communion in glory with his Father (v.5). The first part of the prayer (vv.1-8 with vv.1-3 as an introduction) mainly concerns his relationship with his Father and his mission. Yet his petition for "glorification" (v.1) is an unselfish prayer for it is not just a prayer for himself but it is also a prayer "for" the Father and for disciples, for "those whom you have given him." Both Jesus and the Father are glorified when their life is revealed and communicated and when disciples respond in faith to Jesus as a Son of the Father. This prayer for glorification (v.1) is also a petition that the disciples may "know" both Father and Son in an ongoing, loving and life-giving communion with them (v.3). But in this communion through faith and love, the Father, the one true God (Is 37:20; Ex 34:6), is known in and through Jesus. Furthermore this glorification will take place when Jesus has passed through "the hour" of his death and resurrection to his Father in glory (v.5).

Jesus, then, reflects on his mission not only in relation to his Father (v.4) but also in relation to his disciples (vv. 6-8) and this now leads to his praying for these disciples (vv.9-19).

A PRAYER FOR COMMUNION.
17:9-19.

> [9]"I am praying for them; I am not praying for the world but for those whom thou hast given me, for they are thine; [10]all mine are thine, and thine are mine, and I am glorified in them. [11]And now I am no more in the world, but they are in the world, and I am coming to thee. Holy Father, keep them in thy name, which thou has given me, that they may be one, even as we are one. [12]While I was with them, I kept them in thy name, which thou hast given me; I have guarded them, and none of them is lost

but the son of perdition, that the scripture might be fulfilled. [13]But now I am coming to thee; and these things I speak in the world, that they may have my joy fulfilled in themselves. [14]I have given them thy word; and the world has hated them because they are not of the world, even as I am not of the world. [15]I do not pray that thou shouldst take them out of the world, but that thou shouldst keep them from the evil one. [16]They are not of the world, even as I am not of the world. [17]Sanctify them in the truth; thy word is truth. [18]As thou didst send me into the world, so I have sent them into the world. [19]And for their sake I consecrate myself, that they also may be consecrated with truth."

Jesus, the man for others, prays for them and thus the main part of his prayer is an intercession with his Father for present (vv.9-19) and future (vv.20-23) disciples. But before he intercedes for them Jesus gives three reasons why he is praying only for them (vv. 9-11). First, they belong to the Father and everything that belongs to the Father belongs to him too. Besides, disciples are the Father's gift, for they "were" the Father's (v.6) and now they belong to Jesus as well. Therefore, they are precious to Jesus. Secondly, they are precious for personal reasons also: "I am glorified in them," that is, they both share in his life and love and also they acknowledge Jesus in faith for who he is. Finally, since he is leaving them behind, he is concerned about them and how they fare when he goes. Therefore, he now wants to pray to the Father for them (v.11).

It might seem that Jesus is setting limits to his love when he excludes "the world" from his prayer (v.9). But later he prays that the world of those without faith may come to believe in him (vv.21,23). Also, if the "world" means those forces of evil opposed to Jesus (cf. p. 231) then the hope for this area of unbelief would be that it ceases to be "world" altogether. In addition, this is a special prayer for intimate friends: "I, your Son, am praying for these men who are faithful to you."

However, there is one thing he prays for, one special gift he requests from his Father throughout this prayer for disciples: the gift of a life of intimacy, of communion with himself and his Father and he expresses this one petition in various ways. The first expression of this request is: "Keep them in your name . . ." (v.11). Now the name is the person of the Father in so far as he communicates himself, that is, his life and love, to the Son. Not only are disciples to be "kept from" the force of sin and unbelief (called the "world"), from the "evil one" (vv.14-15), but they are also to be "kept in" the name which the Father has given his Son, in that vital sphere in which Father and Son share life together. Jesus' request, then, is that they remain in a communion of life through faith, through the word they have received (v.14), with himself and the Father. In this way disciples will be united ("one") through their communion with God.

When Jesus addresses his Father as "holy" he is following an Old Testament way of describing God. According to that tradition holiness is not just one quality of God among others; it constitutes the essence of God, for it is that which makes him God - his uncreated life, his love and his power. Though totally other, God manifested his holiness to his people Israel. He is "morally" holy, too, because he is infinitely raised above sin, above all that is weak and reprehensible. Here Jesus calls his Father "holy," for the Father manifests his holiness when he draws disciples, through Jesus, into the area of his own love and life and shares his life with them and thus he keeps them apart from the forces of sin and unbelief. In this way he makes them holy or "sanctifies" them (v.17). Jesus, too, is holy for he is the "Holy One of God," a Messiah who is also a Son who shares fully with his Father in a communion of life and consequently reveals and communicates the life of God (6:69).

Jesus asks the Father to continue to do for disciples what he had done for them in his mission (v.12). By maintaining them in discipleship and in a life of companionship with himself through his word (v. 14), he had succeeded in guarding them and strengthening their faith — all except Judas, the "son of perdition," who is "lost." This is not a statement about the eternal loss of Judas, for the gospel does not record his death. But the meaning is: whereas other disciples remained in communion with Jesus, Judas by his betrayal severed himself from a life-giving communion (3:15-16) with Jesus during the time of his passion. Besides, his act of betrayal, his separation from his friendship with Christ, belongs to God's plan as reflected in Scripture (13:18; Ps 41:9). His name "son of perdition" is a Hebrew idiom for "the man destined for perdition" or "the man under the influence of the power of destruction," which is the more likely meaning here since John sees Judas as acting under the influence of Satan (13:2, 27). Thus Judas represents and symbolizes the power of evil, just as the "son of perdition" in 1 Thess 2:3 is a sort of incarnation of evil, one in whom the devil has absolute sway.

In contrast to the darkness of betrayal and the sadness of disciples at the prospect of his departure, Jesus consoles them (v. 13) and he hopes that his message and promise about the life of communion with himself and his Father may be a source of joy for them, and also that they may experience his divine gift of joy (like peace), which comes through a life of communion with him (15:11; 16:20-24).

"Sanctify them in the truth" (v. 17): the "truth" is the self-revelation of the Father in the person of Jesus. Jesus petitions again that disciples may live in a communion of life with himself and his Father. As children of God they share through the "word" of faith in the life of the Father and the Son. Already Jesus has addressed his Father as "holy" (v. 11) for it is he who "sanctifies" disciples in drawing them into a life of communion with himself through Jesus, and the "truth" in which they are to be sanctified is the love and life of the Father revealed in Jesus. This divine life and love of the Father and Son is a kind of sacred area in which disciples live, protected from evil and unbelief (vv. 12-16) and it is this communion with the Father and his Son which makes disciples holy so that they belong completely to them. This communion is also a necessary condition for disciples to carry out their mission and to prolong in the world the mission of Jesus himself (v. 18).

In his mission Jesus belonged fully to his Father and in this way he was "sanctified" (consecrated: the same word is used throughout vv.17-19). Thus he dedicated himself, offered himself constantly to his Father all through his life in loving obedience to him and especially in his death. Besides, his loving obedience and filial communion with his Father is the model and source for disciples ("for their sake"), who are sanctified by leading a life of communion, through faith, with Jesus and the Father (v.19). The climax of Jesus' loving obedience to the Father is his death leading to resurrection, through which he shows that he belongs fully to the Father. Thus he sanctifies himself or offers himself fully to his Father through his death. Likewise, disciples are sanctified not only by the word of Jesus but also by his death since they enter into a life-giving communion of faith and love through the Spirit who is given through the death and resurrection of Jesus. But sanctification does not exclusively refer to the death of Jesus for it embraces the whole mission of Jesus through which Jesus expressed his dedication to his Father, including his death in loving obedience to him.

'THAT THEY MAY BE ONE.'
17:20-23.

> [20]"I do not pray for these only, but also for those who believe in me through their word, [21]that they may all be one; even as thou, Father, art in me, and I in thee, that they also may be in us, so that the world may believe that thou hast sent me. [22]The glory which thou hast given me I have given to them, that they may be one even as we are one, [23]I in them and thou in me, that they may become perfectly one, so that the world may know that thou hast sent me and hast loved them even as thou hast loved me."

The petition for future believers concerns communion with Jesus and the Father once again, but is spelled out in more detail than in v.11: "That they may all be one; even as (*because*) you, Father, are in me and I in you, that they also be *one* (to be added to the RSV version) in us" (v.21). Thus the community of life between Jesus and the Father is not only the model but it is also the source and the cause of the communion of christians with Christ and with one another. "I in them and you in me" (v.23): this sums up the reality and source of christian communion with God: disciples are not only drawn into communion with God through Jesus but they are also integrated into a communion that exists in God himself, into that community of life between Father and Son so that they share in the "glory" of Jesus, that is, the richness and power of God's own life which Jesus received from his Father (v.22).

In addition, the communion with the Godhead is creative of communion or community among christians themselves. Thus the core of johannine "mysticism" is that communion with God means man's integration into community within God, through which life in human community is radically changed. "That they also may be one in us": the focus is not so much the oneness of believers with one another, for the gospel does not view unity in terms of distinct "vertical" (union with God) and "horizontal" (union with one another) categories. Rather the communion of believers with the Father and Son and their communion with one another originate from the life and love that is shared beween Father and Son.

The resulting oneness relationship of believers with Jesus and with one another is not merely internal or spiritual. It is also manifested concretely and perceivably in fraternal love. Besides, the mention of love (vv.23,26) and the similarty (v.21) to Jesus' command of love (13:34) implies that the oneness among believers is manifested in love. But this love is not just "horizontal" or due to human effort alone; rather it is a gift of God transmitted by the Father and his Son to believers because they have been drawn into the divine life and love, and this love disciples manifest in their life together.

"So that the world may believe . . ." (v.21): this oneness among believers is a witness and yet it does not follow that people will accept Jesus but, at least, christian believers will offer to the world the same type of challenge that Jesus offered - a challenge to recognize God in the one whom he sent, Jesus. Besides, this oneness among believers, manifested in love, will show not only that Jesus is sent by the Father but also that God has loved them "even as you loved me" (v.23), for God the Father, who is the centre of this prayer, has taken into his own love those who believe in his Son. Thus christians are his children, living with that very life Jesus has from his Father (6:57;16:27). Why would he not love these children as he has loved his own Son?

FINAL REQUEST.
17:24-26.

> [24]"Father, I desire that they also, whom thou hast given me, may be with me where I am, to behold my glory which thou has given me in thy love for me before the foundation of the world. [25]O righteous Father, the world has not known thee, but I have known thee; and these know that thou hast sent me. [26]I made known to them thy name, and I will make it known, that the love with which thou hast loved me may be in them, and I in them."

Jesus' final request for disciples, who here represent all christians, is again for communion for he prays that disciples may enjoy an eternal life of communion with him in the glory of his Father, although a present life of communion with the Father through faith is also intended. Addressing his Father as a saving and loving Father ("righteous"), Jesus reminds him that in his mission he was always in loving communion with him, so that he could reveal his Father to believing disciples (v.25). Thus he did not cease, and will not cease, through his Spirit, to reveal and communicate the love and life of his Father (his "name") to disciples and this will lead them together in loving communion with himself and his Father. The final promise of Jesus is that he will continue to be the mediator of his Father's love and to realize God's abiding presence among his people (v.26).

This prayer is essentially a prayer of communion, for out of communion with his Father, Jesus prays that disciples may be drawn into and remain in communion, through faith, with himself and his Father, in communion with one another and, finally, that they may enter into eternal communion in glory with them. Therefore, it is a prayer of intercession based on his own communion with his Father which finds expression in a word of special intimacy: "Father." Jesus also looks forward to communion in glory with him. In fact, the prayer contains the kernel of the evangelist's theology of communion and summarizes, in addition, many of the gospel themes.

It is also a prayer of the "hour" of Jesus (v.1) - of his death and resurrection. Jesus appears as if he were still facing death (vv.13,19) and yet already glorified (vv.4,11,12,18), as if he were still in the world and as if he had just left it. The fact is that Jesus is on his way to the Father through death and resurrection and this is his prayer as he crosses the threshold of eternity into a life of communion in glory with his Father. Thus, as he enters into this communion through death and resurrection in his hour he prays for disciples that they, too, may receive what he is accomplishing in his hour through his death and resurrection—communion with God. Therefore, the traditional name of the prayer - "the priestly prayer" also catches the essential mood: while on his way to the Father, about to offer himself to the Father in the most supreme expression of his love, Jesus intercedes for disciples as a mediator and requests that they may receive through his death, leading to resurrection and through the gift of the Spirit, this communion of life with himself and his Father.

The "World" in the Gospel

The "world" (*kosmos*) has very diverse meanings in the gospel, all of which appear in this prayer. Seldom enough it is the created universe (17:5,24) but more often it is the world of man, mankind, which is loved by God and to whom Jesus reveals himself (17:21,23;3:16). Then this world of man as a kind of "area" is contrasted with the transcendent "area" of God, from where Jesus comes (17:15;1:9).

Further, the world is not exclusively the world of man as such but also mankind concretely experiencing itself as sinful, in need of God's saving love, in need of his life, salvation, light and faith (17:21,23). Finally, the world in its fully negative sense is identified with those who have turned against Jesus, influenced by the power of Satan. Thus a strong note of hostility accompanies the use of the "world," particularly in the second part of the gospel as the opposition mounts and the essence of this meaning of "world" is hostility to Jesus who is the light, and rebellion against God (15:18-19; 17:9, 14). This negative sense of "world" is to be understood in the light of the situation of the johannine community. Their "world" of Jew and gentile was experienced as hostile because of the conflict with the Jewish synagogue and also because of the unbelief they encountered among gentiles (cf. introduction: III(i), (ii)).

C. JESUS LAYS DOWN HIS LIFE: PASSION NARRATIVE.

18:1-19:42

ARREST.

18:1-11.—*Master of the Situation.*

18 When Jesus had spoken these words, he went forth with his disciples across the Kidron valley, where there was a garden, which he and his disciples entered. ²Now Judas, who betrayed him, also knew the place; for Jesus often met there with his disciples. ³So Judas, procuring a band of soldiers and some officers from the chief priests and the Pharisees, went there with lanterns and torches and weapons. ⁴Then Jesus, knowing all that was to befall him, came forward and said to them, "Whom to you seek?" ⁵They answered him, "Jesus of Nazareth." Jesus said to them, "I am he." Judas, who betrayed him, was standing with them. ⁶When he said to them, "I am he," they drew back and fell to the ground. ⁷Again he asked them, "Whom do you seek?" And they said, "Jesus of Nazareth." ⁸Jesus answered, "I told you that I am he; so, if you seek me, let these men go." ⁹This was to fulfil the word which he had spoken, "Of those whom thou gavest me I lost not one." ¹⁰Then Simon Peter, having a sword, drew it and struck the high priest's slave and cut off his right ear. The slave's name was Malchus. ¹¹Jesus said to Peter, "Put your sword into its sheath; shall I not drink the cup which the Father has given me?"

NOW THE ACTUAL events of the "hour," of Jesus' return to his Father are described. However, our reading of the passion (chs. 18-19) should not be separated from all that has gone before, since already the gospel has given us many reflections on the meaning of Jesus' death. For example, the suffering of Jesus is an expression of love, for the good shepherd is on his way to lay down his life for his friends out of love (10:11,15;13:1;15:13). Not only the love of the Father (3:16) and of the Son for the world, but also their own mutual love shine through and transform a most poignant and mysterious moment in world history (10:17; 18:11). Besides, Jesus' death is a pass(ing) - over to the Father so that death and resurrection are inseparable (13:1). In the Synoptics, but especially in this gospel, the light of the resurrection penetrates suffering and gives it meaning and thus already in the passion the evangelist anticipates the victory of the resurrection. Consequently, Jesus is presented as triumphant, as one who has been "lifted up' (3:14;8:28;12:32).

Therefore, Jesus is also seen as master of the situation - he is in control, fully aware of what is going to happen to him, he takes the initiative in the events that lead to his death and under interrogation it is he who puts the questions (18:21) and dominates the dialogue (19:11). Also, there is a prolonged reflection on the kingship of Jesus on two levels (18:28-19:16): while Jesus is accused of claiming to be king, the real situation for believers is that he is king and Lord of our lives. Furthermore, his last word from the cross is a cry of triumph (19:30) and some grim details of certain brutalities, described by the Synoptics, are omitted by John in order to focus on the dignity and power of the suffering Jesus on his way to glory. And yet the humiliating aspects of his suffering and the stark reality of his rejection are not overlooked, since Jesus is not only a transcendent Son who overcomes death but also the broken and humiliated "man" (19:5) and a crucified "Jesus from Nazareth" (19:19).

The garden is the place of conflict between the powers of darkness, represented by Judas, the betrayer (cf. 13:27,30) with soldiers and officers, and Jesus, the light, along with his disciples. This contrast is underlined by the mention of "lanterns and torches," which are absent from the other passion accounts. Yet Jesus is master of the situation, for he is aware of all that is going to happen to him and he goes forward to question and to hand himself over to his captors. Thus he is the powerful character of the drama. "I am he": on one level, he identifies and hands himself over. But the words also say to the believing reader that Jesus is the transcendent revealer of God who is now intervening in the history of man's salvation (8:24,28;13:19). Also, before him the forces, which oppose God and persecute a just sufferer, a Messiah, "fall down," that is, are powerless (Pss 27:2;56:9; Is 11:4; Ezek 1:.8). Then by saving his disciples he is laying down his life on behalf of others, since at the moment they have not sufficient faith to endure death along with him (vv.8-9;6:39;17:12).

Surprisingly, the suffering destiny of Jesus, which is symbolized by the "cup," is a gift from the Father to his Son (v.11) as the Father invites Jesus to lay down his life and loves him for doing so (10:17). Jesus, in turn, accepts suffering in loving obedience to him. Peter, however, who has not grasped the meaning of Jesus' death as the Father's gift, violently tries to prevent Jesus from going his way. Once more Peter acts out of false enthusiasm and lacks true understanding of Jesus (13:37-38) and this will lead to his failure in discipleship. Still, he and the other disciples in the garden are companions of Jesus and are also the Father's gift to him (v.9). They are the protected ones of Jesus who stay with him and do not run away at this moment of conflict.

DENIALS AND INTERROGATION.
18:12-27.

> [12]So the band of soldiers and their captain and the officers of the Jews seized Jesus and bound him. [13]First they led him to Annas; for he was the father-in-law of

Caiaphas, who was high priest that year. [14]It was Caiaphas who had given counsel to the Jews that it was expe-
dient that one man should die for the people.

[15]Simon Peter followed Jesus, and so did another
disciple. As this disciple was known to the high priest,
he entered the court of the high priest along with Jesus,
[16]while Peter stood outside at the door. So the other
disciple, who was known to the high priest, went out and
spoke to the maid who kept the door, and brought Peter
in. [17]The maid who kept the door said to Peter, "Are not
you also one of this man's disciples?" He said, "I am not."
[18]Now the servants and officers had made a charcoal fire,
because it was cold, and they were standing and warming
themselves; Peter also was with them, standing and
warming himself.

[19]The high priest then questioned Jesus about his
disciples and his teaching. [20]Jesus answered him, "I have
spoken openly to the world; I have always taught in
synagogues and in the temple, where all Jews come
together; I have said nothing secretly. [21]Why do you ask
me? Ask those who have heard me, what I said to them;
they know what I said." [22]When he had said this, one of
the officers standing by struck Jesus with his hand,
saying, "Is that how you answer the high priest?" [23]Jesus
answered him. "If I have spoken wrongly, bear witness
to the wrong; but if I have spoken rightly, why do you
strike me?" [24]Annas then sent him bound to Caiaphas
the high priest.

[25]Now Simon Peter was standing and warming himself.
They said to him, "Are not you also one of his disciples?"
He denied it and said, "I am not." [26]One of the servants
of the high priest, a kinsman of the man whose ear Peter
had cut off, asked, "Did I not see you in the garden with
him?" [27]Peter again denied it; and at once the cock
crowed.

Whereas Peter denies Jesus before others, before the
high-priest Jesus publicly reveals himself. Here, unlike the

Synoptics, the evangelist does not describe a public "trial" of Jesus before Caiaphas and the Sanhedrin. While Jesus is on his way to give his life, Peter is unable to follow Jesus and to give his life for Jesus. Moreover, the repeated use of the word "disciple" throughout this scene (vv.15,16,17, 19,25) shows that what Peter denies is true discipleship of Jesus. Previously Jesus had warned him that, in spite of his promises, he will have inequivocally ("three times") denied Jesus by early morning (by cockcrow: 18:27;13:37-38). The reasons for Peter's failure have already been made clear: his lack of understanding and trust in his own false enthusiasm (18:10-11;13:36-38). But the true basis of discipleship, of witnessing to Christ, is the understanding of Jesus and the strength of faith communicated by the Holy Spirit (15:26-27). Whereas the Synoptics (Mk 14:72 par.) mention Peter's tears of repentance and conversion, this is absent here for later on there is a detailed account of Peter's reconciliation (21:15-19). As yet the story of Peter is incomplete. Here he stands alongside another disciple, probably the Beloved Disciple, who does not deny Jesus. Peter, too, has a representative value and his denials are a warning to all disciples not to think that the following of Jesus and witnessing to him depend on man's good will.

The confrontation of Jesus with Annas is also a conflict with the forces of unbelief. Sometimes, too, the gospel mentions "blows" to which Jesus is subjected (v.22;19:3). But the interrogation is a farce because the interrogator has obviously made up his mind already (v.21). Yet the power of Jesus dominates this conflict as he dictates the dialogue by leaving questions unanswered and by his refusal to enter into a discussion (v.21). He had often called for faith and warned his hearers that one day it would be too late (7:33-38; 8:21-24). Now the time of his open revelation to the world is over (v.20). However, there remains the opportunity to accept the testimony or word about Jesus from those who have followed Jesus in faith, who have "heard me" (v.21). But Jesus has nothing more to say to Annas and he is innocent and does no wrong since he fulfils his Father's will always (v.23;8:45-51). The roles are also reversed as Jesus becomes the accuser and Annas the accused (v.23). Besides, Jesus reduces him to silence and shows himself both as Lord of his passion and as God's authoritative revealer for the whole "world" (v.20). Therefore, he must speak out "openly" God's decisive words for man (cf. Is 45:19).

Jesus the King and the Jews Before Pilate 18:28-19:16.

THE ACCUSED, 18:28-32.

[28]Then they led Jesus from the house of Caiaphas to the praetorium. It was early. They themselves did not enter the praetorium, so that they might not be defiled, but might eat the passover. [29]So Pilate went out to them and said, "What accusation do you bring against this man?" [30]They answered him, "If this man were not an evildoer, we would not have handed him over." [31]Pilate said to them, "Take him yourselves and judge him by your own law." The Jews said to him, "It is not lawful for us to put any man to death." [32]This was to fulfil the word which Jesus had spoken to show by what death he was to die.

The trial before Pilate is staged dramatically in seven scenes which shift from inside to outside the Jerusalem fortress of Pilate. Besides, the action takes place on two stages: there is the front stage where Jesus appears outside with Pilate. Here, outside the praetorium, Jesus does not address one word to the crowd, for the time of his public ministry and revelation is over (cf. v.20). But inside, backstage, Jesus communicates with Pilate (18:36-37;19:11). This conflict between Jesus and unbelief comes to a head in the mounting hostility and final rejection of Jesus as king (19:15). Also, the scene always moves on two levels of meaning. For example, Jesus has been handed over to Pilate and his death is demanded under the pretext that he claimed to be a king (19:12), but ironically this constitutes for the evangelist a proclamation that Jesus is a true king. This type of situation is so characteristic of the gospel that it has been named "johannine irony": the meaning of a scene or a statement is the very reverse of what one would suppose to be the meaning at first sight.

First of all, a brief introduction (v.28) sets the stage and presents the place, the time and the actors of the drama: Jesus, Pilate, the soldiers ("they") and the Jews. The time indication also expresses the crucial importance of the drama - it is "early," the break of that day when the task given to Jesus by the Father is accomplished (19:30) and this day of fulfilment and glorification has arrived. Then, outside, the crowd accuse Jesus of doing evil without specifying his crime (vv.29-32). However, the decision had already been taken to have Jesus put to death; otherwise recourse would not have been made to Pilate, who wants further information: "What crime can you impute to this man who claims to be king of the Jews?". According to this account (v.30), the Jewish supreme council (the Sanhedrin) had power to condemn a man to death but to carry out this sentence there was need of a decision or, at least, permission from the governor. In any case, Jesus is going to his death fully aware of his destiny as a suffering and exalted Son of Man, since he had proclaimed himself in this role earlier (12:32).

A TRUE KING.
18:33-38.

> [33]Pilate entered the praetorium again and called Jesus, and said to him, "Are you the King of the Jews?" [34]Jesus answered, "Do you say this of your own accord, or did others say it to you about me?" [35]Pilate answered, "Am I a Jew? Your own nation and the chief priests have handed you over to me; what have you done?" [36]Jesus

answered, "My kingship is not of this world; if my kingship were of this world, my servants would fight, that I
might not be handed over to the Jews; but my kingship
is not from the world." [37]Pilate said to him, "So you are a
king?" Jesus answered, "You say that I am a king. For
this I was born, and for this I have come into the world,
to bear witness to the truth. Every one who is of the truth
hears my voice." [38]Pilate said to him, "What is truth?"

Alone with Pilate backstage Jesus says he is king and he
explains why and how. He also assumes control of the
dialogue by pointing out to Pilate the ambiguity of his
question: if Pilate speaks from his Roman understanding
of kingship, then Jesus is not a political king, still less a
political subsersive. Jesus then describes the origin, quality
and meaning of his kingship: it is not of "this world" and it
is related, to the "truth." No human authority has legalized
his "office" as king, since his power is "from above" and
superior to all human power (3:31) and yet he is a king who
exercizes power in this life over those who believe through
his truth. For Jesus is the "truth" in so far as he reveals God
in his person, words and action (14:6). Thus the disciple who
responds to the truth, the self-revelation or the word of
Jesus, especially to his supreme manifestation of himself
in love on the cross and lives out this "truth," is "of the
truth." If, then, christians base their lives on Jesus' self-
revelation, Jesus becomes Lord of their lives, a king. The
questioning answer of Pilate which follows (v.38) is not a
philosophical inquiry but rather a realization and proclamation of what Jesus has already said, and Pilate's question
has revealed that he certainly is not "of the truth" for it
shows he is ignorant and lacks understanding of him who is
the truth. Thus no neutrality is allowed before Jesus who is
the truth, whereas Pilate yields more and more to those who
reject Jesus and allows them take the initiative. Though
Pilate is a witness to the innocence of Jesus (v.38) the fact
that he does not free Jesus springs from his decision against
the truth, God's own revelation in Jesus.

FACING A CHOICE.
18:38-40.

> After he had said this, he went out to the Jews again, and told them, "I find no crime in him. [39]But you have a custom that I should release one man for you at the Passover; will you have me release for you the King of the Jews?" [40]They cried out again, "Not this man, but Barabbas!" Now Barabbas was a robber.

Onstage again Pilate offers a choice between the true Messiah, leader and king, and Barabbas, a "robber" or leader. This name was used also for guerilla leaders in Palestine who led revolts against the Romans. Thus the whole irony of the situation is that people reject him who embodies all their messianic hopes and dreams in favour of a false leader.

PUNISHED AND CROWNED.
19:1-3.

> **19** Then Pilate took Jesus and scourged him. [2]And the soldiers plaited a crown of thorns, and put it on his head, and arrayed him in a purple robe; [3]they came up to him, saying, "Hail, King of the Jews!" and struck him with their hands.

Pilate hopes to satisfy those who cry out for the death sentence by punishing Jesus with the less radical punishment of scourging. In this scene some humiliating and mocking brutalities, recorded by the Synoptics, are omitted (Mk 15: 16-20 par.) and those elements are highlighted which symbolically point to Jesus' kingship - a crown of thorns and a purple garment. While Jesus wears the signs of his dignity and kingship, he also receives blows which are signs of unbelief and rejection.

'WHAT A MAN!'
19:4-7.

> [4]Pilate went out again, and said to them, "See, I am bringing him out to you, that you may know that I find no

crime in him." ⁵So Jesus came out, wearing the crown of thorns and the purple robe. Pilate said to them, "Behold the man!" ⁶When the chief priests and the officers saw him, they cried out, "Crucify him, crucify him!" Pilate said to them, "Take him yourselves and crucify him, for I find no crime in him." ⁷The Jews answered him, "We have a law, and by that law he ought to die, because he has made himself the Son of God."

The brutalized king is led out before the crowd wearing the symbols of his kingship and he is solemnly presented to them by Pilate in words that express the broken humanity and yet invincible transcendence of Jesus: "Look at this poor broken man - the ridiculousness of this pretender. There's nothing to be feared from him and yet you have been causing such an uproar about him" (v.5). But the evangelist sees, beyond the appearances, a deeper meaning, namely, that Jesus is not only a humiliated "man"; he is also a powerful "Son of Man" on his way to glorification (12:23-24). Therefore, those who call for his death are sending him on his way to the Father. While he, a transcendent, divine Son is accused of blasphemy because of his claims, yet in actual fact it is his accusers who are acting blasphemously against God in demanding the death of a king and Son of God (v.7; cf. Lev 24:16; Jn 5:17-18; 10:33-35).

'WHERE ARE YOU FROM?'
19:8-12.

⁸When Pilate heard these words, he was the more afraid; ⁹he entered the praetorium again and said to Jesus, "Where are you from?" But Jesus gave no answer. ¹⁰Pilate therefore said to him, "You will not speak to me? Do you not know that I have power to release you, and power to crucify you?" ¹¹Jesus answered him, "You would have no power over me unless it had been given you from above; therefore he who delivered me to you has the greater sin."

> [12]Upon this Pilate sought to release him, but the Jews cried out, "If you release this man, you are not Caesar's friend; every one who makes himself a king sets himself against Caesar."

Inside there is a second interrogation by Pilate, this time about a key issue and vexed question throughout the gospel: the divine origins of Jesus (7:27;8:14). Once again we have a reversal of roles and we get the impression that Pilate is in Jesus' power (v.11) as Jesus becomes the judge of his judge. Pilate merely registers a vague, superstitious fear (v.8) and curiosity about Jesus and yet he is afraid to lay violent hands on someone who claims to be God in human form. Jesus at first refuses to reply to one who is not open to the "truth" (18:38) but then he tells Pilate that his power over him comes from the Father. Thus it is through Pilate that the Father disposes of Jesus in his divine plan. While it is true that this account, as compared with Mark's (15:6-15), tends to exculpate Pilate, yet the point of Jesus' reply (v.11) is not to explain Pilate's lesser guilt, but rather to accuse in no uncertain way those who are responsible. However, Pilate is not open to the "truth" for here he is hesitant and lets himself be trapped between two fears: a vague, supersititious fear of Jesus and a fear of those who are pressing for his death. Thus, having rejected the truth, he is powerless against, and lets himself be caught up by, the forces of unbelief and he is helpless against those who threaten his one and only security - the fact that he is and must remain a faithful servant of the Roman emperor (v.12). Therefore, he refuses to give allegiance to someone who, in his opinion, falsely claims to be king.

THE MOMENT OF DECISION.
19:13-15.

> [13]When Pilate heard these words, he brought Jesus out and sat down on the judgment seat at a place called The Pavement, and in Hebrew, Gabbatha. [14]Now it was the day of Preparation of the Passover; it was about the sixth hour. He said to the Jews, "Behold your King!"

> [15]They cried out, "Away with him, away with him, crucify
> him!" Pilate said to them, "Shall I crucify your King?"
> The chief priests answered, "We have no king but Caesar."

This is the climax of the trial as Jesus is dramatically
presented and proclaimed to the crowd as king by Pilate
(v.14). First, the details of time and place give special
weight to the scene at Gabbatha, meaning the "high place"
- a name that underlines the dignity and power of Jesus, the
king. Also, the mention of "Passover" here and at the
beginning (18:28) brings us closer to the death of Jesus
who is a Passover Lamb offered for mankind (cf. 19:36).
Here the passion account, which describes the confrontation
between Jesus and the forces of unbelief (the "world,"
represented by "the Jews" in v.14), reaches a climax as
Pilate proclaims Jesus king from his "judgment seat" (v.13).
For some the meaning is that Jesus "was made sit down" on
the judgment seat and he is therefore the "judge." But
apart from linguistic difficulties the emphasis is on Jesus
the king. In either case, this is a moment of "judgment"
when, in a confrontation between Jesus and unbelief, those
who reject Jesus condemn or "judge" themselves (3:18;
12:31). Thus they are rejecting their own messianic hopes,
their very belonging to God's people which, in fact, is
founded on the expectation of a messianic king.

At the Cross of Jesus
19:16-37.

A PLACE OF HONOUR.
19:16-18.

> [16]Then he handed him over to them to be crucified.
> [17]So they took Jesus, and he went out, bearing his own
> cross, to the place called the place of a skull, which is
> called in Hebrew Golgotha. [18]There they crucified him,
> and with him two others, one on either side, and Jesus
> between them.

There is somehow more peace and calm on Calvary than at the praetorium as the scene shifts from the strident atmosphere of the "high place," which reached its moment of greatest intensity with the ultimate rejection of Jesus and his simultaneous proclamation as king. Also, the to and fro movement at the praetorium gives way to the relative stillness of Calvary and there are five "still" snapshots of Calvary which invite the reader to contemplate the cross of Jesus from five different "angles."

The introduction to these scenes (vv. 16-18) does not describe the details of the crucifixion but only baldly states the fact (v. 16). Yet it does insinuate the sovereignty and freedom of Jesus in his suffering, in so far as he does not need anyone to help him carry "his own cross," since there is no Simon of Cyrene as in the Synoptics. Then Jesus is crucified along with two others, "between them," literally, "in their midst." In contrast with Mark's account (15:32) nothing is said about them or by them in order to save all the attention for Jesus and to highlight the power and dignity of the crucified king, for the place in the middle is a position of honour (Mk 10:37; Mt 25:33).

A TITLE OF HONOUR.
19:19-22.

> [19]Pilate also wrote a title and put it on the cross; it read, "Jesus of Nazareth, the King of the Jews." [20]Many of the Jews read this title, for the place where Jesus was crucified was near the city; and it was written in Hebrew, in Latin, and in Greek. [21]The chief priests of the Jews then said to Pilate, "Do not write, 'The King of the Jews,' but, 'This man said, I am King of the Jews.'" [22]Pilate answered, "What I have written I have written."

The first picture takes in the title on the cross: Jesus of Nazareth, the king of the Jews, which is written in all three main languages of the known world, Hebrew, Greek and Latin and thus proclaims the kingship of Jesus to the people of Jerusalem, "urbi et orbi" - to the whole world and for the whole world. Besides, this title is retained by Pilate and thus on a deeper level of meaning Pilate is presented as one who refuses to change, unknowingly, the truth of Christ's kingship into a lie and who bears witness officially but unconsciously to the dignity of Jesus (11:50;12:3). Thus protests cannot change the reality of Jesus' universal kingship, which rests secure because of Pilate's firm and providential decision.

ULTIMATE DEPRIVATION.
19:23-24.

> [23]When the soldiers had crucified Jesus they took his garments and made four parts, one for each soldier; also his tunic. But the tunic was without seam, woven from top to bottom; [24]so they said to one another, "Let us not tear it, but cast lots for it to see whose it shall be." This was to fulfil the scripture.
>
> "They parted my garments among them, and for my clothing they cast lots."

The spotlight now turns from the title on the cross to the soldiers beside it who draw lots for Jesus' clothing. These soldiers, as the agents of the chief priests who handed over Jesus to be crucified (19:15-16), are ranged on the side of those who reject Jesus (cf. 19:2) and the indignity Jesus suffers at their hands belongs to God's plan as reflected in Scripture (Ps 22:18). Perhaps it is implied that Jesus is deprived of all, and in death gives up his whole self, all that he is and possesses. But some see in the undivided garment of Jesus either a symbol of the unity of the Church (the garment is not "torn," cf. 11:51-52;21:11) or a symbol of the priesthood of Jesus is so far as Jesus' death is sacrificial and we are reminded of the garment of the high-priest. However, the account does not seem to emphasize unity here or give any clear pointers to a priesthood of Christ.

THOSE WHO STAND BY JESUS.
19:25-27.

> [25]So the soldiers did this. But standing by the cross of Jesus were his mother, and his mother's sister, Mary the wife of Clopas, and Mary Magdalene. [26]When Jesus saw his mother, and the disciple whom he loved standing near, he said to his mother, "Woman, behold, your son!" [27]Then he said to the disciple, "Behold, your mother!" And from that hour the disciple took her to his own home.

The group in this picture contrast with the soldiers—the mother of Jesus and some women who "stand by" the cross of Jesus along with the Beloved Disciple. These are believers who are close to Jesus, for they "stand by" him, that is, they are loyal faithful followers, whereas unbelievers are those who "go away from" Jesus (6:66-67). But this group of women also represent all those who confess faith in their crucified Lord and who, through faith, overcome the scandal of the cross. Then the message of Jesus from the cross to his mother and the Beloved Disciple is not just a question of a Beloved Disciple looking after the mother of Jesus when he dies (vv.26-27); otherwise the words of Jesus to him alone would have sufficed.

"He took her to his own home" - this translation restricts the meaning of the phrase which has a more general sense: he took her into a special relationship with himself. There was a tradition that John the Apostle took Mary to his own home but this is not the message of Jesus' words nor is it clear from the gospel that this disciple is John the Apostle. Also, the relationship between the mother of Jesus and the Beloved Disciple is not in the "material" order of caring, since it concerns the life of faith which is part of Jesus' work of salvation (19:30), resulting from his death and resurrection in his "hour." What, then, is the nature of this relationship?

There are many interpretations among which the following two are selected as the more significant:

(a) The relationship of Mary to Jesus (as "woman") and to the Beloved Disciple (as "your mother") on Calvary is linked with the Cana scene (pp. 60-61). Both at Cana and to a more radical degree on Calvary her relationship to Jesus as a mother in the flesh is transformed. Here she "stands by" him as a faithful follower and is now influenced by him in a relationship of faith, whereas once she had influenced him as a mother. Thus she is influenced by his death because, as a believer by the cross, she receives new life from her Son who completes his life-giving work and confers this gift of life, symbolized by the water that flows from his side (19:30,34). Furthermore, the dignity of her transformed relationship is expressed by Jesus when he calls her "woman."

Thus Mary is the new Eve who receives life from a man, her Son (Gen 2:23). But Eve is also called "mother of all living" and Mary, too, becomes mother in a new sense for she is constituted mother of the Beloved Disciple, who represents all beloved disciples or all believers (v.27). As the physical mother of Jesus, she had represented the people of Israel out of whom Jesus was born but now that her physical motherhood is transformed, she represents a new people who are the church. The Beloved Disciple, too, has a representative role in so far as he stands for the individual christian who receives the life of Jesus in and through the church which Mary represents. Mary is, therefore, the new Eve and symbol of the church. Besides, at Cana she had encouraged others to be docile in faith to her Son (2:5) and here again on Calvary she is an example to believers as one who "stands by" her Son in faith. Consequently, it is implied that as one who leads others to faith in her Son, she is "mother of the faithful."

(b) Another interpretation sees the Beloved Disciple as the central figure in this scene since he assumes a more important role throughout the gospel. The stress is rather on what he does for Mary since the final statement of the passage underlines his action (v.27b). Thus the sense of Jesus' message from the cross is: "Woman, here is your son who is *to take care of you* . . . There is your mother whom *you have to take care of*." On Calvary Mary is more than a mother of Jesus since, because of her relationship of faith to Jesus— with the other women here she represents believers—she has an added dignity, expressed in the special, solemn title: "Woman." Besides, in the scene at Cana (2:1-6) she is a believer and has the same title. Therefore, the meaning of the relationship between her and the Beloved Disciple is: Jesus entrusts his mother, Mary, representing the believing community for whom the Fourth Gospel was written, to the Beloved Disciple in so far as his witness is found in the gospel. Thus the words of Jesus refer to the relationship of faith between the community, represented by Mary, and the Beloved Disciple whose testimony to Jesus is contained in the Fourth Gospel. In other words, all believers are referred in faith to the Beloved Disciple's message about Jesus.

MISSION COMPLETED.
19:28-30.

> [28]After this Jesus, knowing that all was now finished, said (to fulfil the scripture), "I thirst." [29]A bowl full of vinegar stood there; so they put a sponge full of the vinegar on hyssop and held it to his mouth. [30]When Jesus had received the vinegar, he said, "It is finished"; and he bowed his head and gave up his spirit.

A fourth picture describes the end with the final words of Jesus. First of all, his "thirst" (Pss 69:22;22:16) is more than physical, for it also symbolizes his desire to fulfil the Father's wish, to drink the "cup" (18:11) and to complete in death the "work" of salvation (4:34;6:35;7:37). Secondly, his last word is a cry of triumph as he has carried out to the full the most supreme expression of love, the work the Father gave him to do (4:34;13:1): "My work is brought to its perfect completion." Probably the "giving up" of "his spirit" is a reminder of the Holy Spirit who is "given" by Jesus through his death and resurrection (7:39). Therefore, in a double sense Jesus "hands up his Spirit" in this scene which is a theological picture: Jesus dies and through his death communicates the Holy Spirit.

BLOOD AND WATER.
19:31-37.

> [31]Since it was the day of Preparation, in order to prevent the bodies from remaining on the cross on the sabbath (for that sabbath was a high day), the Jews asked Pilate that their legs might be broken, and that they might be taken away. [32]So the soldiers came and broke the legs of the first, and of the other who had been crucified with him; [33]but when they came to Jesus and saw that he was already dead, they did not break his legs. [34]But one of the soldiers pierced his side with a spear, and at once there came out blood and water. [35]He who saw it has borne witness—his testimony is true, and he knows that he tells the truth—that you also may believe. [36]For these things took place that the scripture might be fulfilled. "Not a bone of him shall be broken." [37]And again another scripture says, "They shall look on him whom they have pierced."

The final Calvary scene describes the effects of Jesus' death, in particular, the blood and water flowing from the side of Jesus, which, however, does not interest the evangelist as a medical phenomenon, because he is a "witness" - he sees a deeper meaning in a physical reality and in his account he reveals something which can be grasped only in faith (v.35). Here the blood symbolizes Jesus' death (6:51-54) and water the new life communicated by the Spirit (7:38-39; cf. the background of this symbolism p. 119), which comes to man from his death. Thus the death of Jesus (blood) is a source of new life (water) for believers. On a further level, this new life is communicated to believers through the sacraments of eucharist (blood) and baptism (water: cf. 1 Jn 5:8). Furthermore, the bones of Jesus are not broken, although this, in fact, would have been an act of mercy hastening his death, because Jesus is a Passover Lamb given over in death for the salvation of the world (Ex 12:46; Ps 34:2). Zechariah (12:10) had spoken of a lamented shepherd king whose death would be a source of purification and conversion. Similarly, all those who look with the eyes of faith and respond to that love manifested by their Lord crucified and lifted up in triumph on the cross (3:14-16) will receive the gift of new life through him (v.37).

EPILOGUE OF THE PASSION.
19:38-42.—*Burial for a King.*

> [38]After this Joseph of Arimathea, who was a disciple of Jesus, but secretly, for fear of the Jews, asked Pilate that he might take away the body of Jesus, and Pilate gave him leave. So he came and took away his body. [39]Nicodemus also, who had at first come to him by night, came bringing a mixture of myrrh and aloes about a hundred pounds' weight. [40]They took the body of Jesus, and bound it in linen cloths with the spices, as is the burial custom of the Jews. [41]Now in the place where he was crucified there was a garden, and in the garden a new tomb where no one had ever been laid. [42]So because of the Jewish day of Preparation, as the tomb was close at hand, they laid Jesus there.

The atmosphere becomes even more peaceful as Jesus is taken down from the cross where he had been lifted up and pierced. He is now laid in a tomb by believing disciples, by Joseph, and also Nicodemus who has passed through successive stages of development and is now a true follower of Jesus (cf. 3:1;7:50-52). This is a quiet burial of a king by believers who are contrasted with the soldiers at the cross (v.34) and yet very special honours are accorded Jesus in burial: expensive and plentiful ointments (cf. 12:3-7), a new tomb (it was customary to pay these honours to a king in death) - all this suggests the dignity of Jesus as king.

The "Jews" in the Gospel

The passion account and sometimes the rest of the gospel, too, seem to show up the Jews most unfavourably and give the impression that the whole people, at least of Jerusalem, want to do away with Jesus. For example, the "Jews" want him put to death as they opt for Barabbas and want Jesus "away" (18:31,38;19:12,14) - and all that so soon after he was acclaimed king in the city (12:12-19). Also, Jesus is often in conflict with "the Jews" who "persecute" him (5:16;7:1) while he tells them that they are "of the devil" (8:44,48).

But this title "the Jews," which is used much more frequently in this gospel than in the Synoptics (about seventy times), has many shades of meaning. It does not univocally describe a national grouping hostile to Jesus, for "many of the Jews" came to believe in him (12:11) and the Saviour of the world is to come "from the Jews" (4:22,42). Besides, they are sometimes mentioned in a neutral way (18:20) but frequently "the Jews" has a negative and hostile sense (cf. chs. 18-19) because the gospel envisages the situation of the johannine community in conflict with "the Jews" of the synagogue (cf. introduction: III(i)).

Finally, the name sometimes transcends ethnic considerations because it belongs to the vocabulary of conflict between Jesus and the forces of sin and unbelief (the "world"). Consequently, "the Jews" become a group, not a whole people, who represent all those who reject Jesus and the evangelist in referring to the Jews in this hostile sense does not condemn a race but only opposition to Jesus. Thus he could be reproving our own failure to accept Jesus.

D. JESUS TAKES UP HIS LIFE AGAIN: RESURRECTION. 20:1-21:25.

AT THE TOMB OF JESUS.
20:1-10.—*The Beloved Sees and Believes.*

20 Now on the first day of the week Mary Magdalene came to the tomb early, while it was still dark, and saw that the stone had been taken away from the tomb. ²So she ran, and went to Simon Peter and the other disciple, the one whom Jesus loved, and said to them, "They have taken the Lord out of the tomb, and we do not know where they have laid him." ³Peter then came out with the other disciple, and they went toward the tomb. ⁴They both ran, but the other disciple outran Peter and reached the tomb first; ⁵and stooping to look in, he saw the linen cloths lying there, but he did not go in. ⁶Then Simon Peter came, following him, and went into the tomb; he saw the linen cloths lying, ⁷and the napkin, which had been laid on his head, not lying with the linen cloths but rolled up in a place by itself. ⁸Then the other disciple, who reached the tomb first, also went in, and he saw and believed; ⁹for as yet they did not know the scripture, that he must rise from the dead. ¹⁰Then the disciples went back to their homes.

THE RELIGIOUS EXPERIENCE communicated in this chapter is the "coming" (vv. 19,24,26) of the risen Jesus to his disciples. It also reflects the Easter faith of the early christian community: "Come, Lord Jesus" (*Maranatha*). The main theme of the gospel continues, too: Jesus reveals himself, this time as the risen "Lord" (vv.2,18,20,25,28) and disciples respond in faith - they "believe" (vv.8,25,27,29,31), that is, they commit and attach themselves to their risen Lord in faith. Besides, they "see" him (vv.18,20,24,27,29), they become aware of his presence and grasp the mystery that he is their risen Lord.

But this faith is not a sudden, once and for all response, for it is a gift of the risen Jesus and it grows through the experience of his absence, through fear and doubt (vv.13-16, 19,26-29). Thus the three main scenes - at the tomb (vv.1-18), Jesus' coming to the gathered community (vv.19-23), and finally to Thomas (vv.24-29) - all describe the Easter faith of disciples and the meaning of the presence of the risen Jesus. At the end there is a crescendo of faith culminating in the credo of Thomas: "My Lord and my God" (v.28).

The darkness (v.1) before the dawning of Easter conveys that the light of Jesus' presence is gone for disciples. Thus Mary Magdalene suffers a profound sense of absence as she is deprived of her Lord who has been "taken away" (vv.2,13,15). Then there is growth from darkness to "seeing" and "believing" (v.8) in Jesus as risen. For the Beloved Disciple Jesus is physically absent from the tomb and all that he "sees" physically is an empty tomb with some cloths (v.6). But he comes to "see" in faith and "believe" (v.8). He is sensitive through faith and love to the presence of his risen Lord and he detects in faith the signs of his presence even without previous knowledge that Scripture has to be read in the light of the resurrection of Jesus (Ps 16:10; Hos 6:2).

This Beloved Disciple certainly is a real individual of flesh and blood and as the basic source of the traditions they received about Jesus, he is specially important in that community for which the gospel was written. But he also represents the christian disciple who is sensitive to the presence of the risen Jesus in faith and love, and he contrasts with Thomas, who wanted a special sign from Jesus (v.25).

However, the Beloved Disciple did not "see" Jesus at the tomb in the same way as Thomas experienced him. Yet given just an empty tomb with some cloths, he "sees" in faith that Jesus is risen. The description here of two disciples racing to the tomb does not suggest any rivalry between Peter and the Beloved Disciple who gets there first and waits for Peter to let him have the first look but it is all part of a dramatic build-up to the punchline of the account: "He saw and believed" (v.8). Furthermore, the "cloths" and the "taking away" (vv.2,13,15) of Jesus reflect some rumors that had been circulated in the community about the stealing of his body from the tomb. On the contrary, it was highly unlikely that his body was stolen if the cloths were still there.

MARY AT THE TOMB.
20:11-18.—*A Promise of Intimacy.*

¹¹But Mary stood weeping outside the tomb, and as she wept she stooped to look into the tomb; ¹²and she saw two angels in white, sitting where the body of Jesus had lain, one at the head and one at the feet. ¹³They said to her, "Woman, why are you weeping?" She said to them, "Because they have taken away my Lord, and I do not know where they have laid him." ¹⁴Saying this, she turned round and saw Jesus standing, but she did not know that it was Jesus. ¹⁵Jesus said to her, "Woman, why are you weeping? Whom do you seek?" Supposing him to be the gardener, she said to him, "Sir, if you have carried him away, tell me where you have laid him, and I will take him away." ¹⁶Jesus said to her, "Mary." She turned and said to him in Hebrew, "Rabboni!" (which means Teacher). ¹⁷Jesus said to her, "Do not hold me, for I have not yet ascended to the Father; but go to my brethren and say to them, I am ascending to my Father and your Father, to my God and your God." ¹⁸Mary Magdalene went and said to the disciples, "I have seen the Lord"; and she told them that he had said these things to her.

There is also an intimate, affective quality about this scene in which Mary Magdalene, who "stood by the cross of Jesus" (19:25), now becomes a witness to his resurrection. Now she feels very deprived because "my Lord" had been taken away (vv.2,11,13) and she laments his absence just as Mary of Bethany lamented the loss of her brother. But she "seeks" Jesus in faith like the first disciples who also "seek" Jesus and come to faith in him (v.15;1:38), and through a special faith-experience she comes to "see" Jesus as her risen Lord (vv.16,18). Her faith, however, is a gift of Jesus for he leads her to recognize him in faith (v.16) and she shares this faith in her "Lord" with other disciples (v.18). This difficulty in recognizing Jesus reflects the mystery of a "risen body" (1 Cor 15:44) as Jesus is transformed and somehow different because of his resurrection. Then he calls her by name ("Mary"), that is, he leads, invites her personally to faith in him as her risen Lord (vv.13,16;10:3). But the mention of a gardener as well as Mary's constant lament that Jesus has been "taken away" (vv.2,3,15) probably recall some accusations circulating in the early community that Jesus' body was stolen either by disciples or by a gardener.

Mary longs for an intimate communion in faith with Jesus (v.17) and she wishes to worship him as exalted with the Father but Jesus stops her: "Do not try to cling to me like that." "Clinging" expresses the notion of intimate attachment to or communion with Jesus and he assures her that she will receive this gift of intimate communion when he has "ascended" to his Father, i.e. when he goes to his Father and sends the Holy Spirit. It is through the Holy Spirit that christians enter into an intimate, life-giving communion with Jesus, the Son of God, as their brother and also with God as the Father. Now the risen Jesus is transformed and he will communicate himself in a new and more intimate way through his Holy Spirit. Through faith, the gift of the Spirit, disciples share in the divine life of the Father as his children and this life is present in Jesus. Thus the Father of Jesus becomes the Father of believers.

In this account (vv. 1-18) as also in the Synoptics (cf. Mt 28:8-10) the disciples' experience of the risen Jesus is linked with the empty tomb. Yet their Easter faith is not founded on an empty tomb but rather on their special experiences of faith, i.e. appearances of the risen Jesus. Thus in the light of this Easter faith, the early christian community came to understand the empty tomb as a sign that Jesus was risen (20:8). Perhaps, too, by the time this gospel was composed the tomb had already become a place of christian worship.

JESUS COMES TO DISCIPLES.
20:19-23.

> [19]On the evening of that day, the first day of the week, the doors being shut where the disciples were, for fear of the Jews, Jesus came and stood among them and said to them, "Peace be with you." [20]When he had said this, he showed them his hands and his side. Then the disciples were glad when they saw the Lord. [21]Jesus said to them again, "Peace be with you. As the Father has sent me, even so I send you." [22]And when he had said this, he breathed on them, and said to them, "Receive the Holy Spirit. [23]If you forgive the sins of any, they are forgiven; if you retain the sins of any, they are retained."

Everything in this scene focuses on the person of the risen Christ, on what his presence means and brings to disciples. He "comes" to the frightened community of disciples and he is transformed because he is no longer restricted by material conditions (v. 19). But they grow from a state of fearfulness, as they lacked the courage of faith, to belief in his risen presence and this presence also brings them peace ("peace *is* with you") and joy (vv. 19-21). This peace, a divine gift promised often in the Old Testament for the coming days of deliverance, arises from the awareness of the presence of Jesus who has over-come death (16:33). Joy is also a gift, very similar to peace, "life" or salvation, which Jesus had promised disciples for the time of his resurrection (16:20-22).

By communicating his Spirit to disciples, Jesus enables them to continue his own mission which he had received from his Father. Now Jesus, described at the beginning of the gospel as a "baptizer with (i.e. who communicates) the Spirit" (1:33) gives, "breathes" on them this Spirit for their mission. Just as God had created man by breathing life into them (Gen 2:7; Ezek 37:3-5), now by his Spirit Jesus effects a new creation in and through disciples. Therefore, he communicates to them the life of his Spirit for mission while they, in turn, will pass on the life-giving power of the Spirit of Jesus to others who come to believe in him. They will also continue his mission to forgive sin which he exercises as the Lamb of God (1:29) and this power they receive is associated with that Holy Spirit who gives life and purifies (Ezek 36:25-27;37:3-7) and who probably also illumines those who exercise it in Jesus' name. However, it is not clear whether the power refers to forgiveness through baptism or penance or both. In any case it is a power over sin resident and exercised in the community.

DOUBTS ABOUT EASTER.
20:24-29.

24Now Thomas, one of the twelve, called the Twin, was not with them when Jesus came. 25So the other disciples told him, "We have seen the Lord." But he said to them, "Unless I see in his hands the print of the nails, and place my finger in the mark of the nails, and place my hand in his side, I will not believe."

26Eight days later, his disciples were again in the house, and Thomas was with them. The doors were shut, but Jesus came and stood among them, and said, "Peace be with you." 27Then he said to Thomas, "Put your finger here, and see my hands; and put out your hand,

and place it in my side; do not be faithless, but believing."
[28]Thomas answered him, "My Lord and my God!" [29]Jesus
said to him, "Have you believed because you have seen
me? Blessed are those who have not seen and yet believe."

Elsewhere in the gospel Thomas is a keen follower of
Jesus but he is slow to grasp the mystery of his person
and he looks for concrete and clear "proofs" of faith
(11:16;14:5). Here he is still a pre-Easter disciple as he
is taken up with establishing the miraculous or marvel-
lous aspect of Jesus' appearances (cf. 4:48). Yet he is like
Nathanael in his firm scepticism which eventually is turned
into a supreme confession of faith in Jesus after he had
received a special experience of Jesus (v.28; 1:45-49). Like
Nathanael he rejected the faith of fellow-disciples who
had "seen the Lord" (v.25;1:45-46), but he is brought to
"see" the risen Jesus, that is, to realize that he is "my
Lord and my God." "Lord" and "God" (Yahweh Elohim)
are Old Testament names for God (Ps 35:23) and thus the
Easter faith of Thomas recognizes God in the risen Jesus.
The response of Thomas in his confession of faith recalls
Jesus' words to himself and Philip: "If you have known
me, you will know the Father. He who has seen me has
seen the Father" (14:7,9).

This confession of faith at the end of the gospel links
with the prologue (1:1): what God is, the Word is, for
Jesus is the Word who has now returned to the glory he
had with the Father before the world began (17:5). Thus
the circle, the whole movement of the gospel is complete.
However, Thomas is remembered more for his doubting
than for this supreme expression of faith. But Jesus'
reply (v.29) does not find any fault with his expression
of faith, for it simply contrasts two different and valid
ways of faith. On the one hand, disciples who had been
with Jesus came to "see" him and believe in him as risen
through special faith experiences, that is, appearances.
But the community of disciples down through history
have not experienced the risen Jesus in the same way.

Yet they, too, have received the gift of faith and they are in this respect equally praised and blessed by God.

EPILOGUE.
20:30-31.—*A Book of Signs.*

> ³⁰Now Jesus did many other signs in the presence of the disciples, which are not written in this book; ³¹but these are written that you may believe that Jesus is the Christ, the Son of God, and that believing you may have life in his name.

The "signs" of the gospel invite readers to grow in faith: "so that you may *continue* to believe" (rather than "so that you may believe") in Jesus as the expected one of his people and a divine Son. Through this ongoing commitment of faith in Jesus who revealed himself (his "name") as Messiah and Son, christians have a life-giving communion with Jesus who shares with them the life of his Father. These two titles constitute the double credo of the gospel (cf. 11:27): Jesus is the Messiah for he realizes the expectations of his people in the history of salvation. But Jesus is the Christ who comes from the Father, who is in close relationship with him as the Son of God.

The first part of the gospel (chs. 1-12) had given a special place to the signs of Jesus' public ministry. But what immediately precedes, namely, the resurrection appearances of Jesus, are also "signs" because they are miraculous events which reveal the truth about Jesus. The disciples penetrated beyond the startling appearance to believe that Jesus is Lord and God. Besides, these signs manifest that Jesus is glorified and gives eternal life to those who believe. The risen, wounded Jesus is a source of new life and of the Spirit (19:30,34;20:27,29) and thus, the glorified, the dying and risen Lord is himself a sign, for he is the source and symbol of that new life and of the Spirit which come to us through his death and resurrection.

The communication of the Holy Spirit to disciples (vv.20-22) only partially realizes the promises of the Paraclete and Jesus' baptizing with the Spirit, because the Paraclete becomes effective only when Jesus has gone and when disciples come to understand the mystery of Jesus on a deeper level (16:7,12-15). Yet the resurrection of Jesus and his appearances are a beginning of the days when Jesus will continue to pour out, to baptize with the Spirit. This Spirit will strengthen faith and lead christians into the fullness of the truth, into an ongoing, life-giving communion of faith with the risen Messiah and Son of God. This will take place when Jesus has gone; as yet he is present with disciples (20:19-29) who still have to grow further in faith (16:13).

The risen Jesus, showing his wounds, gives the Spirit (20:22), even though he has already given the Spirit in death (19:30,34). However, the two scenes consider the same event from different points of view. In ch. 19 we have a comprehensive picture of all the events of the hour of Jesus—death, exaltation, glorification, his ascent to his Father. Thus in the physical death of Jesus, John contemplates simultaneously the consequences of his death, with particular emphasis on its effects for the life of the church through the mention of blood and water (v.34). He already sees the fruits: the new life and the Spirit which result from Jesus' death and resurrection and which are operative in the sacraments of the church. Thus in 19:30,34 the humanity of Jesus, his bloody self-offering, his crucified flesh are revealed as the source of salvation and from which is born the church in the grace of the Spirit. While the evangelist concentrates on death he also sees its consequences and the whole unity of the "hour" of Jesus. Therefore when Jesus gives the Spirit to disciples (20:22) an aspect of the "hour" is considered apart in a different kind of way, from the point of view of the risen Jesus. The Easter apparition, then, takes up the same complex reality of the "hour" of Jesus and clarifies it in a new way. Thus it represents beyond death another side of this same "hour"—the resurrection of Jesus which brings the gift of the Spirit.

The Theology of the Holy Spirit

Sayings about the Spirit are scattered throughout the gospel, in the first seven chapters (1;3;4;6;7), in the five promises of the Paraclete (chs. 14-16) and in the passion-resurrection narrative (19:30,34;20:22). He is also given several names: Spirit, Holy Spirit, Paraclete, Spirit of truth. There is an even greater variety of images: he is the dove, (living) water, wind and the breath of Jesus, a teacher (14:26) and a guide (16:13). Thus after we have read through the gospel the Holy Spirit could easily become submerged and elude us altogether because of this seemingly disorganized complexity of sayings, names and images.

In fact, the gospel shows a striking unity in its theology of the Holy Spirit. This is, first and foremost, very Christ-centred, for the most characteristic aspect of the Spirit is that he awakens, deepens and strengthens faith in Jesus, in who he is and what he means for believers, both in his relationship to his Father and to the world. "He will lead you into the heart of the truth" (16:13)—this is one of the key phrases in the gospel summarizing the work of the Spirit who leads people all the time into a deeper understanding of Jesus, of his person, achievements and message for daily living.

In his activity the Spirit is directed and oriented towards Jesus just as Jesus himself in his mission is oriented to and distinct from the Father. For John the Holy Spirit is present and active where people are inspired by the example of Jesus and realize more effectively his message in their lives with one another. Thus Christ "comes" to, is more present in, the community whenever christians are receptive to the action of the Spirit who helps them appropriate and realize the message of Jesus through faith and mutual love (14:15-21;15:10-14).

The faith he awakens, deepens and strengthens is not just an intellectual understanding of the meaning of Jesus and his message. This faith is a personal attachment, commitment to Christ, a life-giving relationship with him, for he is a Spirit of "renewal," of a new life which grows through a continued life of faith in Jesus (3:3-10). In the first part of the gospel the becoming of faith is attributed to the "Holy Spirit" (3:5;6:63). Later in the Farewell Discourse he is called a "Paraclete" and a "Spirit of truth" because the deepening, strengthening and keeping of faith in Jesus are more in the foreground. Then the christian community, whose faith is reflected in the gospel, was as keenly aware as today of external pressures that tested their faith. Their experience of God's strengthening power in such situations made them conscious of the presence of a Paraclete-Spirit in their lives.

But the activity of the Spirit is not only directed towards the person of Jesus for he is also a *gift* of Jesus. At the beginning of the gospel Jesus is described as a baptizer with the Spirit (1:33), someone who will communicate the Spirit. During his ministry the Spirit works through his words, and also through his death and resurrection he gives or baptizes with the Spirit (19:30,34;20:22). Thus Jesus continues to baptize with the Spirit whenever his promises of the Paraclete are realized in the christian community. It is he who baptizes us with the Spirit when we are led more and more into the heart of the truth who is himself, when our commitment to him survives and grows under pressures from without, when we realize more effectively his message, particularly his words about fraternal love.

The Spirit continues to act in word and sacrament. Although the Spirit was active in the words of Jesus during his ministry, now his message, his "truth" becomes more effective in the hearts of believers through the power of the Spirit (3:34;6:63;16:13-15), for he constantly gives power to the message of Jesus in new circumstances and situations. Thus he unfolds, interiorizes and actualizes it in the life of the believing listener. Besides, he is the power who helps the christian proclaim the word and christian disciples give witness to Christ through the word out of inner conviction which is the work of the Spirit (15:26-27).

Furthermore, every christian worship of the Father is inspired by the Holy Spirit (4:23-24) and, as the Spirit of faith, he belongs to the sacramental life of the christian. Thus faith is placed alongside baptism (3:5), and the eucharist is an expression and confirmation of faith in Jesus (ch. 6), so that the Spirit is the source of sacramental faith which is directed towards the person of Jesus. Baptism and eucharist, for example, point to Jesus and they are expressions of a faith in him which is evoked in us by the "witnessing" Spirit (1 Jn 5:6-8). But John never presents the Spirit as an effect or gift of the sacrament; rather the Spirit gives effectiveness to the sacraments because he is the Spirit of that faith necessary for participating in them and it is he who creates faith in Jesus (3:3-10;6:63).

This Spirit who helps christians receive and communicate the word is essentially a Spirit for mission, for he "remains" on Jesus, enabling him to carry out his mission and to communicate the power of the Spirit through his life-giving words (1:32-33;3:34). When his mission is complete he gives the Spirit to disciples for the mission of communicating faith in Jesus through Spirit-filled and life-giving words (20:21-22). Thus christian disciples realize their apostolic mission in the world only through the help of the Spirit, just as Jesus himself possesses the fullness of the Spirit for his mission.

But the Holy Spirit is more than a power who works within us. He has more of a "personality" in this gospel than in the rest of the New Testament. While his mission is Christ-centred and directs us towards Christ, yet we can recognize and address him in this gospel as a distinct person, as "someone" who can have a place in our lives. His relationship to Jesus is parallel to Jesus' own relationship with his Father (5:43;14:26). Besides, he comes only when Jesus departs to his Father (16:7). In particular, the five promises of the Paraclete clarify his distinctive role and personality.

Today that belief in the Holy Spirit, which has revitalized the christian life of many, can grow in depth and strength by reflection on the Paraclete and Spirit of truth as he is presented in the Fourth Gospel. He may not be as exuberant, explosive or as ecstatic as the Spirit of Luke, the powerful and prophetic Spirit who "fills," "falls on" and even "seizes" people (Acts 2:4;8:39;10:44), who provokes outbursts of joy and praise (Acts 2:11,46). But he is a very personal, Christ-centred Spirit who leads us into an intimate, personal communion with Jesus in faith and love. All these facets and workings of the one Spirit of Jesus need to be known and experienced by all christians.

LAKESIDE REVELATIONS.
21:1-14.

21 After this Jesus revealed himself again to the disciples by the Sea of Tiberias; and he revealed himself in this way. ²Simon Peter, Thomas called the Twin, Nathanael of Cana in Galilee, the sons of Zebedee, and two others of his disciples were together. ³Simon Peter said to them, "I am going fishing." They said to him, "We will go with you." They went out and got into the boat; but that night they caught nothing.

⁴Just as day was breaking, Jesus stood on the beach; yet the disciples did not know that it was Jesus. ⁵Jesus said to them, "Children, have you any fish?" They answered him, "No." ⁶He said to them, "Cast the net on the right side of the boat, and you will find some." So they cast it, and now they were not able to haul it in, for the quantity of fish. ⁷That disciple whom Jesus loved said to Peter, "It is the Lord!" When Simon Peter heard that it was the Lord, he put on his clothes, for he was stripped for work, and sprang into the sea. ⁸But the other disciples came in the boat, dragging the net full of fish, for they were not far from the land, but about a hundred yards off.

⁹When they got out on land, they saw a charcoal fire there, with fish lying on it, and bread. ¹⁰Jesus said to them, "Bring some of the fish that you have just caught." ¹¹So Simon Peter went aboard and hauled the net ashore, full of large fish, a hundred and fifty-three of them; and although there were so many, the net was not torn. ¹²Jesus said to them, "Come and have breakfast." Now none of the disciples dared ask him, "Who are you?" They knew it was the Lord. ¹³Jesus came and took the bread and gave it to them, and so with the fish. ¹⁴This was now the third time that Jesus was revealed to the disciples after he was raised from the dead.

This chapter, which was composed as an addition to a work already complete (cf. 20:30-31) and published with it, puts more emphasis on the ecclesial or community aspect of Jesus' risen presence among disciples. For example, the miraculous catch of fish suggests the apostolic mission of the Church and the meal at the lakeside recalls the eucharistic presence of the risen Lord in the community. Besides, pastoral authority is conferred on Peter; in fact, the chapter is built around Peter and the Beloved Disciple.

Whereas Jesus "came" to gathered disciples in Jerusalem (20:19,24,26), now by a lakeside in Galilee in a fishing scene (vv.1-8) and at a meal (vv.9-13) the risen "Lord" (v.7) "reveals" himself (vv.1,13) to disciples. The appearance of Jesus is, therefore, an event of his initiative inviting them to faith (cf. 2:11;17:6). He also shows that special knowledge, here about fishing (v.6!), characteristic of him throughout the gospel (1:48;4:16). There is an intimacy and ease about his relationship with the disciples reminiscent of the first day they met him (vv.2,5,10,12; 1:37-39); Nathanael and Peter are mentioned in both scenes. The words of Jesus are familiar in tone, even quite colloquial: "Lads, you haven't caught anything, have you?" (v.5). But the disciples again have difficulty in recognizing him (vv.4,12) for he is the transformed, risen Lord. Though Peter has the more important role (vv.2,3,7,

11), it is the Beloved Disciple who is sensitive in faith to the presence of the risen Jesus and recognizes him (v.7).

The miraculous catch, which is described before the resurrection by Luke (5:1-11), has also a symbolical meaning, for to become "fishers of men" (Lk 5:10) is a call to an apostolic mission. Besides, disciples in the gospels never catch anything without the help of Jesus! Here the great haul of fish (vv.6,11) insinuates the universal and abundant mission which Jesus gives his community of disciples, the church and the net which was not "torn" suggests the all-embracing character of the apostolic mission, gathering people together from everywhere into the community of Jesus (cf. Mt 13:47). Also, the "drawing" in of the net (vv.6,8,11) echoes Jesus' words about his Father who "draws" to faith, and about himself as an exalted Lord who "will draw" all to himself (6:43;12:32). Furthermore, the real meal by the lakeside where Jesus "took the bread and gave it to them" (v.13; cf. 6:11) conveys the meaning of eucharist: the risen Jesus is present among christian disciples and gathers them around himself in a meal of communion.

PETER AND THE BELOVED DISCIPLE.
21:15-23.

> [15]When they had finished breakfast, Jesus said to Simon Peter, "Simon, son of John, do you love me more than these?" He said to him, "Yes, Lord; you know that I love you." He said to him, "Feed my lambs." [16]A second time he said to him, "Simon, son of John, do you love me?" He said to him, "Yes, Lord; you know that I love you." He said to him the third time, "Simon, son of John, do you love me?" Peter was grieved because he said to him the third time, "Do you love me?" And he said to him, "Lord, you know everything; you know that I love you." Jesus said to him, "Feed my sheep. [18]Truly, truly, I say to you, when you were young, you girded yourself and walked where you would; but when you are old, you will stretch out your hands, and another will gird you and

carry you where you do not wish to go." [19](This he said to show by what death he was to glorify God.) And after this he said to him, "Follow me."

[20]Peter turned and saw following them the disciple whom Jesus loved, who had lain close to his breast at the supper and had said, "Lord, who is it that is going to betray you?" [21]When Peter saw him, he said to Jesus, "Lord, what about this man?" [22]Jesus said to him, "If it is my will that he remain until I come, what is that to you? Follow me!" [23]The saying spread abroad among the brethren that this disciple was not to die; yet Jesus did not say to him that he was not to die, but, "If it is my will that he remain until I come, what is that to you?"

Jesus turns his full attention to Peter whom he not only rehabilitates but also entrusts with a special mission. Already the memory of Peter's denials has been evoked by the charcoal fire (v.9;18:18) and now once again by three questions and answers (vv.15-18). However, the repeated question and answer do not imply Jesus' doubts about Peter but rather that Peter's love for him is earnest and that he has the devoted love which is the heart of true discipleship. More important are the three commands to feed "my sheep (lambs)" in which Jesus expresses his trust in Peter and gives him the task of shepherd. In the light of Jesus' description of the good shepherd (10:1-18), this mission entails guidance through teaching and preaching, care for the community of believers, self-giving to the point of laying down one's life.

Peter is to treat the community of believers as "my" sheep but he does not fully replace Jesus, since his authority is not absolute as leader or shepherd: "Tend my sheep as mine not as yours" (Augustine). This kind of authority or pastoral care, after the example of Jesus the good shepherd, does not accent the shepherd's superior position. Rather it has overtones of love and total concern for and dedication to the community. This attitude is clarified by 1 Pet 5:1-4: "Tend the flock of God that is your charge not by constraint but willingly . . . not as domineering over those in your charge but being examples to the flock . . ." But Peter is not assigned this mission because of his special worthiness since it follows after his failure in discipleship and after reconciliation with his Lord. Rather it shows how Jesus works through failing and weak disciples.

Jesus goes on to speak about the futures of Peter and the Beloved Disciple (vv.18-23). Peter's freedom will be taken away as he will be led bound like a criminal to his martyrdom (v.18). Thus he is the shepherd who follows Jesus to the point of laying down his life for his people and through the power of the risen Jesus he will realize what he had previously failed to achieve when he relied on his own enthusiasm: to "follow you," to "lay down my life for you." Therefore, he will realize the assurance of Jesus: "You shall follow me afterwards" (v.19;13:36-38), for he will follow Jesus only after failure, reconciliation and after receiving his special mission. Thus his confession of love (vv.15-18) will be tested by his willingness to die.

However, no confession of love needs to be drawn from the Beloved Disciple who has not denied Jesus (18:16); neither does he receive a commission as a shepherd. Yet both himself and Peter are witnesses to Jesus: Peter's martyrdom is a witness in accordance with his shepherd's duty of laying down his life and the Beloved Disciple has a special destiny also willed by Jesus (v.22). The form of his witness is different since he "remained" as Jesus wished, that is, he lived out a long life in the love of Jesus. Consequently, there is no question of his witness being inferior.

In this final chapter Peter receives a pastoral office as he is called to share in the authority of Jesus himself. The purpose of the inclusion of Peter was to give an interpretation to the ministry of Peter, which was already accepted in the early Church (cf. Mt 16:16-19; 1 Cor 15:5). The editor of this chapter makes it clear through the dialogue between Peter and Jesus that authority must be understood in the christian community in relation to the love of Jesus, even to the point of dying for Jesus and thus for the brethren. On the other hand, the ecclesial function of the Beloved

Disciple is clarified also: he bears witness to the revelation of Jesus. As the intimate friend of the Lord, his witness has value for the johannine community, since the Fourth Gospel is the heritage of the Beloved Disciple and they should accept this testimony as part of Jesus' heritage. If Jesus has given him the office of witness, he continues this function in the Fourth Gospel for the community.

SECOND EPILOGUE.
21:24-25.—*Unfinished Symphony.*

> [24]This is the disciple who is bearing witness to these things, and who has written these things; and we know that his testimony is true.
>
> [25]But there are also many other things which Jesus did; were every one of them to be written, I suppose that the world itself could not contain the books that would be written.

This second epilogue attributes the whole gospel ("these things") to the Beloved Disciple who is a witness in faith to what has been recorded. Yet he is distinct from those who "know that his testimony is true." In any case, the Beloved Disciple is an "author" who has "caused these things to be written"; his authority stands behind the traditions communicated in the gospel. The final comment (v.25) is a type of hyperbole, an accepted literary convention of the time, explaining why no attempt was made to include all the other things thatJesus did and expresses that no story can communicate the infinite and unfathomable riches of Jesus (Col 2:3) since he is beyond human categories, words and books. Already the unending flow of writings and commentaries on the Fourth Gospel as well as the present writer's limited contribution confirm the last words of the gospel: much has to remain unsaid because no number of books will exhaust the "New Testament Message" and the mystery of the Word made flesh.

SUGGESTIONS FOR FURTHER READING

1. "Introductory" works on the gospel

R. Kysar, *The Fourth Evangelist and His Gospel.* Minneapolis: Augsburg, 1975. An analysis of contemporary johannine scholarship and a reference work for the study of individual themes and problems in the Fourth Gospel.

G. MacRae, *Faith in the Word: The Fourth Gospel.* Chicago: Franciscan Herald Press, 1973. An essay on some of the major questions about the gospel and some of its major themes.

F. J. Moloney, *The Word Became Flesh.* Dublin, Cork: Mercier Press, 1977. A brief account of the origins of the gospel and of the main aspects of its Christology.

P. Perkins, *Gospel of St. John.* Chicago: Franciscan Herald Press, 1975. A help to readers to reflect and pray on the gospel.

2. Commentaries

A. The following commentaries are written with the scholar in mind:

C. K. Barrett, *The Gospel according to St. John.* London: SPCK, 1967. This requires some knowledge of Greek.

R. Brown, *The Gospel according to John, I-XII (AncBi 29), XIII-XXI (AncBi 29A).* New York: Doubleday, 1966/70. Provides an extensive commentary on the gospel; it also deals with many gospel themes and problems concerning the gospel. Full bibliographies on every passage.

R. Schnackenburg, *The Gospel according to St. John. Vol I: Chs. 1-4.* New York: Herder, 1968. English translation of *Das Johannesevangelium. Kap. 1-4 (HTKNT IV, 1).* Freiburg: Herder, 1965. *Vol. II: Chs. 5-12.* London: Burns and Oates, 1980 (translation of *Das Johannese-*

vangelium: Kap. 5-12 (HTKNT IV, 2), 1971. The remaining volume has not been translated: Vol. III: *Kap. 13-21* (HTKNT IV, 3), 1975. A very comprehensive work, which also deals with the theology of the Evangelist.

B. Commentaries aimed at the general reader:

B. Lindars, *The Gospel of John.* London: Oliphants, 1972. For the non-specialist, yet comprehensive; based on the RSV.

P. Perkins, *The Gospel according to St. John: A Theological Commentary.* Chicago: Franciscan Herald Press, 1978. A brief, up to date commentary, presenting the theology and literary aspects of the gospel.

3. Books

M.-E. Boismard, A. Lamouille (ed.), *L'Évangile de Jean: Synopse des Quatres Évangiles en français, III.* Paris: Cerf, 1977. An important attempt to reconstruct the stages of the composition of the gospel.

R. Brown, *The Community of the Beloved Disciple.* New York: Paulist, 1979. An attempt to sketch out the history of the johannine community: treats of the gospel and epistles of John.

J. Comblin, *Sent from the Father: Meditations on the Fourth Gospel* (English translation of *O Enviado do Pai*: Petropolis, Brazil: Vozes Ltds., 1974). Dublin: Gill and Macmillan, 1979. A series of reflections on the gospel in the light of the missionary experience.

C. H. Dodd, *The Interpretation of the Fourth Gospel.* Cambridge: University Press, 1953. Informative, detailed work on the relationship between John and Jewish-Hellenistic traditions.

——————————. *Historical Tradition in the Fourth Gospel.* Cambridge: University Press, 1963. Detailed investigation of the traditions behind the gospel and of the relationship with synoptic traditions.

J. T. Forestell, *The Word of the Cross: Salvation as Revelation in the Fourth Gospel.* Rome: PIB Pontifical Biblical Institute, 1974. Study of John's view of salvation.

P. B. Harner, *The 'I Am' of the Fourth Gospel.* Philadelphia: Fortress Press, 1970. A study of the "I am (he)" sayings of Jesus in the gospel and their background.

R. Kysar, *The John the Maverick Gospel.* Atlanta: John Knox Press, 1970. Deals with the main themes and problems of the gospel, using effective pedagogical methods.

J. L. Martyn, *History and Theology in the Fourth Gospel.* New York: Harper & Row, 1968. Deals with the debate with Judaism as reflected in the gospel.

——————————. *The Gospel of John in Christian History.* New York: Paulist, 1979. Attempts to reconstruct johannine church origins.

J. P. Miranda, *Being and the Messiah: The Message of St. John.* (English translation of *El ser y el mesías.* Salamanca: Sígueme, 1973). New York: Orbis, 1977. Places the message of the Fourth Gospel in relation to contemporary philosophy. Marxism and questions of poverty and justice.

F. J. Moloney, *The Johannine Son of Man.* Rome: LAS, 1978 (second ed.). A comprehensive and original study of the johannine use of the 'Son of Man' title.

S. Pancaro, *The Law in the Fourth Gospel. Supplement to Novum Testamentum, vol. XLII.* Leiden: Brill, 1975. A study of the Law in the gospel with special attention to the situation of the johannine community with reference in relation to the synagogue.

I. de la Potterie-S. Lyonnet, *The Christian Lives by the Spirit*. English translation of *La Vie selon l'Esprit*. Paris: Cerf. A series of essays on the theology of St. John and St. Paul. Two of these deal with the promises of the Holy Spirit and with the dialogue of Jesus with Nicodemus. They present the theology of John in the context of these topics.

M. Taylor, *Companion to John*. New York: Alba House, 1977. A selection of articles, previously published, by well-known scholars on major johannine topics.

4. Articles

N. Flanagan, *The Gospel of John as Drama*. Bible Today, 19 (1981), 264-270.

G. MacRae, The Fourth Gospel and Religionsgeschichte. Catholic Biblical Quarterly 32 (1970), 13-24.

W. Meeks, *The Man from Heaven in Johannine Sectarianism*. Journal of Biblical Literature 91 (1972), 44-72.

J. F. O'Grady, *The Role of the Beloved Disciple*. Biblical Theology Bulletin 9 (1979), 58-65.